"*The Monster in the Cave,* by David Mellinger and Steven Jay Lynn, is a remarkably good self-help book that explores in detail how you can cope with many different common and uncommon aspects of anxiety. It tells you all you wanted to know about handicapping fear, everything you might ask about it, and just about everything that you can do to overcome it. Exceptionally well done!"

> —Albert Ellis,
> author of *A Guide to Rational Living*

"*The Monster in the Cave* provides state-of-the-art guidance for helping people overcome panic attacks, phobias, and other anxiety-related problems. Based solidly on science, it is nevertheless engaging, lucidly written, and accessible to the general reader."

> —Richard J. McNally, Ph.D.,
> professor of psychology, Harvard University,
> author of *Remembering Trauma*

"Mellinger and Lynn's book is a gift to the mental-health profession and its consumers. The authors present a detailed, simple to follow, scientifically grounded self-help program for anxiety. It is a must-read for those who suffer from anxiety as well as for those who treat patients with anxiety."

> —Maggie Bruck, Ph.D.,
> professor of psychology,
> Johns Hopkins School of Medicine

THE MONSTER IN THE CAVE

How to Face Your Fear and Anxiety
and Live Your Life

DAVID MELLINGER, MSW,
and STEVEN JAY LYNN, PH.D.

BERKLEY BOOKS, NEW YORK

B

A Berkley Book
Published by The Berkley Publishing Group
A division of the Penguin Group (USA) Inc.
375 Hudson Street
New York, New York 10014

Copyright © 2003 by David Mellinger, MSW, and Steven Jay Lynn, Ph.D.
Cover design by George Long.
Text design by Tiffany Estreicher.

PRINTING HISTORY
Berkley hardcover edition / Septmeber 2003
Berkley trade paperback edition: August 2004

Berkley trade paperback ISBN: 0-425-19639-9

The Library of Congress has cataloged the Berkley hardcover edition as follows:

Mellinger, David.
The monster in the cave : how to face your fear and anxiety and live
your life / David Mellinger and Steven Jay Lynn.—1st ed.
p. cm.
Includes bibliographical references and index.
ISBN 0-425-19169-9
1. Fear.   2. Anxiety.   I. Lynn, Steven J.   II. Title.

BF575.F2M45 2003
616.85'22—dc21   2003052353

PRINTED IN THE UNITED STATES OF AMERICA

10 9 8 7 6 5 4 3 2 1

This book is dedicated our wives,
Sharon Marie Mellinger and Fern Pritikin Lynn,
and to our daughters,
Ariel Marissa Mellinger and Jessica Barbara Lynn,
with love.

Acknowledgments

DAVID MELLINGER: Many people have taken part in this rich journey. Benjamin Crocker gave me a scintillating education about anxiety disorders that first inspired me to help fight fear, and Cathy Costa helped actualize and support our first anxiety treatment program. Thanks to Thomas Shiovitz, Marc Graff, and Michael Agress for generously sharing their knowledge of anxiety; and to Chris DeHaan for her feedback and astuteness in reviewing early versions of our work. I deeply appreciate the rigor, wit, and gusto with which Len Sushinsky, a scholar of behavioral science and my clinical program manager, has tackled questions of treatment of every sort of anxiety problem. Thanks also to my father and stepmother, Morris and Collette Konqui Mellinger, and to Laurie Gertz for their support and help. I am boundlessly appreciative of and delighted with the love, enthusiasm, and tolerance my wife, Sharon, and my daughter, Ariel, grace me with, and grateful to all of my clients who shared their deep feelings, insights, and hopes as they took up the challenges of overcoming their fears.

STEVEN JAY LYNN: My wife, Fern Pritikin Lynn, my "soul and inspiration," was not only an unstinting source of strength, support, and good will throughout this project, but her astute judgment and detailed editorial comments contributed immensely to the clarity and "down to earth" quality of *The Monster.* As always, my daughter, Jessica Barbara Lynn, lit up my life with her very presence. My thanks to Kelley Shindler and our editor, Denise Silvestro, for their valuable comments and feedback on the book, and to our agent, Audrey Wolf, for her support and encouragement.

Contents

Introduction

The people of a little town bordered by the tall spruce of the North Woods avoided Old Hillside Road for decades. Children walked the extra half mile home from school to skirt the marshy bottomland of the abandoned Skinner farm rather than running the fool's errand of walking past the Dark Cave. One icy winter, legend has it, a monstrous beast on a foraging expedition took up residence in the cave and stole food. After it wreaked havoc on the hunters who sought to kill it, townspeople came to shun its lair. Infrequently and with trepidation, they would follow an overgrown track past the mouth of the cave bearing Holy Bibles and flashlights, beating on skillets and shaking noisemakers for "monster protection." For the most part, though, everyone kept away.

Then one May a newcomer family moved into the Skinner place. Lacking fluency in English, the two sons didn't learn the tall tales and legends before school let out for the summer. Early one evening they ventured deep into the Dark Cave, shining the way with their flashlights. The main tunnel opened into a vast chamber, cool and musty, where in one corner their beams illuminated the sole sign of life, present or past, in the whole place—a bunch of moldering animal bones, which they scooped into a sack.

Meanwhile, their sister told her new girlfriend where her brothers had gone. The friend told *her* brothers, who told their father. And so a nervous group of armed townspeople were fretting at the mouth of the cave as the boys emerged, nonchalantly carrying their booty. People were relieved to see them and astonished that they'd encountered nothing but the old bones of a small bear.

Our fears are like the monster in the cave. We squander precious moments of life on fears of objects, people, and situations that actually have no power to harm us. Fears become the basis for avoidance, detours on the maps of our existence, and sponges that soak up vital energy. By failing to confront our fears, they become more real and intimidating, like the mythical monster in the cave. By avoiding our fears the way the townspeople avoided the cave, we relinquish the chance to learn whether they can truly harm us and whether we have the power to conquer them. When we confront our fears, we release the vast energy that lies hidden in their shadows. We mobilize our intelligence to discern the true nature of our difficulties and engineer ways to lay bridges over the challenging areas of our lives.

This book is all about confronting anxiety in an intelligent, step-by-step way. The cutting-edge principles of behavior change and techniques we present in the pages that follow are designed to help you confront your personal monsters—your excessive and irrational fears—and emerge victorious. Before we introduce you to the nuts and bolts of our approach to mastering anxiety, we shall consider the nature and scope of anxiety conditions that bedevil humanity and are likely to trouble you or someone you care about.

How Anxiety Is Experienced

Anxiety is experienced as discomfort, intense confusion, or a sense of imminent disaster. Anxiety hobbles the ability to think clearly and act decisively. Tugging like a tight suit, anxiety robs us of our freedom to enjoy life. When nervous feelings gather momentum and escalate into panic attacks, they can render a person breathless and speechless, sweating and trembling, with a wildly beating heart and a terrible fear of dying or going insane. Recurrent waves of panic that strike with little or no warning can instill a consuming sense of terror and a general fear of many situations. Tension and worry become constant companions of the anxious person.

Anxiety can provoke such strong fear and avoidance that its victims become, among other things, incapable of:

- Attending school, religious services, movies, or sporting events
- Driving on freeways or making left turns
- Using public restrooms
- Getting blood pressure tested by medical professionals
- Feeling comfortable in the presence of dogs or cats
- Being in a closed room
- Receiving injections or dental treatment
- Giving speeches or making presentations
- Being home alone

Thoughts of vomiting, passing out, or uttering unspeakable profanities in public demoralize some people who suffer from anxiety disorders, while for other individuals, everyday worries become more and more consuming, as minor issues of security or safety balloon into major obsessions and doubts about self-control.

Consider the Numbers

For those readers who have not experienced the sting of anxiety and the stumbling blocks it creates, the above description might sound dramatic or even overblown. Yet if you have experienced intense anxiety, even for a moment, you understand something about its potentially crippling effects. And if you suffer from debilitating anxiety, you are not alone. The tentacles of anxiety reach across the social spectrum to afflict the rich and famous, the poor and the homeless.

Recent statistics compiled by the National Institute of Mental Health indicate that more than 19 million Americans ages eighteen to fifty-four suffer from one or more anxiety disorders each year. During a given year, between a third and a half of the people in the United States have at least one anxiety or panic attack—the most widespread of the anxiety conditions—and about 2.4 million people suffer from panic disorders, marked by recurrent panic attacks. An estimated 12.5 million people in the United States suffer so intensely from anxiety-related disorders that they seek mental health help. And for every person with an anxiety disorder, several others experience anxiety that doesn't fully meet diagnostic criteria.

How Much Anxiety Is Too Much?

These numbers reflect an unsettling truth: Anxiety is very much a part of the human condition. It poses a myriad of challenges and ranges from mildly distressing to severely disabling. It therefore seems reasonable to ask the question, "How much anxiety is too much?" Or the related and more personal question: "Do I need help?" If anxiety hampers your social relationships or your ability to work and live productively, then your anxiety is excessive and you need to seek help.

Because anxiety plays an important role in everyday life, you might question whether the anxious discomfort you feel is run-of-the-mill. After all, anxiety equips us with ultrasensitive radar to help us contend bravely with a challenging, complex environment. One of the world's most common negative feelings, it is also the most essential of life preservers. Anxiety activates an automatic biological and psychological program that permits escape from danger—or at least evasion of its sting—through flight, avoidance, or freezing, a kind of paralysis or immobilization in hazardous situations. Anxiety has three important adaptive functions:

1. Anxiety alerts us to risk and danger, so that we may recognize and learn from previously experienced threats. We are warned of imminent mortal danger through an unmistakable sense that the world is dreadfully askew—at the least a gripping tension, an overshadowing cloud; at the most, abject terror.

2. Anxiety permits a lightning-quick response to real or perceived danger.

3. Anxiety buys time to think about what we fear and to decide how to act. It can guide our actions, cue us to situational and social hazards, and steer us away from engaging in illegal, shameful, or harmful behaviors.

While anxiety ensures survival, it exacts a dear price. Although anxiety activates our intuition and vital coping skills, it can cloud the mind and trigger blatantly unbalanced states like panic. Small pangs of vulnerability

When Anxiety Goes Unnoticed

Oddly enough, multitudes of people fall victim to preventable accidents because of problems with insufficient awareness of anxiety. In *The Gift of Fear,* Gavin de Becker, an expert in high-level security and prevention of stalking and violent attacks, observes that thousands of people in the United States are unnecessarily victims of violence and treachery. This tragedy is due largely to denial, a primitive defense mechanism that limits anxious distress by minimizing awareness of threat and impairing the memory of disturbing objects and events in the environment. Victims of rampant violence often have underestimated the potential for others to harm them and overrated their ability to control risky situations. Our capacity to experience and evaluate anxiety allows us to gauge danger and actively plan to cope with it or avert harm.

and hurt get bundled together into big, disturbing waves of emotional pain. Once the grip of anxiety starts to tighten, our physical sensations and mental interpretations and reactions compound the anxious feeling. Disturbing, negative emotional thinking hampers motivation, frustrates, and even terrorizes us. Ironically, anxiety is both the target of recovery and its biggest obstacle. Like all intense, disturbing emotions, anxiety distorts our perception of reality, thereby creating, in the Dalai Lama's words, "a disparity between how things appear and how they really are."

You should be aware of sources of real danger, stay safe, and act in keeping with your personal goals. "Normal" means of relieving and controlling anxiety often work well enough to ease nervousness, fearfulness, and tension. Many people are satisfied with the calming, heartening effects of prayer or affirmation or the rejuvenating power of healthy exercise, or else they successfully "white-knuckle" their way through anxiety-provoking events and relationships. And many people are capable of problem-solving and toning down episodes of stress and can somehow transform excessive anxiety into creativity, energy, and good works. According to a Chinese proverb, "Out of difficulty, opportunity is born." Reasoned analyses of anxious perceptions help people to understand and improve disquieting aspects of their lives. However, if much of your anxiety occurs outside the

ℑt danger prevention and remains inadequately subdued despite your
ℑt efforts to soothe yourself, this book can offer you a wealth of ways to
control and relieve anxious discomfort and its oppression.

Some Examples of Anxiety Symptoms and Disorders

As you read the examples below of anxiety disorders drawn from our clinical practice, ask yourself whether your symptoms or signs of anxiety resemble those of the individuals described. You might also ponder a number
of other questions: Do you make decisions or sidestep certain activities
or people because of your fears? Does your anxiety make sense? Is your
anxiety proportionate to the situations you encounter, or is it an excessive, irrational, knee-jerk reaction that ill serves you and others? And, finally, would your life be improved if you could shed needless tension and
worry?

PANIC

Of all the anxiety symptoms, panic is the most terrifying and unsettling.
Wendy started having panic attacks just when she thought she had overcome her extreme distress at her boss's overbearing harshness. As his executive assistant, she felt pressured ever since the company won a premium
account. She found herself fighting an impulse to make sarcastic remarks
to her boss that she knew she would regret. Her smoking increased, and
she lost a few nights' sleep ruminating about how resentful she felt. Then
one day, on her way out of a mall where she had been shopping, she got
stuck in heavy traffic. Suddenly, she thought she was dying! She felt intense
uneasiness overtaking her. Her stomach churned. She looked everywhere
for an escape route but all she could see was wall-to-wall cars. Her heart
pounded violently in her chest and she started to tremble. These sensations
continued for about fifteen minutes, but they seemed to last forever.

Wendy had just experienced a panic attack. According to the *DSM-IV*, the
authoritative guidebook of psychiatric diagnoses, her symptoms were classic: She had a period of intense fear or discomfort that was accompanied
by multiple physical or mental symptoms of anxiety. In Wendy's case, they
were fear of losing control, abdominal distress, pounding heart, and trembling. Her symptoms developed abruptly, and they peaked rapidly. As is

often the case in a panic episode, Wendy felt a sense of impending doom and an urgent desire to flee.

PANIC DISORDER

Wendy had two more attacks during the next couple of weeks. She thought she recognized a pattern: She was most susceptible when she was in crowded places, so she gave up on Christmas shopping and changed her daily schedule to avoid rush-hour traffic. At this point, she had developed panic disorder. That is, she began to have "recurrent, unexpected panic attacks, followed by at least one month of persistent concern about having another panic attack, worry about the possible implications or consequences of the panic attacks, or a significant behavioral change related to the attacks."

SPECIFIC PHOBIAS

Specific phobias are irrational anxious reactions to very *specific* objects like snakes or bugs or *discrete* situations such as thunderstorms or Fridays the 13th.

Jennifer was fiercely protective of her little dog, Almo. When a neighbor moved in across the street with a feisty young German shepherd, Jennifer repeatedly approached her neighbor to urge him to reinforce his fence. One day, the shepherd jumped the fence and fiercely attacked her dog. Jennifer was injured while she tried to defend Almo. After that time, Jennifer experienced intense anxiety whenever she walked through her own and any other neighborhood with dogs. In fact, the mere sight of even a small dog would provoke an immediate anxiety response.

Jennifer's intense reaction mirrored that of many other persons with specific phobias. However, unlike Jennifer's fear of dogs, which emerged during adulthood after a traumatic incident, many adult phobias are the remnants of fears that have their origin in childhood. Whenever fear originates, it can attach itself to many different objects or situations, ranging from the commonplace to the esoteric. Fears we have treated include the sight of blood, thunder and lightning, bodies of water, bees and spiders, medicines, impure drinking water, loud sounds, people in clown costumes, and cheese (yes, it's true).

AGORAPHOBIA: A GENERAL SITUATIONAL PHOBIA

Randall had endured repeated panic attacks for several months, and his life had changed drastically for the worse. Because he feared he would panic, he quit his job and tried to work from home. He avoided bank lobbies and post offices, and could only shop in the middle of the night, in the absence of crowds.

Randall suffered from panic disorder with agoraphobia. Agoraphobia is defined by anxiety regarding situations where escape might be difficult or embarrassing or where help might not be available in the event of an anxious reaction. Agoraphobia often appears to be the direct result of full-blown panic attacks or milder "limited-symptom" attacks in which one or more panic symptoms such as a racing heart are present. Although some agoraphobics appear not to have such attacks, agoraphobia can make it virtually impossible to enjoy a normal life in all its fullness.

Although agoraphobia is technically a specific phobia, we term it a *general situational phobia* because it is capable of triggering anxious feelings in situations, events, or activities that have certain physical or environmental characteristics in common. Claustrophobia, another general situational phobia, involves a fear of confining spaces, whereas acrophobia involves a fear of high or precipitous places. Interestingly, many, if not most, people with symptoms of claustrophobia also suffer from agoraphobia, as agoraphobia is itself often associated with a fear of closed spaces.

Some, yet certainly not all, agoraphobic persons experience such severe symptoms that they become homebound, making it possible to confuse agoraphobia with other conditions that have quite different causes. For example, a person who has paranoid fantasies and delusions of being followed by the minions of Satan or a secret government agency might well be reluctant to step outside the house. However, the avoidance of a person with paranoia stems not from concerns about experiencing anxiety away from home, but from deeply distorted and unrealistic perceptions of the world.

SOCIAL PHOBIA

For as long as he could remember, Matt was uncomfortable with strangers and groups. As a boy, he tended to stutter in the classroom and when he felt he was "onstage." Although later in life he outgrew his tendency to stutter, in adulthood he came to fear virtually any situation in which he felt he had to perform. Matt saved money to move to Silicon Valley and jump-start his career as a software designer. His goal was to pitch his software design skills to dot-com upstarts. However, as he settled into his apartment, his daily life became fraught with painful inhibition. Although he made a number of professional contacts before he moved, he found that he lacked the nerve to arrange for interviews. He talked himself out of each job possibility, saying it was "not good enough," yet he occasionally had a flash of insight that this was only a rationalization for the fact that he feared he would stumble over his words during the interview and not measure up on the job. He held on to a relationship with an ex-girlfriend because he felt "too uptight" to date.

In the Eye of the Beholder

If it can be said that beauty is in the eye of the beholder, the same can be said for ugliness. Marc was preoccupied with the size of his ears. Though others found them unremarkable, to Marc they were too large and stuck out too far. In the winter he wore hats that covered his ears, and he developed a slap-dash and rumpled appearance because he avoided looking in mirrors for fear of catching a glimpse of his "jug ears." Thoughts about his ears infil-trated his daily life to the point that he often could not concentrate on his work as an accountant.

Surveys indicate that about 70 percent of the college population is dis-satisfied with some body part or aspect of their appearance. However, only about 1 percent of people in the community suffer from Marc's condition, body dysmorphic disorder (BDD)—an exaggerated dislike and preoccupa-tion with a physical attribute (e.g., nose, teeth, hair, size of penis, breasts) that is generally not noticeable to others.

The belief that a body part is ugly or disfigured can lead to intense dis-comfort in social situations. So it is not surprising that more than half of in-dividuals with BDD also meet the diagnostic criteria for social phobia. Yet not all individuals with BDD develop the feelings of embarrassment in so-cial or performance situations that qualify them for a social phobia diagno-sis. Nevertheless, many individuals who feel their body is disfigured or ugly do require a great deal of reassurance from others. Researchers and clini-cians are very interested in determining why some individuals with BDD develop social phobias while others do not.

Matthew is socially phobic: he fears social and performance situations that he associates with embarrassment or humiliation. Social fears can be so strong that a wide variety of situations ranging from appearing in front of an audience to performing specific public actions such as dancing, signing one's name, singing, and eating are avoided or only endured with dread. Of course, certain situations, such as delivering an important speech to a large audience, will ignite fears in most people. Accordingly, in order for social phobia to be diagnosed, the fears must be either excessive or unreasonable. It is worth pointing out that as many as 40 percent of college students describe themselves as shy, and that shyness per se is not problematic unless it begins to interfere with everyday functioning or causes undue distress.

GENERALIZED ANXIETY DISORDER

Unlike specific phobia and social phobia, generalized anxiety disorder (GAD) is a long-lasting, "portable" disorder that is not attached to specific objects, situations, or activities. GAD consists of anxious thinking, tension, and feelings of apprehension that intensify around potential threats.

Robert suffered from some degree of generalized anxiety for most of his life. In the past, work had been a haven for him, a way to channel his nervous energy into productive activity. A lifelong bachelor, his coworkers had become like a surrogate family. However, the closer retirement loomed in Robert's future, the more his work performance deteriorated. He became consumed by worries about avoiding mistakes and by daily apprehensiveness. He thought that retirement was the answer, but he was wrong. Work had served to maintain his feelings of competence and worthiness and also was his primary social outlet. When he did retire, he became more nervous than ever in an expanding variety of situations. Robert's generalized anxiety intensified because of the insecurity he felt in the absence of the validation of his work and the painful isolation of his new existence. Anxiety had become so much a part of Robert's life that he could no longer see himself as anything but a "nervous wreck."

Why Confront Anxiety?

Clinically significant problems at work, in social relationships, and in other important areas of functioning are hallmarks of GAD and of many of the other conditions we have introduced. However, in actuality, there is a tremendous range of anxiety symptoms, and each person imparts a unique negative meaning to anxiety in terms of the kind of limitations it places on his or her life. Indeed, our clients express a myriad of reasons for undertaking anxiety treatment. Yet many, if not all, of the reasons our clients express for initiating the dedicated work of overcoming anxiety are included in the categories we consider in the following section:

1. Keep in sync with peers

2. Fully participate in landmark life events

3. Enjoy liberty and life

4. Experience comfort with natural and normal levels of anxiety

5. Close the door on toxic stress

6. Restore and maintain a sense of general well-being

As you read the following stories of lives beleaguered by anxiety, key into how *your* life can improve when you are no longer burdened by excessive anxiety. Armed with a solid understanding of the payoff for engaging in the activities we present, you can optimize your opportunity to confront and conquer anxiety.

1. *Keep in sync with peers.* Marie, an agoraphobic, was afraid to attend the high school that was located a mile outside her "safe territory." Although bright, attractive, and humorous, she couldn't date because her anxiety became intolerable when she was alone in a car with a boy, particularly when it was far from home. She wasn't able to go to the movies, religious services, friends' parties, or ball games.

Anxiety forced Marie's development path to diverge from that of other teens. At the age of nineteen, when she entered treatment, her motivation to recover was very strong—she wanted her adolescence back! For Marie, overcoming anxiety meant overcoming social isolation, regaining momentum in achieving her goals, and restoring her hopes for a happy future of self-determination. Many challenging steps later, she vanquished her territorial limitations, attended vocational school, developed sophisticated employment skills, became employed and progressively promoted, dated, and married, and now travels quite freely. Marie's motivation for overcoming her fears was getting back in the developmental ball game, a compelling purpose especially common among young people.

2. *Fully participate in landmark life events.* Janine's panics had largely subsided through participation in a panic workshop, but she later returned to treatment as a recently married person, six months into her first pregnancy. Instead of joyously anticipating her baby's birth, Janine worried a lot about the anticipated loss of independence the baby's arrival would bring. The worry increased to the point that it interfered with her sleep and filled her with trepidation about her future. Janine also experienced apprehension and panicky feelings that resulted from constriction of breathing created by the pressure her big stomach exerted on her diaphragm and lungs.

Anxiety like Janine's can easily be stirred up in relation to marriage or weddings, learning how to drive a car, or coping with the illness of a close friend or relative. If untreated at the time, anxiety often precludes full participation in landmark life events. Fortunately, Janine was able to quiet her anxious thoughts by focusing on the joy her new child would bring her, enlisting her husband's support to care for their newborn, and learning to relax and take deep, calming breaths when the pressure created by her stomach created discomfort.

3. *Enjoy liberty and life.* Michael's family lived in a faraway country and was prepared to frequently fly him home to visit. However, this pleasure was rendered exceedingly uncomfortable by his phobia of flying. Actually, his fear of flying did not prove to be as debilitating as his more general fear of being in enclosed places. As you recall, this fear is known as claustrophobia. In fact, Michael was afraid of elevators and of being locked in restrooms as well. In airplanes, the terrible imagery of crashing, combined with his claustrophobic concerns about being trapped in a small place, made visiting his family seem prohibitive. By confronting his fears of confinement in small places, practicing relaxation techniques, and learning to quell his catastrophic thinking, he succeeded in training himself to travel comfortably by plane. With hard work in therapy, he was also able to ride elevators without fear and to use public bathrooms when he traveled.

4. *Experience comfort with natural and normal levels of anxiety.* Esteban suffered from "bashful bladder syndrome," a condition that made it difficult for him to use public urinals and restrooms. His recent job promotion was not without its downside since it required that he make several business trips with colleagues each month. Each time, the specter of embarrassment was raised because he was unable to urinate in restrooms in airports and in airplane bathrooms for fear of people waiting outside.

Long before he went on a trip, his anxiety would surface; and closer to the trip, he would become intensely anxious, knowing that he would not be able to urinate easily and might have to "hold it" for as long as six hours on some occasions. His anxiety in these situations escalated to the point that he contemplated requesting a demotion to a position that did not require travel. Fortunately, with consistent practice of relaxation techniques he was able to desensitize himself to his anxiety, gradually feel increasingly comfortable in public restrooms, and earn a job promotion that also involved occasional business trips. With his bashful bladder problem relieved, Esteban was able to deal with the normal anxieties and frustrations his job promotion entailed.

5. *Close the door on toxic stress.* After twenty years overseeing the operation of her factory's production line, Amanda thought she was cruising toward a comfortable retirement a couple of years down the road. However, her hopes for the future were dampened by the arrival of a "supervisor from hell," the emissary of the new executive team that had come to roost at corporate headquarters. Suddenly, her every decision was scrutinized and Amanda was required to produce copious reports to document and justify every aspect of the operation she had successfully put in place.

After Amanda developed insomnia and gastrointestinal problems and began to worry incessantly about her future, she wisely sought treatment. She recognized that she could either confront her boss head-on and thereby channel her worries and concerns into assertive action, seek employment elsewhere, or retire. Amanda chose to confront her fears and her supervisor as the first step in a plan of action developed in concert with her therapist. Fortunately, the confrontations with her supervisor cleared the air so that they were able to develop a cordial working relationship, after which Amanda experienced considerable anxiety relief.

6. *Restore and maintain a sense of general well-being.* Alice became highly anxious when she felt her heart beating rapidly and erratically during her organic chemistry final. She excused herself from the exam and went to the emergency room, convinced she was having a heart attack. After this episode, during and even before exams, Alice began to hyperfocus on her heart and its sometimes irregular rhythm and experienced nausea and heavy sweating as well. Each time this occurred, she thought she was having a heart attack. After her psychologist told her that she had "anxiety sensitivity," triggered by her focusing on her stress-related bodily symptoms that were not, in fact, truly a threat to her health, she felt much better. She worked actively on getting her anxiety symptoms in perspective, and they diminished in frequency and intensity until she was symptom-free two months later.

Alice was fortunate in that her anxiety episodes were not long lasting and were easily treated. However, for many thousands of people anxiety is persistent, pervasive, and does not remit so easily. Whatever its extent, anxiety gnaws at happiness and constricts the feeling of well-being.

Did you see yourself in any of the examples we presented? Perhaps you wondered whether you would be able to achieve success as each of the individuals depicted did. Overcoming anxiety can require hard work and dedication, yet it is well worth it. Successful anxiety therapy results in empowerment to assess threatening situations and to deal with fear, worry, and panic. Once you learn to cope with your anxious feelings, you can steer your way toward wide-open horizons of liberty and enjoyment of life, and anxiety may never regain the capacity to upset your mind again.

Are Anxiety Disorders Courage Disorders?

Many people with phobias and panic have discovered the excruciating experience of "white-knuckle coping" whereby they endure intense anxiety as they struggle to reenter situations they fear. No matter how courageous or strong their willpower, people with anxiety disorders can seldom take control of anxiety-related behaviors and physical reactions by means of sheer determination. Anxiety is a powerful force, and a sense of lack or loss of control is a central feature of these conditions.

However, anxiety disorders are not courage disorders. During times of grave mortal danger, such as when there is a threat to you or to those you care about, your mind will recognize the reality of the threat, mobilize your resources, and activate your impulses to contend with it. If your courage is called upon, you will discover that your customary level of bravery will infuse you and help you deal with the challenge.

But the mental effects of anxiety disorders make behavioral and physiological control difficult. Why beat a dead horse by persistently and unproductively pushing yourself and wishing for change while continuing to suffer? A much better alternative starts with converting demoralizing, anxious thinking into realistic, effective attitudes and strategies to accomplish your goals.

How Can This Book Help?

We, the authors, have known each other since boyhood and decided to pool our combined fifty years of clinical experience with anxiety conditions into an accessible, reader-friendly book grounded in the latest scientific theories and research. Much of the impetus for writing this book came from the frustration and disappointment we experienced when we learned of the ineffective treatments many of our clients had received. For example, some of our clients spent many unproductive years in treatment dredging up past traumatic memories supposedly related to their anxieties, while the current sources of their anxious discomfort were ignored or minimized by their therapists. Other clients told us their therapists repeatedly exhorted them to "just do it," that is, to confront terrible fears directly, in effect, to "get back up on the horse" after they were thrown, as a means of conquering their fears. Unfortunately, these clients received little or no preparation for doing so, and often were so overwhelmed by their fears that they avoided treatment for many years thereafter. Still other clients' therapists encouraged them to try various dietary supplements that drained their wallets but not their anxiety.

We felt out clients deserved better. This book is written with their needs, and yours, in mind. We provide the background necessary for you to become an anxiety technologist capable of applying a varied menu of techniques to help you face your fears and live your life to the fullest. The techniques we recommend are evidence-based and grounded in up-to-date science. Most research on anxiety disorders has been conducted with adults, but treatment of childhood anxiety is a major contemporary direction of study. Our clinical experience indicates that children as young as nine or ten can benefit from many of the strategies we discuss when assisted by an adult or mental health professional. The anxiety management strategies we present are not self-evident and are generally not taught in schools or even picked up from the School of Hard Knocks.

Novel to our treatment of anxiety is the application of a time-honored technique called *reverse engineering*. By working backward to figure out how to get a malfunctioning device functioning again, we can learn in the process what makes it tick. Reverse engineering helps keep things from children's bikes to artificial hearts running smoothly. When we apply it to anxiety disorders, we analyze catastrophic thinking and the false alarm signals of anxiety, determine what has gone wrong when the danger prevention system stops working properly, and describe techniques designed to systematically reverse the damage and restore healthy functioning. This is done in a straightforward, step-by-step manner by means of clear instructions that constitute an "operations manual" for relieving each disorder.

We describe *self-control training procedures* that attune the mind to think and act in ways that relieve panic and increase mental control, even while one is caught in the throes of anxiety. This powerful tool is essential for building a flexible, durable capacity to cope with anxious physical arousal in a wide assortment of real-life situations. You also will acquire two additional useful tools to contend with anxious thinking and to start dealing with phobic situations: *cognitive self-therapy* and *behavioral exposure techniques*. We ask you to try each intervention on for size and discover what works best for you.

A "Quick Fix"?

Can you expect a quick fix? Probably not. A book that promises a "quick fix" for everyone with severe anxiety is likely to be making a promise it cannot deliver. We make no such promise. It takes hard work, along with equal measures of hope and courage, to overcome anxiety. Not all readers are equally ready to face their fears. According to research by psychologist John Prochaska and his colleagues, people are at various stages in a process of change that unfolds as they surmount life's formidable challenges. We have encountered people with chronic anxiety for whom fear seems so normal that they don't even realize they have a problem. These individuals are at the earliest stage of the change process, *precontemplation*. If you are reading this book, you probably have attained at least the *contemplation* stage of change: You recognize you have a problem, even if you are hesitant to confront your personal monster in the cave. Our approach is designed to accelerate your movement through the *preparation* and *action* stages of change. In the preparation stage, you take tentative steps along the path of recovery, and in the action stage, you confidently implement the strategies and techniques we recommend. The last chapter of the book focuses on developing the skills necessary to *maintain* the gains you achieved and live your life to the fullest.

All treatment ultimately involves "self-help." However, self-help does not preclude the help of others. Because the grip of anxiety can be strong, it may be necessary for you to "work the program" with the help of a skilled therapist or medical practitioner. Just as some people attain peak physical fitness with the assistance of a coach or personal trainer, you may benefit from the support of a therapist or "work buddy." Much of the research on successful treatments we report is limited to treatment protocols in which therapists assist patients. Therefore, you may have the best chance of achieving success with the guidance and structure that a mental health professional can provide. Professional therapy will be especially important if you suffer from serious depression or other long-standing psychological problems unrelated to anxiety or are so overwhelmed by an anxiety disorder that you require medical consultation and medication. In each chapter in which it's relevant, a text box will clearly indicate when you should seek professional consultation.

An added benefit of medical consultation is to ensure that if there are psychiatric and medical conditions that occur side by side with your anxiety, they are recognized and taken into account. Some medical conditions that may occur simultaneously are thyroid or blood sugar imbalances, inner ear conditions, encephalitis, asthma, metabolic conditions such as vitamin B_2 deficiency, congestive heart failure and arrhythmias, pneumonia, hyperventilation, irritable bowel syndrome, and an often-benign heart condition called mitral valve prolapse. Indeed, the first line of evaluation should be your physician if you feel anxious with no apparent reason. In fact, when in doubt, our advice is to seek the help of a mental health professional or physician. Even though some readers will not be able to confront and conquer anxiety on their own, our hope is that reading this book will represent an important milestone on the path to recovery for all readers.

Chapter One

A Brief History of Anxiety
Disorders and Their Treatment

People throughout recorded history have been deathly afraid of snakes and spiders, terrorized by thunder and lightning, and filled with dread by such everyday experiences as being alone in a crowd of strangers. These commonplace fears are probably a by-product of human evolution, since the complete list—including fear of heights, large carnivores, darkness, blood, strangers, confinement, deep water, social scrutiny, and leaving home alone—bears a suspicious resemblance to our earliest ancestors' guide to the hazards of primeval existence.

Twenty-seven hundred years ago in the city-states of ancient Greece, agoraphobia got its name as a condition in which certain citizens, so "phobic" or stricken by fear, couldn't pass through the central city's open-air markets (agoras). Around the same time, the word *panic* came to refer to negative arousal reactions allegedly stimulated by Pan, the legendary Greek god of flocks and herds. A disturbing, intriguing entity, half man and half goat, Pan was reputed to appear unexpectedly and startle and stampede flocks. The music of his panpipes, sounding eerily in the woods at night, terrified travelers and, legend has it, sometimes would scare them to death. Both *anxiety* and *anger* derive from a common root in ancient Greek, namely *anchere*, describing a state of intense emotional disturbance in which breathing is difficult.

After ten thousand generations of considering, agonizing, appraising, obsessing, philosophizing, dreading, arguing, and pondering, people's worries have evolved into something we now refer to as generalized anxiety disorder (GAD), a complex of tension and incessant worry endured by people great and small. A modern-day agoraphobic person is likely to have attacks of apprehension when he is cut off from safety. This most commonly occurs in or near the following physical situations: at shopping malls or supermarkets, when flying in airplanes, riding in or driving cars, riding in elevators, getting caught in heavy street or freeway traffic, attending houses of worship, restaurants, theaters, and sports arenas, or being at home alone.

The great tides of change throughout the world over the past couple of centuries have altered the distribution of anxiety disorders. Urban population density has multiplied literally hundredfold, and many dozens of cities now have over a half million inhabitants. Yet the level of physical closeness in colonial America was greater than it is today. Families and even strangers shared close spaces and slept together in a single room, which they also used for bathing and eating. While the Industrial Revolution and the spread of urbanization have modernized civilization, many more individuals in our twenty-first-century cities feel lonely and insecure. Modern society's complex changes are overwhelming to many GAD sufferers, agoraphobics, claustrophobics, and social phobics, probably because their mechanisms for adaptation are fragile, and emotional oversensitivity increases their tendency to suffer from society's growing pains as if they were their own.

Social phobia, which is also known as extreme shyness, social anxiety, or dating anxiety, has grown in its capacity to impair modern-day people since the world population has grown so dramatically. City dwellers and residents of many other communities are surrounded by strangers with whom they must interact on a daily basis. It's natural that many people would feel painfully uncertain of others' responses.

Overview of Anxiety Medications

ANXIOLYTIC MEDICATIONS: BZDs

Anxiolytic, or anxiety-reducing, medication is often the first line of defense in anxiety treatment. Valium and Librium are two such medications, from a class called benzodiazepines (BZDs) that started being widely used during the 1960s. BZDs are still used extensively today to suppress anxiety

Hikikomori: A Hybrid of Social Phobia and Agoraphobia?

Recent media reports have described a fascinating phenomenon in Japan known as "Hikikomori." Hikikomori, or "those who isolate themselves," are an estimated up to 1 million youths (typically male) who isolate themselves in their bedrooms playing computer games, watching TV, and engaging in other solitary pursuits, often for years. They do not want to be seen and do not want to see others. Many drop out of school. Several of these reclusive youths have committed violent crimes that have attracted a great deal of publicity, but it is not the aggressiveness of a few Hikikomori that is relevant to our discussion, but their feeling that they have to "disappear" because of their shame that they are not "like other people," a strong value in Japanese society. Like severe social phobics, Hikikomori experience intense shame and embarrassment in social situations, and like severe agoraphobics, many express the sentiment that they literally cannot stray far from their established territories without experiencing great discomfort. In one report, a young man retreated even further when his parents ordered him to leave his room. The exact role of anxiety in the genesis of this fascinating phenomenon has yet to be determined. But careful study of Hikikomori promises to shed light on the role of culture in the expression of complex behaviors that bear at least a superficial resemblance to anxiety disorders well known in the West.

symptoms quickly and help restore anxious people's ability to function. Their reputation was tarnished by the specter of their potential addictiveness after Jacqueline Susann published the best-selling *Valley of the Dolls* in 1966, dramatizing the irony of sanctimonious, hypocritical suburbanites getting hooked on BZDs. But Valium and Librium continue to be widely prescribed for relief of tension and anxiety, and many people keep getting addicted.

In 1983, psychiatrist David Sheehan's landmark work, *The Anxiety Disease*, was published. It presented the causes, course, and treatments of "panic disorder with agoraphobia" in easily accessible form and announced a thrilling innovation for anxiety disorder sufferers—Xanax.

Xanax was the first high-potency BZD formulated specifically to stop panic attacks. In essence, high-potency BZDs suppress panic at the point in the brain where it becomes an unpleasant physical feeling. Xanax did its job so well that five years after hitting the drug counters, its manufacturer had sold more of it than any other prescription drug in history. The high-potency, antipanic BZD category has grown to include Klonopin, Ativan, and Serax, and it continues to be immensely popular.

ANTIDEPRESSANTS: TCAs AND SSRIs

Two types of antidepressant medication—TCAs (tricyclic antidepressants) and SSRIs (selective serotonin reuptake inhibitors)—also provide relief of anxiety. They are very different from BZDs in their effects. The anxiety-reducing properties of the TCA imipramine were first studied by pioneer psychopharmacology researcher Donald Klein in the late 1950s, and it soon came to be used commonly for anxiety problems, along with two similar compounds, desipramine and nortriptyline.

Only a few TCAs reduce anxiety, but most SSRIs do. In 1988, Prozac, the first and most famous SSRI, arrived on the U.S. market, followed by a

Medication Misconceptions

In our experience, clients who would benefit from antidepressant medications for the treatment of anxiety are reluctant to take them because they entertain misconceptions about these potentially helpful medicines. To dispel three common misconceptions:

1. Antidepressants are not habit-forming.

2. Depression is not a prerequisite to benefiting from them.

3. The decision to choose either an antidepressant or a BZD for medication treatment of anxiety generally does not depend on the presence or absence of depression.

If you have not taken antidepressant medications for the treatment of anxiety because of one or more of these misconceptions, we urge you to reconsider and talk with your physician or a mental health professional who is knowledgeable about medicines and their effects on the body.

series of other SSRIs and other "new generation" antidepressants with different, often milder side effects. The correct choice of an antidepressant, accurate knowledge of side effects, and the overall course of treatment are more complex than with BZDs, but they are often better treatments for anxiety and panic in the long run. It may be preferable to have them prescribed by a psychiatrist—we also refer to psychiatrists specializing in medication treatment as psychopharmacologists—rather than a nonspecialist M.D. If you are currently taking medications or contemplating a course of antidepressive or anxiolytic medicine, read on, and in chapter 3 you will find a much more detailed discussion of indications for medication, alternative types of medications, and how medications work.

Psychological Perspectives on Anxiety Treatment

The Psychodynamic Perspective

The modern history of psychological treatment for anxiety is often traced to the writings of Sigmund Freud (1856–1939), who originated the psychodynamic point of view. Freud believed that anxiety was associated with psychological conflict.

Have you ever felt a twinge of guilt when you thought of doing something illegal? Have you felt ashamed when you were caught red-handed doing something you were not supposed to be doing? Anxiety can be a product of conflict between the impulse to do something forbidden or illegal and your knowledge that it is wrong to act on the impulse. Embarrassment, shame, and humiliation are powerful feelings that act as a deterrent to engaging in many activities that are tempting, yet socially disapproved.

A moment's reflection suggests that individuals who do not restrain socially unacceptable impulses are likely to get themselves into a great deal of trouble. What if a person demanded sex with whomever struck her fancy? Or lashed out in rage at every person or object of her frustration? Or took possession of whatever appealed to her, even if it belonged to someone else? We suspect that a poorly ventilated jail cell, a cozy room in a mental hospital, or perhaps a worse fate would await such a person.

According to Freud, anxiety serves a valuable function. It prevents certain sexual and aggressive impulses, for example, from ever reaching consciousness or being expressed. Freud's case of Little Hans, one of the first cases of animal phobia to be studied, exemplifies his theory of how mental defenses serve to block feelings and conflicts from awareness. In a nutshell, Freud believed that Hans's fear of horses and being bitten by them actually represented his symbolic fear of retaliation from his father, who was the sole rival for his mother's love and the object of Little Hans's aggressive feelings. Because Hans also loved his father, he was highly conflicted. According to Freud's analysis, this conflict went "underground," and here's how it happened: Hans's love for his mother was repressed from consciousness, and his feelings of hatred for his father were displaced onto the horse, which Hans came to fear. The price of limiting awareness and suppressing consciousness is constriction of the capacity to think about and work through anxiety-provoking thoughts, feelings, behaviors, and situations.

According to Freud, when anxiety materializes, avoidance and repression have proven inadequate as defenses. The person becomes increasingly edgy, panicky, worried, apprehensive, and/or fatigued. The experiences of symptoms or attacks are disproportionately severe and frequent because they are actually reactions to cumulative, unresolved past stresses.

Freudian psychoanalytic treatment for anxiety disorders focuses on recalling and working through inner conflicts that were internalized when parents and significant others frustrated the anxious person's desire to love and be loved. The psychoanalyst's task is to help the patient to create a more meaningful, harmonious sense of self and to clear away the emotional distortions bred by past guilt and frustrations.

Extensive research and clinical experience with anxiety have challenged Freud's explanation of anxiety and demonstrated that an understanding and acceptance of one's emotional history, however deep and gratifying, ultimately does *not* relieve anxiety disorders or symptoms. But despite its very limited effectiveness, until the 1960s, psychoanalysis and other long-term psychodynamic approaches were the preferred treatments for phobias and anxiety neurosis. A precious artifact of psychoanalysis is its emphasis on the importance of recognition of underlying core fears. Another part of Freud's work became the foundation of exposure therapy: his repeated assertion that in order to recover from a phobia a person must be reexposed to situations like the one that initially instilled the fear and learn through treatment to cope with them differently.

THE LEARNING PERSPECTIVE

Although American psychologists have long studied the learning process, it is only in the last forty years or so that they have applied learning prin-

Inoculating Children Against Anxiety Disorders

Although the ideas of the psychoanalysts are intriguing, many have not garnered scientific support to date. However, the idea that childhood experiences are important, even crucial, determinants of character has been highly influential and is widely accepted by modern clinicians and researchers. Today we know that it is possible for caretakers to do much toward inoculating children against excessive fears. If you are a parent or caretaker, here are some things you can do to help your children contend with anxiety and keep it at manageable levels.

- Resist impulses to require young children to conform to adult time pressures.

- Ensure that young children feel secure, particularly when they are alone.

- Limit the extent of children's exposure to aggression.

- Don't smother children with overly protective parenting. Instead, help them develop ways of discussing with themselves, reframing, and manipulating excessively anxiety-provoking situations to reduce discomfort and increase coping skills (see chapters 5, 7, 9, 11, and 13).

- Refrain from frightening children with warnings about dangers in the environment, such as spiders or insects, that adults exaggerate because of their own excessive or irrational anxiety.

- Help children develop social skills, withstand social pressures, and overcome their social anxiety—that is, their fears of embarrassment, self-consciousness, shyness, and performance anxiety.

ciples to the analysis and treatment of adaptive and nonadaptive behaviors symptomatic of psychological disorders.

According to learning theory, fears are not determined by unconscious conflicts. Instead, they are learned. The story of how fears can be learned is nicely conveyed by Watson and Rayner's famous demonstration.

Watson and Rayner chose an eleven-month-old child named Albert as their subject. Albert was very fond of animals, including the small, furry variety. Their goal was to show that through *classical conditioning,* fears that looked irrational and phobic could be learned.

In the laboratory, they closely observed Albert's behavior. Whenever he reached out for a white rat to which he was attracted, a loud noise was created. Not surprisingly, Albert was startled and began crying. After a number of such pairings of the white rat with the loud noise, Albert was terrified whenever the rat was presented to him. Because Albert's reaction generalized to other furry objects as well, Watson and Rayner were able to argue that they had demonstrated that apparently irrational fears (phobias) could be learned through classical conditioning. That is, by pairing a previously neutral stimulus (the rat) with a stimulus that could evoke a strong response (the loud noise) it was possible to obtain a fear reaction to the rat when it was later presented by itself.

The second major mechanism used to explain how anxiety is acquired and maintained is called *instrumental conditioning.* According to a number of psychologists, most notably B. F. Skinner, rewards and punishments are extremely important in understanding the development of anxiety. For example, if a socially awkward girl repeatedly experiences rejection when she asks boys out for dates to the movies, she may become shy and anxious around boys. If this pattern of rejection continues, she might develop a full-blown social phobia. Note that her avoidance of boys is actually rewarding, because it allows her to escape the negative consequences of social interaction with them, thereby pepetuating her avoidance.

In his classics, *Psychotherapy by Reciprocal Inhibition* and *The Practice of Behavior Therapy,* physician Joseph Wolpe described his pioneering experiments in treating psychological disorders, particularly phobias. He helped people learn to overcome intense discomfort by first relaxing in the face of the mildly uncomfortable situations that they had come to avoid. For example, in the case of the socially phobic girl, she might first learn and practice social skills with friends in groups before she confronted the more anxiety-provoking task of dating boys. The technique of gradual, stepwise exposure to a feared situation is known as *systematic desensitization,* a technique you will practice as you master your fears.

During the 1960s, Mowrer's *two-factor theory* guided a great deal of conceptual work in understanding and treating anxiety. In its simplest terms, two-factor theory can be illustrated by way of example. Imagine that a child is bitten by a large black dog and taken to the hospital by his frantic parents. It would be easy to see how the child might come to associate dogs with pain and come to fear dogs by way of classical conditioning. Over time, the child's fears may generalize so that he comes to fear not only the dog that bit him, but also dogs of all sizes and colors; he might even become anxious in a park when dogs are not in sight. It is interesting to note that about half of clinical phobias arise by way of this classical conditioning process.

Yet the crucial question that two-factor theory addresses is: What maintains the phobia? The answer to this question is avoidance or escape, the second factor in the process of learning fear. The unfortunate consequence of this learned response is that by avoiding or escaping situations that involve dogs, the child never learns from direct experience that he is unlikely to be bitten by another dog. In learning theory terms, the fear is never extinguished or unlearned. You will recall that because avoidance or escape reduces anxiety it is reinforced. And as the child continues to avoid dogs, the fear can even incubate and grow.

Two-factor theory provides the conceptual foundation for the exposure techniques. By confronting your fears in a step-by-step, systematic, and controlled way, you reclaim your ability to approach the situations you have learned to fear.

Learning theorists such as Rachman believe that at least some, although not the majority, of fears can also be acquired by:

1. Observing others engage in fearful behaviors and modeling those fearful behaviors (for example, observing your mother's fear of dogs) and

2. Receiving information or misinformation from others that leads to fearful behavior.

You will be interested to learn that regardless of how a fear is learned, exposure seems to be helpful in treating a variety of anxiety-related conditions.

THE COGNITIVE PERSPECTIVE

Cognitive theories explore how a person's attitudes, beliefs, and expectancies about a situation influence subsequent behavior. The cognitive perspective is illustrated by the different reactions people have to the same stimulus or event, a point that is vividly exemplified by the situation described in the box on the following page.

As early as 1955, Albert Ellis, a noted cognitive therapist, applied the

On the Border between Virtual and Actual Reality—What Do You Think?

Picture yourself with two friends, Jason and Mark. You and your friends are trying out a virtual reality device, a contraption consisting of a helmet that fits over your head. This high-tech device operates by simulating real environments and is programmed to move through a sequence of three simulated scenarios.

You each place the helmets on your heads in separate cubicles. In scene 1, a cool salty breeze is blowing. The sun is bright and the sky deep blue. The vast ocean roars from every direction. Incredibly, you discover you're in a bathing suit, poised astride a surfboard "riding the edge"—gliding swiftly along the crest of a long, high breaker wave. Suddenly, the ocean fades away, replaced by scene 2: Dramatic peaks line the horizon; the snow is white and crisp. You ski swiftly downward, dipping and bending with splendid grace, the icy air whooshing past your face.

Next, scene 3: You're alone on a stage, a few feet in front of a cliff above a seemingly bottomless chasm. On the other side, a multitude of people surrounds the stage, talking to one another, waiting for you to sing "(I Did It) My Way," and then to make a speech about your most embarrassing life experiences. The sequence concludes and you find each of the scenes has been invigorating in its own way.

When you discuss your reactions to the different scenes, you discover that Mark particularly enjoyed the surfing and skiing scenes, but experienced abject terror in the face of the audience on the cliff. And then you discover that Jason felt a surge of positive energy singing "My Way," but couldn't wait for the terrifying skiing scene to end.

What explains the two friends' polar opposite reactions? A cognitive therapist would start with an examination of the specific thoughts and beliefs, expectancies, and interpretations related to each of the scenarios that each of the friends brings to the experience. What she would discover was that Mark was the foster child of a couple who had met when they competed in the Olympics. He surfed in the summer and skied in the winter from the time he was a child. However, he was highly self-critical in social situations, believed that he had little or nothing of value to say to others, and predicted a catastrophic audience reaction whenever he was required to deliver a speech.

Jason, on the other hand, was raised in a family of Shakespearean actors, and he'd always enjoyed playing the parts they would make up for him throughout his childhood. Jason once had a terrible accident on his bike when his brakes failed on a steep downhill slope. After this, he anticipated he would lose his balance and fall when he would go downhill. These radically different experiences of the same simulated events illustrate the power of cognitive factors—anticipations, expectations, and interpretations—in shaping our personal reality.

verb *catastrophize* to the way people think when they are anxious. Ellis later coined the term *awfulizing* to describe a tendency to greatly exaggerate the frequency, danger, or unpleasantness of a negative feeling or aspect of the environment that one dislikes. At the heart of awfulizing is the irrational belief that "life proves awful, terrible, horrible, or catastrophic when things do not go the way you would like them to go." According to Ellis, a person can awfulize that feeling anxious is terrible and "panic about panicking"—mentally escalating minor anxiety into a panic attack.

Another irrational belief can serve as a basis for *perfectionism:* "I must prove myself to be thoroughly competent, adequate, and achieving." This belief leads to a tendency to set impossibly high standards and avoid mistakes at all costs. It is related to fears of embarrassment and humiliation, obsessive-compulsive behaviors such as washing one's hands until they are "perfectly" clean, and excessive worry in situations in which performance is scrutinized. If you have endorsed beliefs associated with awfulizing and perfectionism, a cognitive therapist like Ellis would challenge you to modify your "irrational thinking." In fact, these two beliefs are among twelve irrational ideas that Ellis identifies as quite destructive yet nevertheless common in our culture. Ellis's Rational Emotive Therapy (RET) vigorously attacks the client's irrational beliefs and stimulates an adaptive, rational approach to living.

Aaron Beck, another cognitive therapy pioneer, has called attention to "automatic negative thoughts" (such as, "If I give the presentation, I'll make a fool of myself") and their power to generate anxiety. Ellis, Beck, and other cognitive therapists are united in the belief that the linchpins of anxiety—irrational beliefs and negative thoughts—have to be identified, challenged, and changed.

Consider the thought process of a woman who is striving to return to the workforce after raising her children. She dismisses out of hand the opportunity to attend computer classes by telling herself she will not be able to tolerate sitting in a classroom with other students and the teacher blocking her access to the exit.

If left unchallenged, this line of thinking might well prevent the woman from undertaking a highly rewarding activity. Therefore, the cognitive therapist would ask the client to carefully examine the likelihood of the predicted event, assess how overwhelming the feared outcome would be, and encourage her to recognize and develop resources that would make it unlikely to occur. In the upcoming chapters, we introduce you to many such cognitive strategies for becoming "anxiety smart."

Cognitive-Behavioral Treatments

Within the past twenty years or so knowledge of the successes of behavioral and cognitive treatment spread throughout the academic and professional communities, so that by the 1980s, therapists and clinics developed innovative combinations of these approaches, known as "cognitive-behavioral" therapies. Cognitive therapy focuses on changing the specific types of disturbing, apprehensive thoughts and expectancies that occur in connection with anxious discomfort. Behavior therapy, in turn, helps the phobic person develop and implement action plans to relieve anxious feelings. Typically, anxiety psychotherapy includes elements of both cognitive and behavioral techniques.

Unlike classical psychoanalysis, cognitive-behavioral treatment (CBT) is generally brief and cost-effective. A great deal of research has been conducted on cognitive-behavioral psychotherapies, and while they do not help everyone, they are generally beneficial. In one study, 85 percent of people with panic disorder treated with cognitive-behavior therapy and no medication improved after four months of therapy, while only 78 percent of those treated with BZDs and no psychological treatment improved, and the latter group was very apt to rely on the medication for their continued improvement. CBT reduces the risks and overcomes the limitations of medication therapy, but may initially be more uncomfortable, because it does not suppress or immediately relieve physical symptoms. Often medications can be artfully prescribed in the context of effective psychotherapies.

The last decade of the twentieth century has been labeled alternately as the Decade of Emotion and the Decade of the Brain. As psychology and neuroscience strove to attain a profound grasp of human nature, new perspectives emerged that enhanced the range and effectiveness of anxiety disorder treatments. A great many people have recovered from anxiety disorders partially or completely.

In this book, up-to-the-minute information about anxiety from the viewpoints of neuroscience, psychology, and the personal experiences of many people who have recovered from anxiety disorders will build and boost your working knowledge of the most effective treatments. In the chapters that follow, emphasizing the cognitive-behavioral approach, we will give you the means to put these treatments to work to improve your life.

Chapter Two

Fundamental Concepts

What is the difference between feelings and moods? What kinds of stresses are likely to provoke anxiety? Are certain people particularly predisposed to experience anxiety? What is the link between thoughts, feelings, and behaviors? Why is it important to directly expose yourself to the monsters in your cave—your fears and phobias? Answers to these questions are fundamental to understanding the rationale for the cognitive-behavioral techniques you will encounter in the chapters that follow.

Emotional Feelings vs. Moods

It is important to understand the differences between moods and emotional feelings, because each anxiety disorder has its own characteristic blend of feelings and moods. The example that follows illustrates this distinction. Tara took a seat in the room where the anxiety disorders treatment group was being held. This was her first session, so she didn't know what to expect. She was so nervous that she trembled and became tongue-tied when it was her turn to speak. The facilitator helped her relax and soon she was describing the burning sensations she'd suddenly felt all over her head during her best friend's wedding six weeks earlier. She recalled how her heart had pounded until it seemed like it was filling her throat. She had become dizzy and couldn't breathe, and the bright lights of the room had blinded her. These sensations came on very suddenly, one on top of the other. She felt so trapped and helpless that she wished she could disappear. Tara's date saw from her expression that something was terribly wrong, but she couldn't explain it to him. It was all she could do not to burst into tears as they hurried away from the reception. This was a typical reaction for Tara. After every panic, she could think of little but to obey her gut instincts to escape and subsequently to avoid places where attacks occurred. Seldom did Tara feel secure enough to relax a little and enjoy herself.

Paul, a stockbroker, spoke next. He expressed sympathy and astonishment that a young woman like Tara could be so troubled, and then recounted his own history. One afternoon he learned that the Dow-Jones stock market average had dropped precipitously. He got nervous and his appetite disappeared. At home that evening, he became consumed with worry about his wife's and his retirement funds and then began to fret about his whole extended family's finances. Paul started checking the stock prices hourly and turned every family gathering into a chance to harangue his relatives about investment strategies. During the subsequent month, he grew increasingly irritable with his staff and started suffering from tension headaches. His anxious mood, triggered by the market downturn, gradually expanded into a generalized anxiety state—a cloud of worrisome thinking and physical tension.

Let's examine the differences between Tara's and Paul's anxiety problems as well as their similarities. Paul's anxiety snuck up gradually and filled him with uneasiness, while Tara's attacks of intensely uncomfortable panic seemingly emerged out of the blue. Both Tara and Paul realized that they felt threatened, but their respective senses of security were breached by very different experiences with anxious distress. Both had become anxious about the future, too—Tara about having more attacks and becoming even more immobilized, Paul about losing everything in the event of a stock market crash.

Tara and Paul both suffer from anxiety disorders, but their respective presentations suggest that Tara's panic disorder is built around *anxious emotional feelings* while the central feature of Paul's more generalized anxiety is an *anxious mood*. You can see from Tara's account of what happened that she suffers from intense emotional feelings of fear and panic, while tension and apprehensive thinking are elements of Paul's anxious mood.

The contrasting presentations of Tara and Paul illustrate some of the fundamental differences between moods and emotional feelings. Paul's moods lasted longer than Tara's emotional feelings of panic. Short-lived and intense, feelings often trigger actions or embody impulses that can be difficult to resist, as when Tara felt like running out of the room. Tara's feelings of alarm and her urge to escape are the product of her deep-seated, disturbing reaction to stressful situations. In the early twentieth century, Walter Cannon first identified physiological stress reactions and the "fight-or-flight" reaction that Tara suffered as an *emergency response* (ER) to immediate, mortal danger. For the next several decades, physician and endocrinologist Hans Selye studied how this instinctual mechanism triggers intensely negative feelings of fear, anxiety, or anger and explained how these feelings can evolve into extended states of great stress such as anxious moods and chronic anxiety states.

Emotional Feelings
- Are sudden, intense, and often quite brief

- Are associated with "gut feelings"

- Make us want to take quick action or freeze

- Trigger *behavior* toward or away from someone or something

- May not be conscious

Moods
- Have gradual onset and may linger for hours or days

- Involve a measure of tension and a large measure of thinking

- Subtly change the state of readiness to act

- Manifest as *changes in the tone of thinking*

- May involve other negative emotions like depression, irritability, or mortification

A number of panic disorder sufferers fall first into an anxious mood that lowers their panic threshold, and then an attack is ignited. For many others, the intense emotional and physical feelings of panic come out of nowhere, and after the worst has passed, an anxious mood may set in that opens the floodgate of disturbing thoughts. That was the case with Tara: After she panicked, she feared that her attack would turn into a major disaster and that more attacks would follow. Sometimes she would spend many hours drifting among anxious moods in which she convinced herself that her luck had run out and then, as the mood deepened, drew unwarranted, pessimistic conclusions about her future.

Tara's and Paul's distresses illustrate a characteristic of anxious moods—*mood-congruent thinking*. All sorts of negative thoughts arise as moods persist, many far removed from the triggering emotional feeling save for their similarly grim and negative emotional tone. Experts actually classify anxiety as a loose structure of negative feelings and thoughts, so it's not unusual for a person in an anxious mood to get depressed, guilty, or even disgusted. The upside of mood-congruent thinking is that when our moods are good or joyous, all sorts of happy thoughts flow into our minds.

Anxiety Sensitivity

Anxiety sensitivity (AS) is the predisposition to experience anxious discomfort and develop anxiety disorders. Identified by psychologists Steven Reiss and Richard McNally in 1985, AS is nearly as widespread as redheadedness. It is a tendency to react strongly to anxiety-provoking stimuli, so a person with high AS will have a propensity to notice and attend to, rather than ignore, physical sensations. Moreover, she will tend to misinterpret normal bodily feelings as abnormal and thus react to them negatively with worry and distress, in effect transforming physical feelings into emotional feelings. According to Albert Ellis, even slightly disturbed feelings can lead to awfulizing—the experience of anxiety about anxiety—and the conviction that panic is imminent. The anxious distress or mood will often continue long after the original threat dissipates, perpetuated by acute sensitivity to the physical sensations the person associates with anxiety and the belief that "I must be perfectly free from anxiety." In time, even the hint of anxiety can trip wire a full-blown panic attack. Thus, due to anxiety sensitivity *the experience of physical sensation becomes a threatening situation in itself,* and can easily escalate into heightened anxiety.

Panickers get intensely disturbed by physical stress symptoms, while GAD sufferers, agoraphobics, and generalized social phobics (people who are phobic regarding all sorts of social and performance situations, such as parties, interviews, meetings, and dates) anxiously overreact while attempting to cope with stressful interpersonal and environmental situations or events.

But people with all these conditions share the trait of high anxiety sensitivity. AS can be measured by a brief psychological test called the Anxiety Sensitivity Index (ASI). A person who scores high on the ASI is relatively likely to develop an anxiety disorder during his lifetime.

AS is the product of nature, nurture, and experience. Research indicates that AS is partly genetic. Some infants are nervous from birth: A significant portion of sixteen-week-old children fret, cry, and show distinctly high levels of fear, which psychologists conjecture is a product of their inheritance. Unless the parents of these children compensate for their tendency to worry, some children may feel helplessly overwhelmed and unable to cope with nervous situations throughout childhood and into adulthood.

However, by the age of six most children have reached the developmental stage when they have internalized the capacity to reassure themselves in familiar social situations. Fortunately, the anxiety-proneness of many children dissipates by the time they turn seven and a half. Apparently the security and relief that many families are able to provide is sufficient to offset their children's fearfulness.

The news about the contribution of experience to AS is both good and bad. First, the bad news: Adult trauma victims or individuals subject to intense, prolonged stress can become sensitized to anxiety. The good news is that anxiety sensitivity generally decreases significantly when a person gets successful treatment or recovers from an anxiety disorder.

WHAT TRIGGERS ANXIETY?

Three types of events trigger anxiety: increases in physical or mental stress, fractures of important relationships, and events that arouse very intense feelings that alter perceptions of how toxic or frightening a situation or milieu can be.

1. *Sustained increases in physical or mental stress.* Repeated stressors, particularly traumas, strongly impact individuals with low thresholds for anxiety. The highest-impact stressors are conditions that affect the ease or effort with which mental or physical actions can be executed. Physical stress could take the form of severe or prolonged discomfort, such as pain or infection, which prevents thinking or sleeping or weakens a person beyond the point where he or she can work or socialize. Mental stress is provoked by situations that don't appear to resolve, problems that seem unsolvable, and threats to a sense of security. A pattern of uneasy thinking

can develop in which every day seems marked by apprehension, rumination, or obsession.

2. *Fractured relationships.* Anxiety can be triggered by problems in important personal relationships in which trust is breached or support is withdrawn, and insecurity develops. For instance, the relationship between spouses can fracture when one spouse fails to aid and support the other during a serious illness or family crisis. The most vulnerable relations involve parents, spouses, lovers, friends, children, teachers, partners, or employers.

3. *Shocking anxiety-provoking events.* When shocking events occur, familiar or manageable situations can become confusing and overwhelming. Examples include events like a car accident, violent death, mortal illness, natural disaster, a congenial close relationship suddenly turning nasty, or a trusted person being indicted for a crime. In such dire straits, the anxious person may become too confused or shaken to cope.

WHAT HAS TRIGGERED *YOUR* ANXIETY?

Challenging relationships, shocking experiences, and the cumbersome machinery of living sometimes converge upon a person. Tension and worry mount up. A shadow falls across your sense of well-being—the shadow of the monster in the cave.

If you are ready to contend with your anxiety, take a few minutes to consider the sources of your anxious discomfort. Which people, or what situations or activities, stimulate your anxiety? List your answers below. Next to each person, situation, or activity, rate from 1 to 100 points the amount of anxious discomfort you attribute to him, her, or it. Total your ratings, and don't be concerned if they do not equal 100 points.

Now divide each of your ratings by the total in order to convert them into percentages. For instance, Gina listed three items, whose total was 125, and she rated Item A as 25, so that A = 25/125 = 20%; Item B was 38, so B = 38/125 = 30%; and Item C was 63, so that C = 63/125 = 50%. Fill in the blank pie chart on the following page with a slice for each item, sizing each slice proportionate to the percentage you calculated for it. Gina's pie chart is illustrated on the left. By filling in the pie on the right with the sources of your anxious discomfort, you will heighten your awareness of the role that anxiety plays in your present life.

Worksheet 2.1
THE SOURCES OF MY ANXIOUS DISCOMFORT

Source of Anxious Discomfort	Discomfort Rating (1–100)	Percentage of Total
A. _____	_____	_____
B. _____	_____	_____
C. _____	_____	_____
D. _____	_____	_____
E. _____	_____	_____
F. _____	_____	_____
Total:	_____	_____

Sources of Gina's Anxious Discomfort

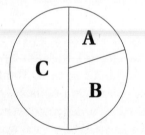

Sources of My Anxious Discomfort

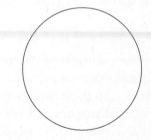

Anxious Thinking

Anxious thinking is a fundamental part of anxiety disorders. People with phobias think anxiously about their inhibitions and ways to avoid what they fear. A claustrophobic person plans how to avoid situations like being in elevators and may also conceal his anxiety from others. Someone with panic disorder gets nervous thinking about the possibility of panicking whenever she feels dizzy or short of breath. The thoughts of a person with GAD are periodically flooded with uncontrollable worry. Frightening thoughts, images, and memories tumble into the spider-phobic person's mind as soon as she peers into the dusty, neglected toolshed and notices all the webs.

Marnie, who suffers from social phobia, is attending an impromptu gathering of a few friends and classmates. She's secretly been rehearsing speaking to groups for a few weeks and decides to take a chance and recount an interesting story she just received in her email. She cautiously launches into it, and her audience seems pleasant and attentive. Then she hears a laugh, loses the thread, and hunts for the source of the distraction. Ted is grinning ear to ear while his neighbor Ben is looking down, struggling to hold back laughter. "I must sound really silly," she thinks, and becomes increasingly anxious and tongue-tied.

Afterward, Marnie confided to her friend Nan how foolish she felt. Nan admitted wondering what had flustered Marnie after such a good beginning. Marnie explained that she felt mortified when the guys laughed at her.

Marnie's reaction was determined by her bias to think in socially anxious ways. She was hypervigilant for signs of ridicule like Ted's laughter, and prone to misinterpreting ambiguous responses, like Ben's expression, as negative. Her social phobia disinclined her from contending strategically with the fear that she was losing her audience—by adding amusing details, for instance—and instead she became distracted, tongue-tied, and self-critical.

Nan's account of Ben's and Ted's actions surprised Marnie. She'd heard Ben whisper to Ted to look at his shoes and glanced down at the same time he did, only to discover Ted had dressed in one black shoe and one brown shoe! Marnie had been certain she'd made a fool of herself, but this alternate account of the events changed everything. She felt very relieved when she learned what Nan had seen. All that had actually changed was the way she thought about the situation, but that was sufficient to alter drastically the way she felt about herself. The reason? An experience or situation does not determine the way we feel. Our thoughts, attitudes, and beliefs about the experience determine the way we feel. This key point provides the rationale for the cognitive-behavioral approach we present in this book.

A person with phobias or untreated panic may function as an ultrasensitive anxiety barometer, a divining rod for subtle stressors and the threatening aspects of situations. She may grow uncomfortable and impelled to withdraw from situations that normally provoke only slight anxiety in others. Anxious thinking may lower the threshold for anxious emotional feelings, opening the way for physical anxiety symptoms and for "social anxiety feelings" like embarrassment or shame

A chronically anxious thinker generally has a high baseline level of tension as well as difficulty relaxing, so that a relatively minor additional stressor can trigger her GAD by making her feel consumed with worry or perhaps tip her over the edge into panic. A chronic sense of uneasiness can also be engendered by perfectionism, the deeply ingrained belief that "I must be perfect, flawless, and not make mistakes." Donny Osmond, Barbra Streisand, and Alanis Morisette are among the celebrities who have had to contend with anxiety related to their strivings for perfection. Consider the distress that acclaimed author Sylvia Plath's confession reflects: "[I] lived under the shadow of fear: fear that I would fall short of some absract perfection (Plath, 1982, p. 178)." Plath committed suicide at the age of thirty. Perfectionism can impede the success of psychological and pharmacological anxiety treatments, and we urge you to seek the support of a mental health professional if the strategies and techniques we recommend prove less than effective.

Table 2.1 depicts the distinctive thinking patterns and features of each disorder. Note that general situational phobias such as claustrophobia are quite different from panic, yet both have elements of GAD thinking—that is, in both the focus is on apprehension about possible bad future events. In the case of panic, this apprehension might take the form of fear of driving to work. A person who is phobic about using elevators might debate whether she could accept an appointment from a renowned specialist with a sixth-floor office. And the GADer is consumed with worry about his son who is using the family car for the first time to take his girlfriend to a concert. Apprehension, phobic fears, and worry are thinking patterns characteristic of anxiety disorders.

Cognitive-behavioral treatment (CBT) of anxiety disorders begins with understanding and developing skills to modify these thinking patterns. The starting point of your CBT can be as straightforward as modifying ways you reason with yourself or coax yourself through certain anxious situations. Sound challenging? Think how much harder it would be to directly control the other features of the disorders, like blocking your physical reaction, for instance. Imagine trying to effectively control panic by telling yourself, "No, I'm afraid this is just too inconvenient of a time for me to panic. You see, I have to pick up a graduation present before three!" Or imagine simply commanding yourself to modify fearful thoughts in the thick of anxious arousal, trying to wish a symptom away by roaring "ab-

Table 2.1
ANXIETY DISORDERS, TRIGGERS, THOUGHTS, AND BEHAVIORS

Anxiety Disorder	Triggers	Physical	Panic Attacks?	Types of Anxious Thoughts	Behaviors
Panic	Negative physical arousal and phobic situations	Acute fear reaction	Yes	Anticipation of future attacks; apprehension about catastrophic outcomes; rumination about mental and physical defects	Seeking emergency help, erratic escaping, paralysis with fear, and avoidance
General Situational Phobia	Feeling cut off from safety and security alone or in public	Anxiety when in or near phobic situations	Yes, except when extensively avoidant	Apprehension of panicking and of catastrophic outcomes; rumination about impairment of coping ability	Avoidance, inhibited behavior when approaching phobic situations, escaping
Generalized Anxiety Disorder (GAD)	Anxiety about work or school, family, health, finances, etc.	Chronic tension and inability to relax	Anxiety attacks in some cases	Unhealthy apprehension, obsession, and rumination about finances, friends and family, chores and work, or health	Fidgeting, procrastination, safety checking, some avoidance
Social Phobia	Anxiety about interpersonal performance or interaction	High tension in or near phobic situation	In some cases	Maladaptive thinking about social and interpersonal performance matters, with dread of scrutiny, embarrassment, and humiliation	Same as general situational phobia, above

solutely no light-headedness! Forget it!" How do you feel when people tell you to quit worrying so much or not to be so panicky? Do you benefit from trying to *force* yourself to relax or to overcome intense nervousness? Wouldn't your purpose be better served by learning techniques of friendly persuasion?

AUTOMATIC THOUGHTS

Do you feel anxious just imagining your phobic situations? Does your anxiety level soar when you think of a worrisome topic or recall a recent anxiety attack? Do waves of anxious thoughts, mental images, or memories sometimes flow into your mind unbidden and affect your comfort level? If so, then you have experienced the *automatic thoughts* that drive anxiety and panic.

Automatic thoughts (ATs) are images of possible physical, mental, or social harm. ATs are part of our evolutionary anxiety system whose purpose is to stimulate us to be ready to take action to protect ourselves from imminent mortal danger. ATs are based on memories, real or imaginary, of past experiences that triggered similar distress. According to cognitive neuroscientist Michael Gazzaniga, our brain cobbles together our past experiences into a coherent narrative that helps guide our present actions and generates predictions. The predictions may be:

- About oneself ("I'm afraid I'm going to throw up" or "I'm losing control of my car")

- Estimations of others' reactions ("They will think I've made a huge mistake")

- Mental images (imagining an adversary is huge and malicious-looking)

These dire predictions spring into the mind with the spontaneity of a flashbulb popping and present themselves as apparently certain assertions—despite the fact that they are often inaccurate and arise without prior systematic reasoning!

How do ATs operate? Because they bypass conscious awareness, they are quicker than rational thoughts. They are action-oriented and urgent ("I've just *got* to *do* something!"). Swiftness and immediacy are made paramount by sacrificing accuracy for speed. Here are three distortions of accurate reasoning characteristic of ATs:

- *Self-confirmation*—ATs highlight data that justify an anxious reaction while fostering suppression or ignoring of memories or facts that could cause self-doubt ("Why let a few bothersome facts obstruct a great action plan?").

- *Overgeneralization*—ATs connect often-dissimilar events, like equating heavy breathing during sex with hyperventilation during panic. As a result of overgeneralization, a person with panic disorder might tend to avoid sex in order to avoid breathing heavily and being reminded of panic or becoming afraid. This distortion is commonly stated as "Better to be safe than sorry."

- *All-or-nothing thinking*—ATs make it sound as if the dreaded event were 100 percent certain to occur and the outcome totally catastrophic, rather than "pretty likely" or "rather bad."

Two additional ways that ATs are inaccurate stem from their integral role in anxiety disorders. When emotionally charged thinking distorts the perspectives of people with anxiety disorders, it commonly does so by *personalizing* the consequences of events—so that the individual's point of view is constricted to focus almost exclusively on feared *personal* consequences. For example: "Everybody's looking at me making a fool of myself," or "I can't breathe in here [despite the fact that nobody else seems to be gasping for breath], so I'm afraid I'll pass out from lack of oxygen." A second distortion characteristic of ATs in emotional disorders—one almost synonymous with "neurotic thinking"—is *reacting to the present as if it were the past*. Brittany, for example, got so sick from eating fish on Catalina Island five years ago that she hasn't eaten fish since.

Anxious automatic thoughts narrow the person's view of the world, inhibit his coping ability, and demoralize him. Although stimuli for automatic thoughts bear little resemblance to the landmark event or situation that triggered the anxiety in the first place, every anxious reaction to a false alarm, where fear occurs in the absence of immediate danger, intensifies the expectancy of panic or adds another trigger for future attacks. With all their capacity to distort thinking in frightening ways, no wonder ATs have such malign power! When ATs hold sway, situations and events that used to feel good, or at least never used to provoke much anxiety, are avoided entirely, while others are approachable only with trepidation.

ANXIETY PROPOSITIONS

Anxiety propositions are quickly formulated, generally inaccurate descriptions of the apparent connection between specific anxiety-provoking events, situations, or activities and specific feared consequences. Understanding anxiety propositions is an important foundation for understanding and relieving anxiety disorders.

Consider the way Doug constructs his anxiety proposition. He becomes nervous as he walks past a yard with a chain-link fence where a dog is barking ferociously. Doug remarks to himself that "dogs are dangerous and are likely to bite me," an anxiety proposition. He would not have to think twice next time before steering clear of ferociously barking dogs.

Although Doug's doggie danger proposition sounds like a statement about reality, it isn't actually a fact but rather a *hypothesis,* a personal interpretation or theory of what the sense of threat means. People unintentionally and often unconsciously "get" these meanings from anxiety-provoking experiences, which then affect their behavior and thoughts.

For example, fear of this volume's namesake—the monster in the cave—originated during a period when the unsettling sounds and sickening odors that emanated from the Dark Cave's mouth were blended together with gory details concocted by one of the town's wags. As a result, a frightening legend developed that daunted the townspeople so that they avoided the cave for decades. The resultant anxiety proposition became ingrained in the local culture: The Dark Cave harbored dangers that could harm living things that entered or even got near it.

Anxiety propositions may become triggers of the sense of threat in their own right. Thus, as a result of their shared anxiety proposition, people would sometimes get anxious when the cave was even mentioned ("When her dog ran away, it nearly ran right into the Dark Cave!"). Similarly, after developing panic disorder, people become fearful and tense from simply *thinking* about a pounding heart. A very effective means of overcoming anxiety consists of recognizing anxiety propositions, examining how they work, and *re*thinking them—reverse engineering.

Some of the pivots around which anxiety propositions revolve include:

- Physical stress symptoms (e.g., pounding heart, dizziness)

- Real-life disconcerting concerns (e.g., barking dogs, heavy traffic)

- Phobic situations, events, and activities (e.g., high places, crowds)

These pivotal anxiety provokers get linked in an anxious person's mind to specific, feared physical or behavioral consequences, such as injury, anxiety symptoms, or panic attacks. For instance, a man may develop the proposition that he could tumble from a steep staircase where he feels dizzy and break every bone in his body, and his fear will generalize to other high places. The pivot points mentioned above may also get linked to emotional feelings like terror or mortification and intensely uncomfortable states of mind such as fear paralysis or a sense of loss of control. A customer may freeze up and feel humiliated when she's unable to locate her checkbook in the checkout line of a busy outlet store and thenceforth become unable to shop at busy stores for fear of mortification. Table 2.2 illustrates this.

Anxiety propositions cut through individual differences to provide a means of discerning common elements in anxiety triggers, identifying types of anxious reactions, and developing and evaluating methods of treatment. As you will see in the chapters describing treatment of each disorder, people's unique constellations of anxiety-provoking situations, experiences, and reactions may be organized into anxiety propositions and then reverse engineered.

THE POWER OF EXPECTANCIES

Our mothers told us that most of the things people fear never actually come to pass. Anxious people often predict that terrible events will happen, even though they have a low probability of actually occurring. If a person thinks an elevator is unsafe and will crash to the ground after he presses a button to go to the thirteenth floor, it is understandable that he will experience an increase in heart rate in that situation. If he expects he will have an anxiety attack when he enters the elevator, it is also understandable that he might panic when he notices his heart race accelerating as he presses the button.

As this example implies, expectancies play an important role in anxiety. Thus, an important means of coping with fears is to change expectancies. You will recall that *agora* is the ancient Greek word for marketplace; so agoraphobia literally means a fear of the market. But the Greek agoras were open-air markets, and the term *agoraphobia* was used to refer to a fear of open places. This was the standard interpretation of agoraphobia until the 1970s. Then two psychologists, Alan Goldstein and Dianne Chambless, introduced a new way of thinking about this disorder. Agoraphobics gen-

Table 2.2

EXAMPLES OF ANXIETY PROPOSITIONS FOR FOUR ANXIETY DISORDERS

Anxiety Disorder	Example of Anxiety-Provoking Event	Specific Anxiety Reactions	Specific Feared Consequence	Anxiety Proposition
Panic	Sudden acceleration of pulse rate	Look for exits, recall phone number of nearest hospital	That I'm having a heart attack	Racing pulse will lead to heart attack.
General Situational Phobia	Squished into plane seat; engine making weird noises	Think, "The plane is going to crash!"	That I will die in this plane	Scary airplane malfunctions herald my imminent death.
Generalized Anxiety Disorder (GAD)	Sees car looking just like one's own, sitting smashed on the other side of the freeway	Racing thoughts, acute aggravation, sweats, tension	That my car could be destroyed or my teenage son is seriously injured	Cars damaged in accidents remind me that my family or I could be gravely harmed in a car accident.
Social Phobia	Waiting to present a progress report at an executive committee meeting	Blushing, trembling, sweating	That I'm going to make a total fool of myself	This attack is my warning that I'll be the butt of everyone's ridicule.

erally avoid a wide range of situations. Goldstein and Chambless realized that agoraphobic patients were not really afraid of the bridges, elevators, or shopping malls they were avoiding. Instead, they were afraid of the panic attacks that they anticipated experiencing in these situations. Agoraphobics suffer from a fear of fear. Theorists like Kirsch and Lynn, one of the authors of this book, believe that agoraphobia is a self-confirming expectancy disorder. Agoraphobics expect to experience panic, and, as we noted earlier, the expectation of a panic attack is frightening enough in itself to induce panic. In the case of socially anxious people, they expect that they will not be competent or likable in social situations and that their inadequacies will lead to rejection or diminished status. In the examples of both agoraphobia and social anxiety, negative expectations produce the anticipated experiences.

Exposure

A common way to diminish expectancies is through a process known as exposure. Treatments for phobias are most effective when they expose people to the situations that they avoid and to a substantial measure of the physical sensations of panic. Before exposure begins, people are provided with accurate, reassuring information that their fears of grievous harm or madness are unfounded and learn techniques for modulating panicky sensations. If the information provided about the experience and gathered during exposures is incompatible with the person's sense of endangerment and uncontrollability, then exposure can result in a changed emotional experience of phobic situations. As individuals come to realize (and expect) that they can tolerate discomfort in situations they once feared, their catastrophic thinking and anxiety diminish as their comfort level rises. This mechanism through which fear is relieved in exposure therapy treatment is known as *emotional processing*. Because of the powerful role of exposure in changing how we think and feel about fears, many of the techniques in the chapters that follow involve exposure and emotional processing of fears.

We have introduced you to the fundamental ways that fear and phobias hold people in their steely grip and given you a taste of the dynamics of anxious thinking. Now let's deepen our understanding of panic and anxiety by delving into the wrinkled gray recesses of the brain itself and unearthing the secrets it reveals.

Chapter Three

The Brain on Anxiety

L isa's brain is on anxiety. She is ready for trouble, too wired to sleep. She has locked all the doors, checked them three times, and turned on all the lights to give the overly curious the impression that she is home. She just returned from a Halloween party where the guests joked and cut up while watching four consecutive horror movies, each more gruesome than the last. Now Lisa is feeling the repercussions of her overexposure to scenes of death and mayhem. There is a sound at the back door, and Lisa starts to panic. Has Freddy from the movie *Nightmare on Elm Street* come to pay her a personal call?

In contrast to the stillness in Lisa's house, her brain and body are roiling with activity. We will introduce you to the ways that neuroscientists have expanded our understanding of the physiology of anxiety by describing what occurs in Lisa's anxiety-fueled brain. According to neuroscientist Joseph LeDoux and his colleagues, the seat of Lisa's anxiety is a region of the midbrain—dubbed the "emotional brain"—that consists of the amygdala, hypothalamus, and hippocampus. Most readers are probably unfamiliar with these brain structures, so an explanation is in order.

- Lisa's swift and intense emotional reaction to any sound outside or in her house is tripped by the *amygdala,* a little almond-shaped organ where vital emotion-laden memories reside and create gut feelings of someone trying to break in.

- The adrenaline rush that Lisa experiences when she hears the sound at the back door is implemented by the *hypothalamus*—the hormonal control center of the nervous system. The hypothalamus is the top link of a mind-body chain reaction that goes from the emotional brain to the adrenal glands that sit on top of Lisa's kidneys. Lisa's brain signals stress to the rest of her body through a linkage known as the HPA (hypothalamus-pituitary-adrenal) axis.

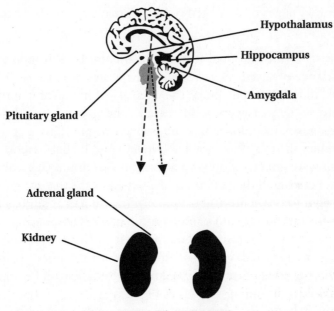

Figure 3.1   The HPA Axis

When the hypothalamus (H) receives signals of mental stress, like fear, excitement, anxiety, panic, or anger, it hooks up with the pituitary gland (P) to release hormones that trigger the physical stress responses. Blood pressure rises and adrenaline (A) is infused into the sympathetic branch of the nervous system that readies Lisa for swift action. When she is startled, frightened, or thrown into a panic, as she is now, alone in her house, her body undergoes the warp drive physical stress response we referred to in the last chapter as the "emergency response."

- The seahorse-shaped *hippocampus* does not refer to a college for aquatic mammals. Many of the brain's long-term memories are stored in the hippocampus, from which Lisa can summon forth her dear uncle's sayings, jokes, and stories. A mere instant after the knock on the door triggered her emergency response, Lisa's hippocampus provided her with her relevant memories as well as the "emergency response cards" of automatic thoughts. More precisely, if she were not too jumpy, Lisa might think, "Oh, that's just my oddball neighbor"; but when Lisa is truly wired, her hippocampus boosts her uneasiness with mental images of deranged prowlers breaking into her house.

Scientists at the National Institute of Mental Health report that when an abundance of distressing emotional experiences from early childhood are stored in long-term memory, the intensity of hippocampal responses to stress and anxiety triggers is increased. The ground for Lisa's edginess about being isolated, alone, and vulnerable was paved by a period early in her life when she felt abandoned and mistreated by her parents.

If Lisa were governed only by her emotional brain, she would be incapable of exercising judgment about the extent of the threat present and devising a plan to deal with it. Fortunately, the human brain has the unique capacity for fathoming and coping with danger. The brain is not only an "emotional brain" but also a "thinking brain." The instant that Lisa's hippocampus tried to make sense of the knock on the door, it opened up a gateway to portions of the cerebral cortex, which Joseph LeDoux refers to as the "thinking brain."

Signals fly back and forth from the emotional and thinking brains like calls between Donald Trump and his broker during a boom on Wall Street. Pressing questions like "Who could that possibly be at this hour?" "Should I call 911?" "Where's my baseball bat?" are answered almost immediately. A moment later, after thinking about it, a more elaborate plan of action occurs to her—speed dialing her brother who lives down the street.

While Lisa focuses on sources of danger, her vital thinking functions make sense of the origin of the stress and work out solutions. Each new development is examined as the course of events unfolds, alternative solutions to the problem are considered, and efforts are directed at refining the coping plan until the situation is stabilized and security is restored. In the meantime, Lisa's feelings have evolved from an initial startled reaction and a sense of threat to anxiety and apprehension.

At one point in the cascade of thoughts and feelings that flood Lisa's consciousness, she has an impulse to climb out the window. A section of the upper brainstem called the *basal ganglia* is signaled when action plans intended to reduce threat are planned or implemented. The basal ganglia, which are linked to the frontal cortex of the thinking brain, where judgments and decisions occur, inhibit Lisa's impulse to jump out of the window. The basal ganglia also feed back information about what Lisa's body is doing to the thinking brain.

The basal ganglia are an integral part of the brain's system to inhibit behavior that could be dangerous to continue. When confronted with threat and anxiety, the basal ganglia may *slow* problem-solving or action planning, *inhibit* goal-directed activity, or *immobilize* the person into a behavioral freeze.

Once Lisa dismisses her impulse to act on her most drastic impulses, she decides to find out who is at the door, while clutching her cordless phone, ready to call her brother for help. Armed with this action plan, she feels more in control and less anxious.

According to new research, different anxiety disorders may activate different parts of the emotional brain—a portion of the hypothalamus in panic, the amygdala in phobias, and parts of the hippocampus in generalized anxiety. At a finer level of analysis, different portions of the amygdala

A Concise Atlas of Anxious Thinking

There are three main types of anxious thinking. During *apprehension,* dire predictions are generated automatically in the emotional brain and shuttle back and forth to a portion of the thinking brain—the frontal lobes—where attempts are made to plan to control the threat. *Rumination,* the rehashing of past losses and failures, is the disheartening product of signals shuttling between the thinking brain and the hippocampal memory banks. *Obsession*—repetitive, intrusive, overdetailed thinking striving to diminish a sense of threat—gets oppressive when the basal ganglia and the frontal lobes fail to moderate the extent to which worries and preoccupations are recycled endlessly.

Table 3.1
EMOTIONAL BRAIN ACTIVITY

Anxiety Disorder	Area Activated	Resulting Behavior Pattern
Panic	Hypothalamus	Flight
Phobias, Anxiety, Obsessive-Compulsive Disorder	Amygdala	Inhibition of behavior
Anxiety and Generalized Anxiety Disorder (GAD)	Hippocampus	Nervous tension and movements

Based on ADAA *Reporter,* Spring 2000

activate different behavioral reactions—flight in panic, freezing (inhibition of behavior) in phobias, and tension in anxiety and generalized anxiety.

Dopamine, Adrenaline, Serotonin & Co.

So far we have talked about changes that take place in the various structures of Lisa's brain. These changes are made possible by the action of neuro-chemicals in her brain. Brain chemicals focus attention, implement creative and rational thinking, intensify and defuse emotions, facilitate memory and learning, and fuel both panic attacks and vivid dreams. Events that trigger strong feelings cause production and transmission of neurochemicals that, in turn, initiate and sustain every emotional reaction. In order to enlarge our understanding of Lisa's reaction to the sound at her door, let us familiarize ourselves with the brain chemistry of panic and anxiety and several of the main ways that neurochemicals work.

The chemicals Lisa's brain uses are "made to order" from raw materials in relatively discrete groups of nerve cells or neurons located primarily in the deepest, most ancient parts of the brain. Most are fashioned from readily available ingredients, like sugar, nitrogen, and oxygen, while others are synthesized out of other brain chemicals. The group of neurochemicals that implement anxiety and panic—dopamine, epinephrine (adrenaline), and norepinephrine (NE)—all originate in the brain stem.

Each brain chemical is responsible for facilitating a number of mental processes. Different chemicals predominate at different times of day and govern various moods and mental states. When we are restless, distractible, tense, or agitated, dopamine is in charge. Dopamine signals parts of the emotional and thinking brains to *inhibit* fight-or-flight behaviors and *evaluate* the threatening situation while the body shifts into a state of tense readiness for action. Dopamine is strongly represented in Lisa's brain when she is too nervous to sleep and at times when she worries too much, and also in the brain of Marnie, the woman with social phobia whom we met in chapter 2.

Norepinephrine (NE) is involved with fear and panic reactions—with fighting or fleeing—but also with alertness and focused attention. If we imagine a scientist with a kit for performing "neurochemical analyses" visiting Lisa when she hears the knock on the door, his lab tests would reveal that much of her emotional brain is flooded with NE.

Serotonin, on the other hand, helps us deactivate and cruise away from consciousness. During the deep, dreamless sleep that serotonin promotes, mental functioning is renewed so that we awaken refreshed. Under serotonin's regime, yesterday's experiences evolve into foundations of deep memories and the building blocks of tomorrow's new perspectives.

The Neurochemicals of Anxiety

- Dopamine predominates during periods of excitement, restlessness, and agitation.

- Adrenaline—norepinephrine (NE) and epinephrine—governs stress responses and the expression of fear and panic.

- Serotonin plays a part in relaxation, reflectiveness, and composure.

HOW DO NEUROCHEMICALS ENABLE US TO PROCESS FEAR?

Brain chemicals affect anxiety in two ways: by functioning as *neurotransmitters* and *neuromodulators*. Neurotransmitters are the media for signals that pass through elongated cells called neurons that link the parts of the brain together for communication purposes. During anxiety, neurotransmitters usually deliver signals that activate a "neuro-neighborhood," a group of receptors uniting for a special purpose. Such purposes include attempting to prevent future danger, reviewing past experiences in an attempt to distill their meaning, and deciding if a threat should be responded to with anxiety or panic. When the brain stem signals the presence of a threat, neurotransmitters facilitate our brains' capacity to deal with it.

Neuromodulation is subtler than neurotransmission. During neuromodulation, the responses of particular neurons are temporarily fine-tuned so they are more likely to react in certain ways. For instance, while you might turn down a steaming bowl of delicious soup on a hot summer day, neuromodulation could change your mind on a chilly wintry evening. The cold, your hunger, or a low blood sugar level could temporarily cause more mental energy to flow toward the parts of your brain that incline or bias you to crave the savory brew. Depending on the circumstances and recent experience, neurochemicals can modulate our responses to situations so that we are calmer or more nervous, quicker or more careful than we have been before. In a number of ways, neuromodulation plays an important part in determining our reactions to fear-provoking situations and in the physiology of anxiety and panic.

During both anxiety and panic, neuromodulation sharpens our alertness so that we can more easily notice threats coming from any direction. The price of this high sensitivity to threat is loss of discrimination, so that distinctions between threats (signals), subtle threats (milder signals), and nonthreats (noise) become difficult to make. The downside of this hypersensitivity is also evident during anxiety states or panic, when it becomes difficult to concentrate or focus on one thing and exclude the rest, rendering concentration on even reassuring matters difficult. For instance, Lisa could not focus on the fact that she had triple-locked her door, her windows were nailed shut, and that she was armed with a cell phone programmed with emergency numbers.

From the moment Lisa entered her house and locked her door, NE and dopamine kept her in a state of readiness to flight or flee. Similarly, chronically anxious people stay rather tense and overreactive as if they need to remain constantly on alert. Primed by the neurochemicals dopamine and NE, acute anxiety can easily recur as a result of the addition of even mild stress.

NE AND SEROTONIN ACTING NICELY

High anxiety hampers performance and clarity of mind. By regulating the neurotransmitter system, a person can be less impeded by anxiety and function better. Medication and therapy can improve the regulation of NE at panicky times so that the signal-to-noise ratio is likelier to be just right, midway between the extremes of obsession (excessive focus) and confusion (excessive noise).

Serotonin can effectively reduce the intensity of fight-or-flight responses that are triggered by false alarms so an anxious person can function with greater composure, reduce acute anxiety, and loosen the tangles of obsessions and compulsions. Thus Lisa's acute anxiety was finally eased when she spotted her best friend through the back window. She opened the door and hugged Marcie, her surprised friend, who remarked, "I knew you'd be glad to get back the sunglasses you forgot at the party, but I had no idea you'd be *this* excited!" The tremendous relief Lisa felt was orchestrated by the breakup of her NE and dopamine by serotonin as soon as she laid eyes on her friend.

Serotonin-enhancing medications like SSRIs (discussed below) and cognitive-behavioral therapy increase the supply of available serotonin and help neutralize negative arousal. As a result, phobic situations, high stress, and physical anxiety symptoms are less likely to trigger panic and anxiety, and attacks may be eliminated.

Meanwhile, in the neurons of the thinking brain, serotonin can help restore the capacity to focus selectively, think systematically and critically, and decide how to contend realistically with anxiety-provoking situations. Later, once distinctions between real threat and anxiety disorders have been established, and anxiety and panic have become controllable through treatment, a balanced serotonin metabolism can help the anxious person internalize and maintain his or her gains.

We have examined the physiological processes of fear, anxiety, panic, and anxious thinking and behavior under "normal" conditions and in the context of anxiety disorders. In the last two sections, we discussed the behavior of our brain chemistry during anxiety, panic, and anxiety disorders. Modifications of the anxious person's NE and serotonin metabolisms help change her thinking as she learns to overcome anxiety and panic and enhance her capacity to deal with anxiety-provoking stress. This, in turn, results in her acting differently—less inhibited and more strategic and confident in anxiety-provoking situations.

As you continue to read, you will be introduced to state-of-the-art cognitive-behavioral therapy techniques that will result in lasting relief and recovery. But first we will discuss antianxiety medications.

Anxiolytic Medications

anxiolytic: (adjective) breaking up or dissolving
anxiety; (noun) a medication with anxiolytic properties

People frequently begin treatment for panic and anxiety by visiting a physician. Once their problem is identified as anxiety, medication is often prescribed to them. *Medication is not necessarily needed for relief of panic and anxiety* but frequently plays an important or central part. If you or an anxious person you knows seeks medication, it's best if the doctor who prescribes it—the psychopharmacologist—is either a psychiatrist or a physician with a lot of experience treating patients with psychiatric medication. When in doubt, ask for his or her qualifications for treating anxiety.

Since knowledge of medicines that affect your feelings and mental functioning is a sophisticated matter, visit a doctor who can inform you about the full spectrum of possible antianxiety treatments and medications. Psychiatric consultation should also ensure that medical conditions that are present concurrently with psychiatric conditions are recognized and taken into account. Some of the most common medical conditions that may occur simultaneously with anxiety disorders—especially panic—are thyroid imbalances, inner ear conditions, and a mild heart condition called mitral valve prolapse.

Medications from the various families of anxiolytics reduce anxiety in different ways, but all can enhance the ability to cope by partially relieving panic and anxious discomfort. Your psychopharmacologist's cornucopia might include:

- High-potency *benzodiazepines (BZDs)*. Alprazolam (Xanax), lorazepam (Ativan), and clonazepam (Klonopin) suppress panic and anxiety attacks.

- The non-BZD anxiolytic *buspirone* (BuSpar).

- *SSRIs*. A class of antidepressant/antianxiety drugs that work largely by increasing the availability of serotonin. Fluoxetine (Prozac), sertraline (Zoloft), paroxetine (Paxil), and citalopram (Celexa) are widely used for panic and agoraphobia treatment. Fluvoxamine (Luvox) is for treatment of obsessive-compulsive disorder (OCD), and Prozac is often used as well.

- *Other anxiolytics. SNRIs,* (selective norepinephrine reuptake inhibitors) like venlafaxine (Effexor) are antidepressant/antianxiety agents that increase the availability of both serotonin and noradrenaline. *Beta-blockers,* such as propanolol (Inderal) and atenolol (Tenormin), interfere with the effects of noradrenaline on the heart and other organs, reduce the resting heart rate, and limit the increase in heart rate during exercise.

- *Traditional tricyclic antidepressants (TCAs).* Desipramine, imipramine (Tofranil), and nortriptyline (Pamelor) have been used to treat anxiety disorders for over thirty years. Clomipramine (Anafranil) is a potent pharmacological treatment for obsessive-compulsive disorder (OCD).

A detailed discussion of the medications used to relieve each anxiety disorder is included in the chapter discussing treatment of that disorder. The National Institute of Mental Health, Anxiety Disorders Association of America, or your local psychiatric association should be contacted, if necessary (see appendix G for anxiety treatment resources), to obtain recommendations of psychopharmacologists skilled in anxiety disorders treatment and to obtain information about medications.

How Do Anxiolytics Work?

Anxiolytics (both antianxiety medications and antidepressants) can enhance the anxious person's ability to cope by relieving panic, apprehension, and other types of anxious discomfort. Medications from any of the three most commonly used medication families are likely to be effective in reducing anxiety, although in different ways and with considerable overlap. Tricyclics appear to help largely by reducing the sensitivity of the brain's anxiety system to NE. They help people get used to experiencing higher levels of stress without becoming overwhelmed, so they can keep more focused and organized despite periodic power surges of panic and general arousal.

Newer, more selective antidepressants include the selective serotonin reuptake inhibitors (SSRIs) and serotonin and norepinephrine reuptake inhibitors (SNRIs) like venlafaxine (Effexor); these are currently the most widely prescribed type of antidepressants. *SSRIs are nonaddictive but should not be stopped without medical supervision.* Side effects of the SSRIs may include nausea, overstimulation, sedation, and sexual side effects such as delayed or inhibited orgasms.

SSRIs and SNRIs function largely by helping anxious people turn down their negative arousal and perhaps to think more clearly about anxiety-provoking situations. We believe that despite the almost immediate effect that SSRIs have on the brain's serotonin metabolism, most patients don't reap substantial gains until they have taken the medication consistently for several weeks so their brains can neurochemically down-regulate the strength of their anxiety and panic reactions. Another contemporary theory—called pruning of ganglia—proposes that medications help "remodel" the nervous system to account for improvements in people's functioning. Whatever the explanation, once an anxious person stabilizes on a suitable medication, he can better discern what made him anxious and begin redirecting energy away from negative arousal, unhealthy worries, and obsessions toward solving problems and restoring his ability to function.

BZDs reduce panic, physical discomfort, and the intensity of urges to escape from anxiety-provoking situations. Doctors hesitate to prescribe BZDs to people with histories of dependency or abuse of drugs or alcohol because they can become addictive. While physiological dependence on these medications may develop in as little as two or three months, they are an important tool in the treatment of anxiety disorders. And the evidence of long clinical experience actually indicates that anxiety patients *without* addiction problems or substance abuse proclivities are *unlikely* to abuse these substances.

Also, a number of other non-BZD medicines, like buspirone (BuSpar) can be helpful. Beta-blockers like propanolol (Inderal) and atenolol (Tenormin) may be used effectively to treat performance anxiety. In addition, medications from an old class of antidepressants called MAOIs (Mono-amine Oxidase Inhibitors), including phenelzine (Nardil) and tranylcypromine (Parnate), may be used to control panic when other antidepressant medications fail, and to relieve social anxiety as well. One the newest medications on the scene is gabapentin (Neurontin), used psychiatrically to treat both general anxiety and irritability. Each type of medication uses a different route for relieving anxiety.

STRAIGHT TALK ABOUT BENZODIAZEPINES

A lot of people with anxiety problems who have little reason to fear becoming drug addicts have difficulty getting and taking BZDs because of the stigma of addictiveness. *BZDs can be addictive but generally are not.* The mythology is the product of four factors:

- *The overprescription era*—Early in the Golden Age of Advertising of the 1960s and '70s, BZDs—especially Valium and Librium (and later Xanax)—were initially marketed aggressively and touted as cure-alls for all sorts of physical and mental problems without proper research to support the claims. As a result they were overprescribed and—in the absence of effective alternative medications—not necessarily discontinued when they appeared to be ineffective.

- *The proscription period*—Overlapping the era of overprescription was the period of popular drug experimentation and overuse of the late '60s and '70s. On the heels of these parallel events in the youth and conventional cultures, the government began outlawing many drugs and broadening the overall class of drugs of abuse. By then, the limitations of BZDs' "powers" were more apparent, as were their clear-cut benefits for treating stress, anxiety, and physical pain; but their addictive potential was also recognized and widely publicized, such as in the 1981 book and 1982 movie, *I'm Dancing as Fast as I Can.* Many psychiatrists term this growing trend of labeling medications good or evil "pharmacologic Calvinism." Monitoring BZD prescriptions by state and federal agencies was deemed necessary in order to prevent abuse.

- *Incorrect choice of medication*—Every medicine has its pros and cons. When certain types of addicts use BZDs, their drawbacks may outweigh their benefits because of their potential to worsen addicts' psychological weaknesses. BZDs probably could complicate many addicts' recovery process by weakening their capacity to develop psychological means of controlling their addictions. That is, while BZDs are likely to be more effective than drugs of addiction in controlling specific anxiety symptoms like panic, one of the fundamental reasons for addictive behavior is that *addictive substances relieve anxiety.* So medication with BZDs would feed into a vicious cycle by simply substituting one anxiety-relieving substance for another.

- *The specter of withdrawal*—Like a lot of other medicines, discontinuation of BZDs should be planned and structured. "Getting off them is predominantly an issue of slow supported taper, which should be consistent, but at a speed the patient controls," explains psychiatrist Benjamin Crocker. A wide range of medicines requires structured discontinuation, and the consequences are normally assumed to be negative if this isn't done. But people may mistakenly frighten themselves away from BZD use by equating it to drug abuse and erroneously equate discontinuation to addictive drug withdrawal, because both must be done gradually in order to prevent adverse reactions. This equation is the result of the first three factors described above.

Like other medications, the best time to taper off BZDs is once the disorder for which they are being taken is relieved and stable. Discontinuation involves gradual decreases of the dosage over weeks to months. Some anxiety will temporarily reappear, often in the form of increased tension lasting hours or maybe days. Professional therapy support helps to contend with this measure of anxiety and sustain improvement after BZDs have been stopped.

BZDs may present more problems than perks for people with certain other mental health problems, such as sufferers from borderline personality disorder. By weakening certain people's inhibitions, BZDs can potentially worsen their preexisting difficulties with thinking in a structured way and/or controlling impulsiveness. For other people who are already unhealthily withdrawn or avoidant, BZDs may cause undesirable enhancement of passivity. So BZDs can be incorrectly prescribed to individuals for whom they're a bad choice, but this undesirable possibility is much more likely when the person's psychological condition has not been evaluated by a mental health professional.

A widespread practice among psychiatrists is prescription of BZDs "prn" or "as needed." Only under three circumstances is "as needed" BZD prescription clearly useful: for brief treatment of people whose panic dissipates within a couple of months; for short-term symptom relief during a relapse; and when a very symptomatic person has to deal with an anxiety-provoking challenge, such as a plane trip or a big test.

Psychiatrist Thomas Shiovitz believes that most anxiety patients who require BZDs benefit from regular dosing during their periods of active panic—that is "x number of y milligram tablets, taken z times a day." In this way, BZDs help actively to protect them from the demoralization and intense anticipatory anxiety that often result from prolonged periods of severe, uncontrollable panics.

In addition, protracted dosing "as needed" with BZDs is counterproductive to treatment of anxiety disorders, because in an important way it subtly enhances, rather than reduces, part of the disorder—a pattern of avoidance of stressful life events. For instance, if a person with panic disorder or agoraphobia takes her Xanax whenever she has to travel by plane or drive into the city, or only takes Ativan whenever her pulse starts to race, these phobic situations and panic sensations retain their power to trigger anxiety whenever they occur. Once the person on his way to facing his fear swallows an "as needed" BZD, the urge to "share the credit" with the BZD for successfully coping with the anxiety situation becomes hard to resist—despite the fact that he may have worked hard to develop psychological techniques and exercised real courage during the event.

Beta-blockers, a type of cardiovascular medicine, is another kind of medication frequently taken "as needed" for acute anxiety. The capacity of these medicines to temporarily relieve physical symptoms of performance or public speaking anxiety is an open secret among public speakers and performers. For the portion of prn beta-blocker users who suffer from clinically significant social anxiety disorders, this way of medicating could interfere with their capacity for long-term therapeutic recovery.

Medicine on a Pedestal?

The urge to attribute much of the power to overcome anxiety to medication is very persuasive but deceptive. When eminent psychologist David Barlow and his colleagues recently researched short-term treatment of panic disorder, they found that combined cognitive-behavioral therapy and medication was more effective than active medication alone; but it did not matter whether the pill combined with the therapy was an active medication (like imipramine) or a sugar pill! This study raises intriguing questions about the psychological processes involved in combined treatment and, practically, is very important, as many patients who enter psychological treatment for anxiety are already taking medication. Commenting on research that indicates that placebos are effective for 20 to 70 percent of people with anxiety disorders, psychologist Michelle Craske speculates that much of this effect may be the result of people's expectations of improvement once they receive medication treatment.

In contemporary clinical practice, people with anxiety are often treated through *polypharmacy*—prescription of two or more types of medication, usually an antidepressant (particularly an SSRI) and a BZD—and encouraged to seek therapy. The BZD provides quick, substantial relief and the SSRI may give additional benefit and is effective in the longer term. Sometimes people taper off their dose of BZDs once acute panic has subsided and the SSRI has taken effect, usually within three to six weeks. Most people are encouraged to stay on antidepressants for at least six months. In our clinical experience, we estimate that the average length of time a client continues on an SSRI medication is about fifteen months. Many clients opt to stay on these medications for years.

The effectiveness of medication treatment is generally enhanced by psychological treatment. Without it, symptoms are much more likely to resume after medication treatment is discontinued. Also, since BZDs effectively "switch off" acute negative arousal, they decrease the ability to discern the effectiveness of every other technique to relieve anxiety. Despite this, many people, especially those with few or mild panic or anxiety attacks, will be satisfied simply to take antianxiety medications for a while, since for them attacks cease being uncontrollable.

Rebound anxiety is the term for a period of increased anxiety and panic that may occur upon discontinuation of BZD treatment. This rebound can usually be treated and relieved through brief psychological therapy known as *relapse prevention*. Relapse prevention involves planned tapering of the medicine, education as to the nature of withdrawal symptoms, and cognitive-behavior therapy to relieve the anxious discomfort that may occur. Psychologically minded individuals may prefer to get extra help from a treatment manual like *Stopping Anxiety Medication* by Michael W. Otto and his associates.

A serious problem occasionally results from overreliance on pharmacological symptom suppression: being too perfectionistic and striving to achieve the unrealistic goal of eternal freedom from all anxiety symptoms through medication. Sometimes people may feel so pleasant and panic-free on high doses of BZDs for many months that they become psychologically as well as physically dependent on these substances.

How can this happen? Continued reliance on BZDs and other controlled substances reduces the person's ability to tolerate emotional discomfort. Before people with this problem lose their motivation to develop other means of relieving anxiety, they should team up with a psychopharmacologist to plan a program for discontinuing the medication. In some cases, a chemical dependency treatment program may be a desirable or necessary means of controlling the discomfort of drug withdrawal.

Nonmedical, psychological techniques and therapies are a vital part of long-term recovery from anxiety; but for many people, the discomfort of acute or severe chronic anxiety is so intense that medication treatment is well justified. For most who choose the anxiolytic path, anxiety disorders get more approachable when medications relieve enough discomfort to permit them to learn and try out coping skills in anxiety-provoking situations. The prospect of dealing head-on with fear can be less daunting when medication makes the risk seem less devastating. For some people, especially trauma victims with post-traumatic stress disorder and other chronically, severely anxious individuals, medication may be maintained on a long-term basis. In either case, this type of treatment works best when planned through consultation with both the psychopharmacologist and the treating clinician.

Chapter Four

How Does Panic Happen?

Have you experienced panic? Panic attacks number among the worst moments of people's lives. *Nobody* should go through such an ordeal.

Even the most psychologically minded of panickers would hesitate to believe that their panic is nothing more than anxiety. "Anxiety?" they say, "Like getting *nervous?* You're kidding! More like dying or going insane!" There's no way some panickers can be convinced that it's all in their minds, either—not with a pounding heart, such difficulty breathing, and visions of dying or total loss of control.

We lead off the treatment part of the book with a discussion of panic for two reasons. Panic is so widespread that at least 30 percent of the general populace experience at least one attack in any given year, while between 1.6 and 3.5 percent meet the diagnostic criteria for panic disorder. As can be seen in Table 4.1, panic attacks can occur as part of every anxiety disorder, as well as in depressive conditions and eating disorders. Also, people who do not suffer from emotional disorders may nevertheless have anxiety or panic attacks before a stressful event.

The other reason that we discuss panic treatment first is because it can snatch away anxious people's attention and undermine their determination more compellingly than any other anxiety symptom or syndrome. *Any anx-*

iety disorder of which panic is a significant component can be tackled more directly once the panic is controlled or overcome.

Table 4.1

THE FREQUENCY OF PANIC ATTACKS IN ANXIETY DISORDER

Anxiety Disorder	Percentage of Sufferers Who Also Have Panic Attacks
Agoraphobia	50–100%
Specific Phobia	31.9%
Social Phobia	23.4%
Generalized Anxiety Disorder	18.1%
Obsessive-Compulsive Disorder	5.3%
Post-traumatic Stress Disorder	3.2%

Antony & Swinson, 2000

The age of onset of panic is typically from the late teens to the late twenties. The youngest new panicker we have treated was a thirteen-year-old who, as a young child, accidentally played a part in causing a relative's death, while the most senior, at eighty, was a retiree who first panicked when he became a widower after a marriage that spanned six decades.

Symptoms of Panic

Panic attacks are intensely disturbing rushes of fear or discomfort that occur in the absence of immediate, mortal danger and reach a peak in less than ten minutes. To meet official diagnostic criteria, an attack must include at least four of the following thirteen symptoms:

Panic Symptoms

- Racing or pounding heart
- Sweating
- Shaking or trembling
- Shortness of breath
- Choking feelings
- Chest discomfort
- Nausea or abdominal discomfort
- Feeling dizzy, faint, or light-headed
- Feelings of unreality or depersonalization
- Fear of "going crazy" or losing control
- Fear of dying
- Numbness or tingling sensations
- Chills or hot flushes

DSM-IV-APA, 1994

Perhaps you notice that physical as well as mental symptoms are listed. Full-blown attacks include symptoms of both kinds,[1] so it becomes easier to understand why many people who panic think their bodies are going out of control and may fear a "nervous breakdown" or even imminent death. Some symptoms, like choking sensations, *feel* entirely physical but are entirely psychological, while others that feel highly psychologically disturbing are normal physical reactions to stress, such as changes in breathing and pronounced heartbeat. As can be seen in table 4.2, panic symptoms may usefully be clustered into four kinds of reactions, each with its characteristic associated fear.

Many of these symptoms ordinarily occur as part of reactions to "bad" stress, such as when we are frightened. Shaking and trembling are both

---

1 Exceptions are two types of relatively mild panic that lack mental symptoms: "simple panic or anxiety sensitivity" attacks, and attacks of panic without fear; they are experienced as almost exclusively physical in nature.

listed because they are subtly different—shaking movements being bigger and broader—and also because in our clinical experience a number of people complain of "internal trembling," a very real mental sense that tremors are occurring *inside* their bodies. Some attacks occur virtually without warning, because the events leading up to them do not seem particularly disturbing, and thus are referred to as "spontaneous." Whatever their apparent points of origin, these panicky thoughts, sensations, feelings, and impulses clearly amount to *attacks*—out-of-the-blue intrusions, stark, frightening, and violent.

Table 4.2
TYPES OF PANIC FEARS

Panic Symptoms	Type of Fear
Shortness of breath and overbreathing, often with activation of the "emergency response"	Fear of respiratory symptoms
Impulses that threaten to cause fainting, sick stomach, or other lapses of control in front of others, along with fear of embarrassment or being a public spectacle	Fear of publicly observable anxiety reactions
Pounding of the heart, heart racing or missing beats, along with activation of the "emergency response"	Fear of cardiovascular symptoms
Mental confusion, flashbacks, a sense of unreality, depersonalization, or fear of going crazy	Fear of losing one's mind

Taylor & Cox, 1998

Although panic and anxiety attacks include physical components, they are nevertheless primarily psychological in nature, so the most qualified help will come from mental health professionals who have training in anxiety disorder treatment, including psychiatrists, clinical psychologists, clinical social workers, and licensed mental health counselors.

Can Panic Develop from Thinking About It Too Much?

Like college students who take introductory psychology courses or first-year medical students, anxious people who read about panic symptoms or anxiety disorders or who enter treatment may start "diagnosing" symptoms or syndromes that they don't have and may even experience a temporary increase in anxiety. These effects are simply the result of interpreting everyday experiences of uneasiness, worry, and physical tension as panic symptoms. If you are in doubt about whether you have an anxiety disorder, consult a mental health professional.

Panic Disorder

Panic disorder is a diagnosis that consists of a pattern of unexpected attacks along with apprehension about their recurrence. *Panic is a fear of bodily sensations,* particularly physical symptoms of stress responses, along with the expectation that attacks will recur. To meet the formal *(DSM-IV)* diagnostic criteria, multiple attacks must occur over a span of at least a month. The individual must be concerned about having more attacks and apprehensive about larger physical or mental consequences, such as loss of health or psychosis. Alternately, or additionally, he must alter his functioning to contend with the fears. Such alterations may include avoidance of certain events, places, or activities. The person may be avoidant except when accompanied by other people, such as spouses, friends, or children whose presence increases the sense of security, or when carrying a security object or talisman like a cell phone or a water or medication bottle.

"Anxiety attacks" are technically referred to as *limited-symptom panic attacks.* They simply involve fewer and somewhat less intrusive symptoms than full-blown attacks and therefore may not meet the formal criteria. All sorts of additional physical symptoms fall into this less specific category—sleep disturbance, prickling sensations in various parts of the body, fear of losing bladder or bowel control or of vomiting in public settings, stress headaches, and an array of other anxiety-generated disturbances.

Panic disorder is usually preceded by both unsettling events and triggering incidents. Typical antecedents are major adverse or stressful life events. Accidents or illnesses, romantic or financial setbacks, parenthood, and starting or terminating a job are examples of likely forerunners of attacks. An anxiety-sensitive individual who goes through a stressful major event or episode is likely to experience lingering, heightened anxiety and is at increased risk of erupting into panic.

Panic is triggered initially by a situation, activity, or event that usually leads to a sense of vulnerability and escalates into acute anxiety. On occasions subsequent to this "primary triggering," anticipation of the triggering event or the onset of physical anxiety symptoms become "secondary triggers" in their own right. Once an individual's "triggering mechanism" is cocked, he or she is likely to suffer attacks unless the problem is solved or the trigger disarmed by means of treatment.

Take Russell, for instance. His mother and sister both had histories of panic disorder. At twenty-four and physically healthy, he used to enjoy working as a contractor until a sarcastic coworker who disliked him was promoted to lead position and proceeded to make his job miserable. The stress of contending with his new boss elevated Russell's level of anxiety, which made him vulnerable to panic.

One night Russell and his friends smoked marijuana to get in a euphoric mood and then went to a nightclub. Seemingly out of nowhere, he was struck by panic. He started breathing hard and suddenly became confused. Everyone and everything became unreal. From that night on, he avoided going out with his friends, fearing that he'd have another one of these attacks.

In this case, the primary trigger for his initial attack was the disturbingly confusing and paranoid reaction Russell had to being high on marijuana in the club. He felt like he was falling apart in front of his buddies that night. From then on, every time his friends suggested that he hang out with them he found himself getting nervous and reluctant. Hanging out with his friends had become a secondary trigger for Russell's panic.

Mindy felt like she was managing her substantial stresses rather well and didn't expect any trouble. At the time she was in the process of finalizing her bitterly contested divorce, and then she had a minor car accident, literally adding injury to insult. She still felt in control until she started teaching her teenage daughter to drive. Mindy went through intense apprehension before each practice, and when her daughter put the car in gear, it triggered a panic reaction. Although her daughter was a willing learner, Mindy's anxiety rattled her to the point that both agreed that somebody else should do the teaching. Mindy continued to struggle with a lesser degree of panic every time her daughter would drive out on a lesson, because the anticipatory anxiety was her secondary trigger. In the next

Did You Have Chest Pain?

If your chest is painful or tight during an episode of apparent panic, get a physical examination right away. Many people are unable to distinguish panic from heart attacks from non-cardiac chest pain, so avoid taking needless chances with your heart! During or after the incident, if you haven't already paid a visit to your physician and so much as suspect a heart problem, go to the doctor. Since panic feels physical—and actually *is* partially physical—why not?

chapter, we will help you to identify your personal anxiety.

Although panic is most commonly a reaction to negative stress, fortune is so fickle that people actually develop panic disorder after winning the lottery or falling in love. We have treated a number of people whose panic emerged as a "complication" of retirement. Occasionally, the side effects of otherwise effective medication treatment of an illness trigger panic, or it develops during the aftermath of successful surgery.

Joyce, for example, had mixed feelings about taking care of her ailing father in her home. He really had nowhere else to go, but she was already a working mother. So this new responsibility added quite a bit of stress, but she naturally justified it by her devotion to him. One evening, while waiting impatiently in a slow-moving checkout line at the local supermarket, she felt an asthma attack coming on, the first in many months. Almost as soon as she inhaled the prescription adrenaline spray she always used, she felt very strange. Her heart started pounding violently and she began to tremble. Psychologically, she experienced these symptoms as a sudden loss of control and was swept up in a full-blown panic attack.

Panic and anxiety are often precipitated by medical symptoms. Two anxiety disorders—panic disorder and generalized anxiety disorder—can be diagnosed as "due to a general medical condition" if they develop when the individual is suffering from a medical condition, going through a medical procedure, or after suffering side effects (or aftereffects) from either a procedure or a medication treatment. According to the diagnostic manual, the main types of conditions that can precipitate these anxiety disorders are:

- Endocrine (e.g., thyroid or hypoglycemia)

- Cardiovascular (e.g., congestive heart failure, arrhythmia, or supraventricular tachycardia)

- Respiratory (e.g., asthma attack, pneumonia, or hyperventilation)
- Metabolic conditions like vitamin B$_{12}$ deficiency
- Neurological conditions like inner ear problems and encephalitis

A Working Model of Panic

In the introduction we introduced the concept of reverse engineering. The corollary of the popular phrase, "If it ain't broke, don't fix it," is, "If it is broke, find out why, and how, and repair it!" What is broken in the case of anxiety and panic attacks? How can we reverse engineer the damage and restore healthy functioning? What follows is a working model of panic disorder that lends itself to ways of modifying panic symptoms by reverse engineering.

Panic begins when an individual who has been under stress has a first attack. An attack can appear to emerge spontaneously from out of nowhere, but it actually is an escalation of the emergency response triggered either by a *sensation* or by the tension engendered by a *phobic situation.* Sensations are often physical stress symptoms but may be other unusual feelings, like feeling sped up by a cold medicine or bee sting venom, light-headedness due to the flu, or becoming overheated on a hot day. Phobic situations are settings such as freeways, airplanes, shopping malls, and elevators, all of which have the capacity to stimulate stress reactions among certain panic-prone people.

Once the brain's fear mechanism is thus engaged, a wave of physical and mental symptoms ensues that crescendos within a span of about ten minutes, but seems like an eternity. The person experiences this array of symptoms (cited in the Panic Symptoms list on p. 66) as a frightening loss of control, accompanied by intensifying fear of what is going on and what is to come. Psychologist David Barlow calls this bewildering state a "false alarm," since the fear is experienced in the absence of real danger.

People who have begun to panic often become very apprehensive. While endeavoring to do their utmost to guard against recurrence of attacks, they become so vigilant that they react anxiously to physical symptoms that *even slightly* resemble the triggers of their first attack. Similarly, many panickers whose attacks were engendered in phobic situations become painfully sensitized to seemingly similar situations, activities, and events. That uneasy "pre-panic feeling" is stirred, and they may begin to generalize their anxiety by avoiding a widening circle of anxiety-provoking settings.

In the last chapter we learned that the physical symptoms of panic, known as the emergency response, are actually components of our stress response system. The emotional brain and the "panic and anxiety branch" of the HPA axis (also discussed in chapter 3) implement a flight or a freeze response to cope with anxiety-provoking stresses. The panicking person feels impelled to flee or escape from the stressor or else is immobilized even to the point of virtual paralysis with fear. During the "flight" response, the heart rate and breathing speed up and the muscles ready for swift, forceful action (like rushing out of a movie theater during a panic attack). During a "freeze," the person's body tenses in preparation for contending with a threat that psychologically he feels too petrified to engage with (like feeling too consumed with fear to even enter an elevator or merge with traffic traveling on a freeway), and often a pattern of avoidant behavior emerges. Researchers tracking the hormones that trigger these reactions have found that people's systems can "learn" to release these hormones when they are embroiled in situations that seem unpredictable and uncontrollable.

This "learned alarm" reaction to physical sensations and phobic situations evolves largely outside of conscious awareness. Indeed, we only become conscious of panic once an attack has already begun and, like a runaway train, is difficult to control. For a time after an initial panic attack, life may seem to have returned more or less to normal. But under the surface, the emotional brain is attempting to field the barrage of uneasy feelings and uncomfortable situations that are evolving. Panic's physical sensations and frightening, intrusive emotional feelings are morphing into anxious moods—longer-term, more general, and less acutely disturbing, but fraught with tension and thoughts of impending misfortune. This anxiety, in its turn, increases the chance of panic attacks that can blaze with renewed force.

In order to learn to contend with panic, we may usefully divide it into thinking, physical, and behavioral components. Once panic disorder has set in, the person's thinking during attacks becomes frightening, indeed catastrophic, consisting of alarm about escalating physical symptoms and intrusive automatic thoughts about dreaded outcomes. The panicker is apt to be acutely fearful of loss of control, going insane, or dying.

Treatment: Reverse Engineering Anxiety and Panic Attacks

Effective treatment targets the "hot button" processes that animate and sustain panic:

- Escalation of the emergency response and the scary misinterpretation of its causes and consequences
- Apprehension about the attacks before they begin and exaggeration of their destructive potential as they happen
- Feelings of loss of control
- Avoidance of situations where attacks could be triggered

One of the first steps in treating and reverse engineering anxiety and panic attacks is to recognize that in the midst of fear, things are not what they seem. When the emergency response or physical situations where attacks could be triggered are dangerous at all, the danger is by definition exaggerated: it is neither mortal nor imminent. Persons with panic also tend to exaggerate the negative impact of attacks and underrate their ability to cope with situations.

The reverse engineering of panic is straightforward. Because panic involves an activation of the emergency response, relaxation strategies can be implemented to counter "bad stress" reactions and strengthen self-control. To reengineer the feelings of loss of control that accompany panic, at the beginning of the next chapter we will introduce you to our Self-Control Relaxation Training techniques that will help you to refocus on the present moment rather than dire future possibilities, gain control of your muscular tension level, and develop the capacity to regulate your breathing.

For many people, when the emergency response engages, respiration becomes rapid and shallow as a panic attack begins. This observation led psychiatric researcher Donald Klein to theorize that a central mechanism of panic is the frightening mental sense of a shortage of the air supply. A great deal of clinical experience and cutting-edge research have proven the potency of breathing retraining as a component of panic treatment and for the easing of phobia avoidance. Accordingly, rapid and shallow breathing can be reverse engineered by slowing and regulating the breathing, a technique you will learn in the next chapter.

Waves of fear that occur early in panic attacks can lead to an acute sense of loss of control: *The very idea* of being consumed with terror—the expectation of panic—can trigger negative automatic thoughts that cause one to react by recoiling from what is feared. As the emergency response escalates and automatic thoughts of disaster explode in the panicker's mind, he temporarily loses the capacity to regain his composure or evaluate his situation rationally. You will learn to implement cognitive-behavioral strategies to reverse engineer apprehension, automatic thoughts, and panicky thinking by identifying anxiety triggers and analyzing and challenging dysfunctional thoughts and then replacing them with realism and coping thoughts.

Acute physical reactions have a central role in panic disorder. You will learn to sharpen your self-control relaxation skills when you are *not* overwhelmed by stress, and then become more and more proficient at reducing your stress response in the face of increasing anxiety and challenges to your composure. As you develop the capacity to roll back fear and apprehension, you will begin to regain clarity and confidence in your ability to resume coping with the situations, events, and activities from which panic and fear has excluded you.

Chapter Five

Conquering Panic

s you might surmise from the last chapter, or know all too well
from your own experience, panic consists of very disturbing,
unusual feelings that are mystifying and disheartening to contend
with. Whenever attacks are part of your anxiety condition, overcoming
panic becomes top priority, since it is so demoralizing and disorganizing
that it limits progress and focus on any other emotional problem. Treatment consists of learning to understand and control the intensely disturbing symptoms and impulses and replacing negative thoughts with realistic
coping thoughts.

In Order to Overcome Panic, What Must I Learn to Control and Relieve?

- Escalation of physical tension

- Catastrophic interpretation of bodily symptoms

- Physical reactions to stressful situations

- Mental overreaction to the impact of anxiety and panic

- Emotional discomfort in anxiety-provoking situations

Self-Control Relaxation Training

Physical symptoms of panic make people feel like jumping out of their skins. Panickers are flooded with fear and tension during attacks until their capacity to concentrate and think rationally all but evaporates. A top priority, then, is development of skills for reducing such acute tension.

Self-control training, or SCT, has an important role in panic and anxiety reduction. SCT helps focus your attention, increase mental awareness, relieve stress, and gain control. SCT also helps alleviate anxiety-stimulated physical tension and quiet disturbing thoughts and impulses until they eventually dissipate.

In order to acquire the techniques of self-control relaxation, read the following sections and start practicing the exercises on a regular basis *at times of low stress*. By building your skills in this way, you will have the opportunity to concentrate on the techniques and practice them until you get confident in your abilities to induce relaxation.

Each of the three self-control relaxation skills you will learn imparts different skills for working to relieve anxiety. The breathing technique will enable you to become more composed and focus your attention. Learning to focus on sensory impressions will help you stay in the present, thus combating the tendency to focus on the past (a hallmark of depression) or fear the future (a common root of anxiety). Practice in progressive muscle relaxation increases awareness of the level of your physical tension and activates your capacity to control it. Self-awareness and focused attention can be scarce commodities during episodes of anxious distress. When attained, they light up your path to composure like a beacon in a storm.

Each person experiences anxious emotional feelings differently, so a unique set of relaxation techniques will prove most suitable for each individual. If you've had good experiences with yoga, breathing exercises, progressive muscle relaxation, or meditation, you will probably notice techniques containing elements of these practices are comfortable and useful for you.

Start your self-control relaxation training now. *Shut your eyes* for a minute and *notice* what occurs in your mind and body. Be aware of thoughts, sensations, behaviors, and emotional feelings. As you stay with your breathing and focus on bodily sensations, you will notice that your thoughts change a great deal from one moment to the next. Just let whatever thoughts arise come and go. You might imagine your thoughts moving like ships on water across your line of sight, coming and going in and out of your awareness.

Accept all of your thoughts as nothing more than thoughts. If an emotion accompanies a thought, accept that, too, and know that it, like the thought, will pass. Continue to focus on your breathing and direct your mind to stay with it regardless of the nature of your thoughts and feelings. Describe your experience in writing:

Next, close your eyes again for a couple of minutes and pay attention to your breathing. Jot down what you notice:

Continue your practice *at least twice a day for the next four days*. Notice what appears on your mental "movie screen" and focus on your breathing. You may devote every session to both the techniques. To benefit the most:

- Find quiet times and situations to practice when you are unlikely to be distracted or interrupted.

- If you find that you are too uneasy to close your eyes, practice at first with your eyes open. Focus your gaze downward. Close your eyes if and whenever you become comfortable enough to do so.

- Remember to notice your breathing. *Control your awareness* (the noticing, focusing part of the process) more than the act of breathing.

The following technique uses elements of slowed, diaphragmatic breathing, progressive muscle relaxation, and present-moment focus on bodily sensations. By practicing this technique once or twice a day for one to two weeks, you will become skillful at decreasing anxious tension.

It can be helpful to record the SCT relaxation exercise on a tape recorder, pausing long enough between instructions to allow time for them to be followed. If someone you know has a voice that you would prefer to listen to, you might ask him or her to record the instructions instead. Complete instructions for the induction of deep relaxation are provided in appendix B, and you will find instructions for relaxation and breathing from a meditation tradition in appendix D.

A Breathing Cure

Scientific opinion holds that panic is frequently accompanied by altered breathing that usually results in an increased carbon dioxide level that can cause numbness, tingling, and light-headedness. In most cases, *consciously slowing and regulating the respiration will remedy panic breathing.*

Begin by sitting up straight with your eyes closed, feet flat on the floor, and palms resting on your legs. Take a breath, hold it a moment, and then exhale s-l-o-w-l-y. Take another breath, hold it, and exhale slowly, thinking the word "calm." Now take three more of these calming breaths.

Continue to breathe slowly and regularly. Turn your attention to your hands. Curl your fingers into fists and tighten them. Spread the tightness to your forearms and then your upper arms. Press your arms tightly against your sides. Lift your shoulders like you are shrugging, tighten them, and hold the tension. Study the tension for several seconds. Then relax. Drop your shoulders. Let your arms drop away from your sides. Relax your upper arms and forearms. Let your fists uncurl and release all the tightness from your fingers. Study the relaxation.

Now for your facial muscles and neck: Purse your lips and clench your jaws. Tighten the muscles along the back of your neck. Squeeze your eyes shut. Wrinkle your forehead and crease your brow like you're frowning. Make all the tight parts tighter, very tight. Hold the tension, and study it for several seconds. Now relax. Release the tightness in your neck and jaws and lips; smooth your forehead and relax your brows; relax all the muscles around your eyes. Maintain and study the relaxation for twice as long as you held the tension.

Continue to breathe slowly and regularly. Shift your attention to the places on your body where you feel physical pressure. Notice the pressure sensations from the seat pressing against your bottom and the backs of your legs. Feel the pressure of the seatback on your back and of the floor where your feet are resting. Study the pressure sensations.

Then let yourself be aware of sounds. Listen to the sounds from nearby, from other people, and from outside or away in the distance. Notice low-

and high-pitched sounds, their steadiness or intermittence, and the smoothness or roughness of the tones. Simply listen, expanding your attention to include all the sounds around you. Continue to breathe slowly and regularly.

Then place one hand on your solar plexus, the soft area near the top of the stomach, just beneath the upside-down V of the sternum bone, and rest it there lightly. Notice the motion as you breathe. As you breathe, pretend that your hand is resting on a balloon. The balloon inflates when you inhale and deflates when you exhale. The area beneath your solar plexus expands and thrusts out with each inflation, contracts and pulls in with each deflation.

In order to help maintain a good rhythm in balloon breathing, count down slowly from ten to one, inflating the balloon by inhaling with each count. Each time you are about to exhale, say the word "calm" to yourself and deflate the balloon.

At the end of this exercise, open your eyes.

Remember: to train effectively in relaxation, plan to practice consistently *at times of relatively low stress* until you become skillful. After at

Table 5.1

Balloon Breathing

	Breathing In	**Breathing Out**
Action	Breathe in on each count. Count down from ten (or five or twenty—your choice) to one.	Say the word "calm" or "smooth" to yourself each time you are ready to breathe out.
Image	Inflating the balloon	Deflating the balloon
Physical reaction	Solar plexus expands outward	Solar plexus contracts and pulls inward
Effect	Lungs fill with air and diaphragm drops, pushing stomach outward	Lungs contract and expel air as diaphragm rises

Worksheet 5.1
EVALUATING SCT TECHNIQUES

Technique	Portion of Practice Time Spent on Technique (Total = 100%)	Effectiveness (Rate Low to High)
Diaphragmatic breathing		
Progressive muscle relaxation		
Focus on present-moment sensations		

least five days of practice, complete the worksheet above. Which exercises seem the most effective for you?

CUE-CONTROLLED RELAXATION

You will soon learn to apply SCT relaxation at selected times of stress. To prepare, start learning to relax on cue. Begin by practicing at will at times of minimal discomfort. Cue yourself by mentally saying, "Relax!" "Calm!" or "Breathe through!" and then spend between a half and two minutes trying to get maximum effect from your favorite SCT relaxation technique. For instance, when you start to feel restless in the doctor's or dentist's waiting room or while waiting your turn to get your hair cut or in a checkout line, take a few calming breaths, tense and then relax your hands or jaws, or else shift your focus to the sounds, sights, and aromas of the present. Another easy, yet effective technique for regulating your breathing is simply to close your mouth. Then you will breathe more regularly through your nose. The relaxation induction in appendix B also includes instructions for relaxing on cue.

At this point we recommend you devote your energy to identifying mildly stressful moments—such as when you feel a little impatient, restless, or irritated—cueing yourself to relax, and trying to relieve as much tension as you can by implementing the technique of your choice. By this means you will fortify the power of SCT to serve you as a tool for tackling anxiety and panic. Try to resist the temptation of enlisting cue-controlled relaxation to contend with major episodes of panic or anxiety until you have added a few more therapeutic arrows to your anxiolytic sling.

Become a Personal Anxiety Technologist— Learn, Experiment, and Evaluate

Knowledge is power. This adage is especially apt for knowledge about the realm of anxiety, whose reign of terror is largely maintained through fear of dire possibilities of the unknown. Supercharged clouds of dread and confusion can be neutralized and dispelled by knowledge and understanding. Since science creates new vistas of understanding, the scientific method is germane to arriving at a deep comprehension of anxiety. From automated tellers to microwaves to TV satellite dishes, most people fit new technology and high-tech devices to their needs and improve their quality of life. Similarly, scientific research and discoveries in psychology, psychiatry, and neuroscience have resulted in great strides in anxiety therapy.

Self-control relaxation training and the other cognitive-behavioral techniques that we advocate are rooted in scientific research and provide a powerful means of recovery from anxiety disorders. While protocols have been created for treating various symptoms and disorders, everyone is unique, so you will benefit most by actively fitting the techniques to your personality and lifestyle. Become a personal anxiety technologist by *learning* how the best techniques work, *experimenting* with them to determine how potent they are in relieving your anxious discomfort, and *evaluating* their overall effectiveness.

How should we think scientifically about anxiety? According to the late Richard Feynman, a highly regarded physicist, three considerations are paramount:

1. *Scientific reasoning must be disciplined.* Discipline in a scientific context entails making a firm deal with yourself to perform experiments that utilize specific techniques to cope with particular situations. Consistently follow your plan for dealing with your targeted thoughts, feelings, or behavior.

2. *Observation must be careful.* Notice what you do to contend with anxiety, how long you do it, and the results. Imagine which events

and shifts of your moods and feelings would be observed if a camcorder could record your practice from start to finish, while instruments measured your level of tension.

3. *The results of observation should be considered objectively.* Can you arrive at a reasonable theory that accounts for changes in your thoughts, feelings, or behavior that resulted from the particular way you handled situations, events, or activities? What patterns do you discern after careful consideration of your observations?

Adapted from *The Meaning of It All*, 1998

Recognizing and Redefining Physical Panic Symptoms

As you learned in chapter 3, the physical portion of panic and anxiety attacks is known as the emergency response. The ER is a negative activation response that resembles a fear reaction. In similar ways, the anxious or frightened person readies himself to take swift, forceful action to escape danger. But since immediate mortal danger is seldom present during panic and anxiety attacks, the ER is a *false alarm*.

Panic attacks are disabling largely because of their capacity to besiege the panicker with these confusing, disturbing symptoms. Acute awareness of these bodily sensations adds to the apprehensiveness by acting as mental radar that signals the brain that anxiety is on the rise as soon as the ER symptoms begin and feeds the panicker's confusion by continuing to sound the alarm as long as they remain uncontrolled. Thus, the ER is both a false alarm and truly a trigger for panic attacks.

A powerful way to counter this disturbing sense of endangerment and uncontrollability is through recognition of the ER symptoms as merely the false alarm of an anxiety or panic attack and accurately relabeling their true causes. Read through the following checklist of emergency response symptoms (portions of which are adapted from Otto et al., 1996) and check off all that you have experienced, even if only occasionally. Then carefully reread about the real cause of each item you've checked. From now on, *every time an ER symptom occurs over the next few weeks, identify it as anxiety and state its real cause to yourself.*

Emergency Response Symptoms

❏ **Tight chest**   One of the first ways our anxious brains activate our bodies for swift response to perceived danger is by automatically tightening up the chest muscles. Tightened chest muscles also force us to engage in rapid, shallow breathing.

❏ **Rapid breathing and heartbeat**   "Panic breathing"—rapid, shallow breathing that sharply increases the body's supply of oxygen—results from tightening the chest muscles. Extra oxygen is accumulated in the lungs, assuring extra stamina and healing power in the event of a struggle to survive. As oxygen accumulates and is blended into the bloodstream, the heart beats extra strong in order to circulate this high-octane blood to the parts of the body where it's needed most.

❏ **Sweating**   This occurs for two reasons. First, both the activation of the heart and lungs and the tensing of muscles for action are hard physical work. The by-product is heat, which the body's cooling system offsets through sweating. Second, sweating makes the skin slippery, which facilitates escape when being grasped or held by an attacker.

❏ **Numbness and tingling**   One source of these symptoms is *piloerection,* where our hair literally stands on end due to fright. Another is that the pattern of blood flow is altered *toward* the big skeletal muscles and *away* from the hands, feet, fingers, and toes. Numbness and tingling result, in much the same way as when a hand or leg falls asleep due to temporarily decreased circulation. See below for the third source of this sensation, whose cause is shared with dizziness or light-headedness.

❏ **Dizziness or light-headedness**   This is a consequence of panic breathing. The extra oxygen that rapid, shallow breathing brings in has a role in light-headedness. In greater measure, the prime suspect is *unexpired carbon dioxide that accumulates at the bottom of the lungs* because of insufficiency in exhaling. Minute increases in the body's carbon dioxide level cause numbness and tingling in the extremities, dizziness, and light-headedness.[1] But keep in mind this

---

1 In anxiety research, air with an increased CO_2 level is sometimes used to precipitate panic attacks. Nonpanicker college students who agree to be subjects of such research are asked to breathe air from tanks with an elevated concentration of carbon dioxide. This usually artificially induces them to have anxiety or panic attacks in the research setting so their responses can be studied scientifically.

comment by noted anxiety expert Richard McNally: "There are three things you can be sure of in life—death, taxes, and that you'll never faint during a panic attack." The basis for this strong assurance rests on the fact that blood pressure rises and heart rate *increases* during a panic, while fainting is caused by a *drop* in blood pressure and heart rate.

❐ **Nausea or upset stomach**   While we are contending with imminent danger, our brain shuts down all unnecessarily energy-consuming processes. The energy devoted to digesting food is redirected to ensuring survival. Consequently, digestion alters and may cease, and stomach acidity may change, resulting in "butterflies" and other feelings of stomach upset.

❐ **Bright vision and oversensitivity to noise or a sense of unreality** The brain of a person who feels endangered turns his senses of sight and sound way up in order to optimize their input about the proximity of threat. The pupils dilate in order to expand peripheral vision and enhance visual discrimination in case the light gets too dim. Consequently, in the absence of real danger, many panickers report discomfort from oversensitivity to light. Similarly, at times of danger the brain sets the "volume control" of the auditory nerves on high in order to permit detection of faint sounds that foreshadow peril. During panic, this enhanced sense of hearing amplifies insignificant noises that can add to the irritation and distraction. Intensified sight and sound may also contribute to a sense of unreality.

❐ **Choking sensations and dry mouth**   The sensation of choking comes from two sources. When tense and anxious, the muscles around the throat commonly tighten up but—do not fear!—cannot close off our throats. Also, rapid, shallow panic breathing sets up a tide of moving air that blows the throat dry. This symptom is also experienced as a lump in the throat, known in the psychiatric literature by the term *globus hystericus*—indicating that the lump is emotional rather than physical in nature.

❐ **Heavy legs, achy chest muscles, and trembling**   All these sensations and symptoms are produced by the muscles tensing in preparation for action. Just thinking about physically demanding activities produces a degree of tension. When we are mentally readying to cope with a threat, as we do during panic and anxiety attacks, the chest, leg, and other big skeletal muscles tense up. In addition, tightening of the chest muscles is an "occupational hazard" of sustained panic breathing (see "tight chest" above), but it will cause achiness. Whenever we tighten a set of muscles and hold it, a tremor can eventually result.

Explain your ER symptoms to yourself *every time* they occur. Start keeping track of the symptoms and discomfort you experience on the worksheet on page 86. Continue to practice and to customize the self-control relaxation techniques for at least a couple of weeks, until you find that you can consistently lower your tension level shortly after beginning a session. Once you've attained this skill, continue regular, low-stress practices often enough to maintain it.

USING THE SUDs SCALE

There is a scale for measuring anxiety. The Subjective Units of Discomfort (SUDs) scale is widely used to rate the discomfort experienced during negative experiences and the amount of relief achieved through therapeutic techniques. Psychologists call these 0–10 ratings *subjective units* because the individual scores his or her personal or subjective estimation, rather than using an outside objective standard. SUDs may be used to evaluate any specified kind of anxiety. To rate panic, recall the unique sense of nervousness and physical tension you felt in specific panic-producing situations. A 0 represents no panic at all; a 5 is moderately panicky, when the nervousness is definitely there and getting disturbing; and a 10 is the worst panic attack you've ever experienced.

1. *List* the ER symptoms that you associate with your panic attacks in the first column of worksheet 5.2 below.

2. In the column for each week, rate the *average* SUDs for each symptom.

3. Next to it, write in parentheses the *highest* SUDs rating, indicating the maximum discomfort the symptom caused you during the week.

Example: Since every one of Jim's attacks this week begins with a very disturbing pounding of his heart, he gives this symptom an average rating of 6. It occasionally becomes severe, so he rates the highest level as a 9. Thus, on the worksheet he lists his "pounding heart" as symptom 1 and the first week's entry as 6 (9), indicating that it's very disturbing at every occurrence (and thus averages 6), and once during the week got severe (and so reached a 9). The second week his panic was milder, because of the treatment he was receiving, so the average severity dropped to 4 and the worst incident hit only a 7. See how these scores are recorded on worksheet 5.2 below.

As you redefine your symptoms and practice SCT relaxation, your SUDs ratings are likely to decrease in both average and maximum intensity.

Stress, Anxious Thinking, and Panic

Recall from chapter 3 that every stress reaction utilizes the HPA (hypothalamus-pituitary-adrenal) axis to make the "mind-body stress connection"

Worksheet 5.2
THE PATTERN OF MY PANIC SYMPTOMS

Symptom	Week 1	Week 2	Week 3	Week 4	Week 5	Week 6
1. Jim's pounding heart	6(9)	4(7)				
2.						
3.						
4.						
5.						
6.						

Six Tips for Immediate Relief of Panic

- Remember: You are not your anxiety.

- Conscious slowing and regulating of your breathing will remedy hyperventilation and shortness of breath.

- Your feelings are not harmful, dangerous, or stupid; they are just an exaggeration of your normal stress reaction. Do not try to fight them or wish them away.

- Do not add anxiety to your panic by thinking about what "might" happen. Stay in the present and notice what really is and is not happening to you.

- Rate your fear level from 0–10 and watch it rise and drop. Notice that it only stays high for a relatively short time.

- When the fear comes, expect and accept it. Allow it time to pass without running away from it.

that results in complex changes in the physical state of readiness. The *amount* of HPA activation can range from slight tension and increased effort to triggering of the emergency response.

Many common situations will produce HPA arousal, such as:

- Having an argument
- Running up a flight of stairs
- Getting up suddenly from bed, an easy chair, or the dinner table after a big meal
- Rushing to finish a project
- Watching an action or police drama
- Fast dancing
- Aerobics
- Lifting or carrying a heavy object

These common stressors are not life threatening or dangerous. They don't stir mortal fear or blind fury. Nor, for that matter, do the stressors that lead to panic: phobic situations or emergency response symptoms. But once a person with panic disorder misinterprets her HPA arousal as threatening, her thoughts quickly become extremely disturbing and hard to control, so that these panic-triggering stressors may *seem* very dangerous.

Every stress—brief or lasting, positive, negative, or toxic—stimulates HPA arousal. There is no objective difference between the kinds of arousal that positive and negative stresses stimulate, and in fact many "positive" stress situations are acceptable or normal parts of daily life. *Anxious thinking* makes all the difference between the rather negligible arousal that usually occurs during positive or commonplace stress and the negative arousal that may trigger panic.

MINI-PRACTICES: USING SCT TO RELIEVE REAL-LIFE TENSION

Mini-practices will help you build an ability to relieve HPA arousal due to negative stress by controlling it through use of SCT relaxation techniques. By "mini-practicing" relief of your stress responses, you can gain a measure of control over reactions to everyday stress and create the headroom to start modifying your beliefs and expectations about the power of stressful events to trigger panic.

Prepare for mini-practices by refreshing your memory of the relaxation techniques you prefer. Review the ratings you made in the worksheet on page 86 and read the description of cue-controlled relaxation below. Next, think about various situations that you often encounter during daily living that cause you some negative arousal, like impatience, annoyance, aggravation, embarrassment, or overstimulation. Don't forget that even good stressors like playing sports, cheering for our team (or razzing theirs), and making love can lead to stress responses. Choose a number of mildly negatively arousing situations that would earn an SUDs rating between 2 and 4 as targets for your mini-practices.

Discover how SCT relaxation techniques can help you cope with these situations better by using the cue-controlled relaxation you've already begun practicing to conduct mini-practices. When you enter a target situation, briefly employ your favorite technique to relieve the stress. Rate your SUDs and then *cue yourself to relax* by mentally saying "Relax," "Calm,"

"Breathe through," or another signal of your choice. Then *intentionally* initiate an SCT technique and try to achieve maximum relaxation and control for between thirty seconds and two minutes. Finally, rate your SUDs again.

For example, cue yourself to relax, and then take three calming or balloon breaths while waiting for your date or your ride to show up. Or instead of waiting impatiently for a traffic light to change, tense your hands on the steering wheel, hold and study the tension, and then relax. During a lull in a heated debate at your restaurant table, focus on the aromas, sights, and sounds. In your role as personal anxiety technologist, do at least ten mini-practices per day for the next two weeks. Remember to rate your panic SUDs at the beginning and end of every practice, so you can measure whether and how much it changes as a result of mini-practicing. As your level of confidence in cue-controlled relaxation gets stronger, try to utilize it in gradually more challenging situations.

By reverse engineering your negative stress responses, you are learning to use a power tool for dealing with the physical symptoms and focusing on problems of anxiety and panic attacks. What anxiety-provoking sensation, thought, or behavior are you working on today? How is your practice affecting it?

This Calls for Outside Help

Seek professional help if any of these is true:

- You continue to believe that your disorder is physical, not psychological

- Your panic symptoms are severely disabling or terrifying

- You do not progress through use of this or other self-help programs, or if you get worse

- You feel like you're losing ground and your livelihood or welfare is in jeopardy

- Some disturbing physical symptoms seem not to be part of a panic or anxiety disorder

Catastrophic Thinking and Panic

When you started to have attacks of anxiety or panic, physical panic symptoms gained the capacity to start your apprehension radar beeping. The immediate trigger for panicky thinking is a kind of negative arousal caused by either a physical panic symptom or a phobic situation. At highly tense moments panickers automatically form catastrophic anxiety propositions. They can hold great sway over our feelings until we size them up for what they are.

When a danger is real, automatic negative thoughts serve on a potent, compelling cognitive "SWAT team" that helps us mobilize swiftly for survival, but they are equally compelling during false alarms of acute anxiety or panic. During panic attacks, automatic negative thoughts distort the panicker's thinking and contribute to the sense of uncontrollability.

Panicky thinking is *acute catastrophic thinking.* Most times, when the possibility of madness, a heart attack or respiratory arrest, a fainting episode, or other form of public incapacitation crosses the panicker's mind and produces apprehension, such a bad event is neither likely nor realistic. If episodes of these kinds of incapacitation will impact an individual's life at all, they are not especially likely to occur in restaurants, while attending a sporting event, sweating on a hot day, or alone in a shower. *True catastrophes are not likely to occur in phobic situations or panic attacks.*

People with panic disorder occasionally find that one or two of their anxiety symptoms remain quite disturbing even after months of practice. For physical panic symptoms that persist in this way, a different procedure, called interoceptive exposure, is likely to be useful. See pages 155–156 to learn about this technique.

Table 5.2 illustrates the first step in the process of cutting through catastrophic thinking—"taking a bite out of the fear," as psychologist Thomas Borkovec puts it, and stating clearly what one is afraid of. Each person's automatic thoughts are enclosed in parentheses in the right-hand column, followed by his or her anxiety propositions—specific statements of what is feared and the physical symptoms or situation that triggered it.

Table 5.2
STATING WHAT I'M AFRAID OF

My Situation	Anxiety Trigger	(Automatic Thought) Anxiety Proposition
Mr. A: I'm dressed in my cheap clothes	Going for drinks with my coworkers	(I'll never fit in.) No one will talk to me because I don't look hip or cool.
Ms. B: Dr. R moved his office to that new high-rise building	Riding in a crowded elevator	(Gonna lose it.) I'll get light-headed and feel like passing out while waiting for the elevator door to open.
Mrs. C: We need new linens; I have to go shopping.	Being in a very busy store during white sale	(Never get to make my purchase; I'll run straight for the bathroom.) I'll feel like I'm going to lose mental control in that crowd.
Ms. D: I'm home alone with the baby.	Spouse out of town and I feel insecure	(History of strokes in my family, and I'm about to have one!) My heart's pounding and I'm light-headed and dizzy—aren't these stroke symptoms?

Cognitive Panic Therapy: Realistic Thinking about Catastrophic Fears

Cognitive panic therapy (CPT) is a three-component system for releasing the panicker from the clutches of anxious thinking. The first component is monitoring and recording the thoughts that lead up to panic and occur during and after attacks. Next, you will learn to analyze your thought records and discern the specific ways that anxiety alters your viewpoint and panic hobbles you. Finally, we will help you to reverse engineer your panic by reframing your acute catastrophic thinking. You will learn to think more realistically about anxiety-provoking situations and systematically gain control of panic so that you can face your fears and live your life.

KEEPING A PANIC RECORD

On the Panic Record below (worksheet 5.3), start entering the details about each episode of panic or acute anxiety. What was the situation in which it occurred? Note who else was there, when the episode took place, and how long it lasted. How severe was the panic at the worst moment, and what specific physical panic symptoms did you feel? During anxious episodes, automatic negative thoughts compete with disturbing images and impulses in clamoring noisily for our limited attention, so observations should be made in a careful, disciplined way. At a minimum, try to record memory-jogging notes shortly after each episode.

Act as a personal anxiety technologist by treating every episode of acute anxiety or panic as an opportunity for scientific observation. Record any instance of even moderate anxiety rather than limiting it to only bad attacks. At the time or later, write out whatever automatic negative thoughts came to your mind as completely as possible. Include thoughts, mental images, or memories. A few times a week, establish regular periods of at least twenty minutes for doing this written portion of your therapy. You will find additional copies of the Panic Record in appendix A.

Remember Mindy? In the last chapter, we learned that the final stage of her divorce and a minor car accident stressed her, and her panic disorder crystallized when she started to teach her daughter to drive. The episode of acute anxiety she experienced while trying to give the lesson made a good entry in her Panic Record.

Fill in a row of this Panic Record whenever you experience panicky feelings. The more observations you record, the quicker you can get a clear understanding of the emotions, physical feelings, and anxious thoughts that drive your panic. Don't expect your automatic thoughts to make logical sense: After all, if you were thinking rationally in panic-provoking situations, you'd feel far better than you do! Automatic thoughts may be *self-statements,* like "I'm afraid I'm going to throw up" or "I'm about to lose control of my car"; *estimations of others' reactions,* like "They'll think I've made a complete fool of myself"; *mental images,* like "always" being overwhelmed by the sheer intensity of the sights and sounds of a professional

Worksheet 5.3
PANIC RECORD

Situation: Who, What, When, Where?	Length of Time of Attack	SUDs (Rate 0–10)	Physical Symptoms	Automatic Thoughts	How Would I *Rather* Think?
I took Brittany for a driving lesson on Tuesday afternoon in a residential part of Shady Hills.	30 min.	7	Rapid heartbeat, dizziness, sweating, shakiness	I think I'm going to faint. (*She* isn't doing anything wrong), but *I'm* afraid she'll kill us both! I'm such a loser!*	

*The statement in parentheses is a realistic thought that Mindy had in the midst of her automatic thoughts. Use parentheses as needed in this column to distinguish your *non*automatic thinking.

athletic event; or *memories,* real or imagined, of past experiences that triggered similar distress. Record them as clearly as possible.

Leave the last column, "How Would I Rather Think?" blank for now.

ANALYZING HOW *YOUR* PANIC AFFECTS *YOU*

Once you have charted several situations, physical symptoms, and automatic thoughts on your Panic Record, see what patterns begin to emerge. You may discover that automatic negative thoughts that lead to panicky feelings often occur in or near phobic situations. You may even realize that you have begun to act phobic. Also, you may have become apprehensive of certain ER symptoms so that panic begins to escalate when they occur.

You might discern that you have developed a pattern of thinking catastrophically. Do many of your automatic thoughts seem to exaggerate the likelihood of a bad outcome for the situations where they occur? Are you perhaps underrating you capacity to cope with possible difficulties or to bounce back if they occur?

Are you really as fragile and vulnerable as your automatic thoughts depict you to be? Natasha, a secretary with panic disorder and asthma who took care of her ailing father, started to fear traveling away from her home. She examined her fears carefully and discovered that she was afraid that she would feel "really awful" by the time she reached her destinations. No matter what good times she planned, she didn't think she could weather the severity of her panic and would somehow have to find a way home.

Once she realized that the dreaded state, severe attacks, and urgent escape plan were her main preoccupations, she could assess her fears realistically. She realized that: 1) her panic attacks no longer lasted any longer than thirty minutes, and in the past three months they occurred no more than once a day; 2) the medication she took for them consistently kept her panics mild; 3) she was delighted at the prospect of getting together with her good friends who lived an hour away and whose innocent invitation had precipitated the latest bout of apprehension and dread; and 4) if, in spite of everything, she actually *did* feel too anxious to drive home, someone would comfort her and—if necessary—help arrange her transportation. After reflecting in this way, Natasha decided she wasn't so fragile after all; so she went, enjoyed herself, and experienced only minimal discomfort.

You can probably clear up these two kinds of thinking errors pretty directly once you identify them:

- *Anxiety that a panic attack is the opening act to a terrible main event.* Since you have already trained in understanding the real nature of panic symptoms and controlling acute negative arousal, you already know that they don't portend heart attacks, respiratory arrest, public humiliation, or the onset of insanity. When you notice these catastrophic misinterpretations of physical symptoms occurring, practice effectively challenging them by countering them with accurate data and scientific explanations.

- *The catastrophic fear that once a panic attack begins, it will last a long time and be very severe.* The next time Mindy took her daughter out for a driving lesson, she told herself that the physical reactions she was having were only panic symptoms, exaggerated stress reactions that were not harmful. She also reminded herself that they would only last twenty minutes or so, regardless of whether she escaped the situation or stayed and faced the music. After a few rough minutes, her discomfort began to subside.

Let's examine more closely how several people with panic disorder have successfully contended with these kinds of anxious cognitions. They practiced challenging their catastrophic misinterpretations of physical symptoms by bringing more realistic, alternative thoughts to mind. First they completed a number of Panic Records and grew familiar with their patterns of physical symptoms and automatic thoughts in a variety of situations. Then, during written cognitive therapy sessions, they arrived at specific alternative ways of thinking about their anxiety, as illustrated on the following page.

Use these examples to start developing your own alternative ways of thinking. Rely on your growing understanding of panic and its tricks to augment your ingenuity and determination. Talk with support people (see pp. 143–145) and a therapist, if available. Continue your panic recording, but *start filling in the right-hand column of your Panic Records* with these challenging alternatives, under the heading "How Would I *Rather* Think?"

In addition to cue-controlled relaxation and reframing physical symptoms, practice self-talk using preferable alternative thoughts *to challenge and modify panicky thinking whenever appropriate and as consistently as you can during episodes of panic and acute anxiety.*

Table 5.3
REALISTIC THINKING

When the automatic thought is:	The alternative thought could be:
Ruben fears he won't be able to breathe.	"The shortness of breath and chest tightening that I'm feeling are symptoms of panic, not respiratory distress. Both symptoms are meant to promote rapid, shallow breathing as an emergency response. They're unpleasant, not dangerous."
Sherri thinks she is going through a catastrophic physical reaction.	"This is a panic attack, *not* a heart attack, respiratory arrest, or acute psychosis."
Eddie thinks that this episode of profuse sweating is going to ruin the whole party for him.	"This physical symptom and the catastrophic thought are parts of an anxiety attack and will last less than a half hour [or whatever is the usual *maximum* length of *your* attacks—check your Panic Records]."
Sara knows it's "just" panic but fears she won't be able to stand all the emotional pain.	"This is a panic attack like the ones I've been controlling lately. Since the SUDs level hasn't exceeded *x* recently [fills in her most recent average SUDs level], it probably won't be any worse right now. In other words, bad, but not unbearable."

REFRAMING YOUR PANIC

Three cognitive reframing techniques will help you think differently and more realistically when you are panicky. Reestimating probabilities, decatastrophizing the worst-case scenario, and planning to cope with the natural consequences of a feared situation may be used separately or consolidated for tackling catastrophic thinking in real-life situations.

Reestimating Probabilities

When apprehensive, we naturally tend to exaggerate the probability that things will come out badly. At calmer moments, we are often eager to dismiss such alarmism as a case of the heebie-jeebies. An anxious person will tend to believe his own inaccurate, alarmist predictions about catastrophic outcomes of panic-provoking situations despite evidence to the contrary. Reestimation will build your skill at modifying predictions that are flawed by anxiety. First, estimate the *anxious probability*—the apparent likelihood that an anxiety-provoking event will turn out badly *on the basis of your point of view when you feel most apprehensive.*

Light at the End of the Tunnel

Can you see a light at the end of the tunnel? Are you approaching the point where you no longer experience SUDs levels above 3 due to panic? If so, congratulations! At this point, many people nevertheless continue to have occasional disturbing panics. Mental habits of predicting catastrophes and fearing loss of control can be deeply rooted and slow to disappear. The advanced cognitive techniques we presented herewith can empower you to loosen the grip of those roots, and—once you become adept—experience a new sense of composure and control.

Anchor this system of ratings by taking a few moments to think of recent or upcoming worrisome matters and rate how certain you are or were that they would come out badly. This *subjective* rating is expressed as a *probability percentage*—0 percent if there's no chance of a bad outcome, 50 percent for a 50-50 proposition, 100 percent for a seemingly certain catastrophe.

A large number of subjects in psychologist Thomas Borkovec's anxiety research program kept diaries of their worrisome negative predictions. Eighty-six percent of the time things came out better than they expected. The other 14 percent of the outcomes were not particularly good, but at least the worriers were satisfied with the ways they coped with what happened.

The next step is to think about this information during your next twenty-minute cognitive therapy practice and try to reestimate the *realistic probability* of the feared outcome of a situation you are avoiding. To do so, ask yourself: Rationally speaking, how likely is the feared outcome to actually occur? In order to be as objective as possible, consider the following:

- How often has this kind of situation come out this negative way before?

- Is this something that generally happens in my life? How likely is it that it would turn out in a negative way for another person?

- What's my recent track record? Is the trend in similar cases toward improvement?

- Is my objectivity being impaired by all-or-nothing thinking? What if I drop all clear-cut demoralizing exaggerators from my self-talk, like "always," "never," and "total failure"?

On the worksheet on the following page, list thoughts that raise your anxiety because they incorporate a prediction of negative or catastrophic outcome and rate their anxious probability. After completing your "reestimation homework," described above, fill in the realistic probability and note the considerations and rationale that led to your reestimate.

Hint: Don't underestimate the realistic probability of a bad outcome in an attempt to be encouraging. You don't need false courage, just a stronger basis for feeling safe or in control.

Decatastrophizing and Planning to Cope with Natural Consequences
- "What's the worst that could happen?"

- "So what?"

The next two techniques will help you to decatastrophize—to manage the actual consequences on occasions when things *do* turn out badly. Much of what remains of panic's dwindling influence over you is its sinister power to infect your imagination with unreasoning dread. In this section, you will learn ways of attaining more active control over the balance of your catastrophic, panic-driven fears, rather than continuing to be victimized by them.

Despite overestimating the likelihood and severity of ominous consequences, people who panic generally have an underlying sense of their capacity to survive adversity. Both psychologists Michelle Craske and David Barlow's worst-case scenario method and psychologist Ronald Rapee's "So what?" technique train the panicker to tap this core conviction and lift it into consciousness where it can fortify him. The Craske-Barlow method accomplishes this by preparing the person to cope with the most catastrophic

Worksheet 5.4
REALISTIC THINKING, WITH PROBABILITIES

Automatic Thought	Anxious Probability	Realistic Probability
I can never go to the mall anymore without feeling frightened.	80%	30% (I've quelled most panic attacks lately and have been successfully mini-practicing in crowds and checkout lines.)
I'll be really scared to drive fifty miles to my mother-in-law's.	95%	50% (I used to love that drive. I think I'm getting more comfortable again, although I'm still pretty doubtful.)

thing that could occur, while Rapee's technique enables the anxious person to consider what will remain after the smoke of the catastrophe clears.

Can you remember occasions when you overestimated how bad you would feel? Your apprehension was costly, wasn't it? Remember how heavily your inhibitions weighed on you, feeling so disheartening, and how daunting it was to put out your best effort? Some outcomes really *are* unpleasant; but what if you discovered that by thinking carefully and systematically about your fears you could get much more objective and dispel many of the remaining frightening shadows?

The first step in decatastrophizing is to ask yourself "What am I truly afraid of?" as soon as you notice that your apprehension is building. Be as specific as possible: Always figure that the fear involves interaction between you, the situation, and physical panic symptoms that you expect to be triggered.

After stating what specifically you are afraid of, apply either of the decatastrophization techniques or a combination of both. Following Craske and Barlow, spell out the worst-case scenario in detail and devote one or more cognitive therapy practice sessions to carefully considering the specific consequences and coping with the measure of discomfort that would result.

For instance, Russell, the young contractor we met in chapter 4, was convinced that he would become psychotic if he tried to resume going out to nightclubs with his friends. He spent a session analyzing his fears. Specifically, he determined, he feared that the overstimulating atmosphere of a club would bewilder and panic him to the point where he would become too immobilized and frightened to function, even to the point of losing the ability to leave and get himself home safely. He enlisted the aid of his best buddy, who agreed to keep an eye on him and promised to escort him to an emergency room if his fears became a reality; and he also enrolled at a local mental health clinic as another means of contending, if necessary, with his apprehension about having a nervous breakdown. After taking these precautions, Russell felt safe enough to begin venturing out to local clubs again.

If the consequences you fear are too terrifying, you have two choices. You could consider how you would expect to contend with the results of this new worst-case scenario and continue doing cognitive therapy with a series of scenarios that evolve, until you reach a point where your reaction stays within the comfort zone. Or, if the fears that emerge as your bottom line are still too potent for you to deal with safely through structured self-help therapy, then seek out the help of a qualified therapist. Here is a modest example of Craske and Barlow–style decatastrophization and a typical sample of Rapee-style decatastrophization.

Example: What's the Worst That Could Happen?

Stacy was afraid she would get stuck in an elevator, that she would try to open the door but it would not open. What's the worst thing that could happen then? She would pound on the door and shout for a while, work herself into a frenzy of panic, and probably start to relax (or at least be exhausted) by the time her rescuers freed her.

Example: So What?

Cal asked himself, "What if I became convinced I was having a heart attack at a Bears game, despite all my worries and precautions? Would my

Worksheet 5.5
Decatastrophization

Panicky Situation	Catastrophic Fear	How to Cope?	So What?
Russell goes back to a nightclub with his friends.	I "go psychotic"—too bewildered and immobilized to leave the nightclub.	Get a friend's help; get taken to the emergency room; call the local mental health clinic hotline.	Nobody will even remember if I get scared. At least I will have tried. If I get *that* nervous, I couldn't enjoy myself anyway.
Stacy rides an elevator.	The elevator gets stuck. I pound on the door and shout for a while, work myself into a frenzy of panic.	Probably start to relax (or at least be exhausted) by the time rescuers free me.	I'd think long and hard before ever taking *that* elevator again. And back to square one in working on elevator phobia. . . .
Cal attends a Chicago Bears football game.	I think I am having a heart attack and become terrified.	Beg someone to call the paramedics or take me to the emergency room.	My friends might be really annoyed with me. But at least I'll see part of the game live.

buddies resent me forever because I clutched my chest or treat
me as an unabashed attention-
seeker for begging someone to
call the paramedics?"

> A final key to success: Treat each inci-
> dent of heightened anxiety as a chal-
> lenge by coping with it strategically
> *every time* it occurs.

If a powerful, pounding heart-
beat played a part in Cal's episode and made him acutely panicky, is it at
all reassuring to know that a galloping heart like this could probably support immense exertion if truly necessary? When he realized he was not dying, only very fearful, would people be more likely to offer their help in a
caring way or to ignore and shun him? If the paramedics helped him
through the worst of his panic and then left, so what?

Perhaps decatastrophization techniques will enable you to relieve even
the most tenacious of fears that are associated with your panic disorder. By
answering either of two questions—"So what?" from the Rapee technique
or "If the absolute worst happens, how would I cope?" from the Barlow
and Craske decatastrophization technique—you can tap your inner determination to cope with daunting fears. Spend a few minutes during each
practice session with both of these techniques and arrive at a narrative or
dialogue. Reverse engineer your catastrophic thoughts: How would you
rather think about the situation if it should occur again?

Recap: How Have You Relieved Your Panic Disorder?

- By controlling your breathing, awareness, and level of physical tension

- By enhancing your self-control in order to focus on present-moment
  sensations

- By improving your capacity to think realistically and implement
  plans for dealing productively with anxiety-provoking situations

- By reaffirming your determination to surmount panic's "dark
  threats" to well-being and liberty

This chapter introduced you to the treatment of anxiety disorders and
enrolled you in a master class for vanquishing anxiety and panic attacks.
The techniques of self-control training and cue-controlled relaxation that

you have learned are versatile "power tools" that will serve you long and well in overcoming the physical tension of stressful living and anxiety disorders. You have become a personal anxiety technologist (add that to your resume!), able to look far below the surface of everyday fears and anxiety attacks and skillfully apply cognitive panic therapy techniques to what you find, until panic and anxiety attacks lose the sharpness of their formerly painful bite.

Chapter Six

The Many Faces of Phobias

Phobias are demoralizing states of anxious avoidance. In a crowd of a hundred people, ten to twelve are likely to have at least one phobia of particular types of events or situations. Throughout history, a dazzling array of fears has been reported. So, we might ask, what fears trouble these unfortunate people? Let's consider a list of possibilities:

Phobic Fears

Dogs	Heights	People dressed as clowns
Thunderstorms	Insects	
Heights	Lightning	Spiders
Contagious illnesses	Supermarkets	Hospitals
The sight of blood	Malls	Earthquakes
Injections	Vomiting	Ocean travel
Planes	Roller coasters	Small closets
Trains	Bridges	Movie theaters
Cars	People with physical deformities	Rooftops
Elevators		

To be sure, there is a large variety of fears on this list, though some of them seem to fall loosely into categories like high places, vehicles, crowded places, and people with striking features. In order to make sense of the many fears that plague humanity, different types and even subtypes of phobias have been identified.

One major type is the *specific phobia*, an anxious reaction to particular objects like snakes or bugs and discrete situations like thunderstorms and Fridays the 13th. Phobic individuals are very likely to report one or more of these fears. Surveys of the general population indicate that out of every nine people, one has a specific phobia. Another notable fact is that between 58 and 81 percent of specific phobics are female.

Specific phobias are classified into five different subtypes in the latest diagnostic manual *(DSM-IV)*. The subtypes and related phobias are listed below, along with examples.

1. Animal: animal and insects

2. Natural environment: storms, darkness, and water

3. Blood/injection/injury: seeing blood, receiving an injection, or other invasive medical procedure

4. Situational: public transportation, elevators, bridges

5. Other: vomiting, choking

As you can see, a number of specific phobias originate with universal fears and superstitions that have not entirely subsided after reigning early in childhood, like fears of the dark, insects, and bad luck. These fears seem to wax and wane in intensity and most disappear by adolescence. Other specific phobias seem to develop out of specific events, such as being bitten by a wasp at an early age or fainting after receiving a flu shot with a very large needle.

The table on the following page shows the ages of onset and lifetime rates of different types of phobias. Phobias of most animals and objects in the natural environment usually pass by childhood's end. Most specific phobias that continue into adulthood persist until the phobic person gets treatment.

As you read the list of fears, perhaps an item or two rang a bell. Maybe you thought, "I am afraid of that," or "That scares me." If so, you might wonder whether your fears or trepidations qualify as a phobia. Phobic fears are by definition excessive, irrational, and unrelated to the actual danger of the situation. A moment's reflection suggests that many fears are

Table 6.1

THE COURSE OF COMMON CHILDHOOD FEARS

Type of Fear	When It Emerges	Lifetime Rates
Animal and insect fears	4–17 years old	22%
Natural environment	Average age of 12	8–9%
Blood, injection, injury	8–17 years old	13.9%

Adapted from Barlow, 2002

adaptive, such as that of contracting AIDS through unprotected sex, since they clearly relate to risk of harm or serious injury and can protect the person who heeds their warning. On the other hand, a person with an injection phobia knows rationally that receiving an injection involves only a moment of pain and protects him against disease, but may nevertheless refuse it even though it is required for employment or travel.

Certain fears, such as those for bugs and snakes, are neither necessarily intense nor uncommon. The once-popular country and western song "I Don't Like Spiders and Snakes" expresses a sentiment that is widespread in our society. In order for a fear to be diagnosed as phobic, according to the *DSM-IV* it must interfere with a person's "normal routine, occupational (or academic) functioning, or social activities or relationships; or there is marked distress about having [it]."

If you return to the list at the start of this chapter, you will note that some of the phobias seem to be focused less on specific objects or situations and more on general classes of situations such as crowded or confining places. These *general situational phobias* include:

- Agoraphobia—fear of open spaces cut off from safety

- Claustrophobia—fear of confining spaces

- Acrophobia—also known as height phobia

A number of differences between general and specific phobias are noteworthy. First, general situational phobias are less common. Agoraphobia, the most widespread phobia of this type, occurs in no more than 5 percent of the population. Second, unlike specific phobias, which emerge most often during childhood, general situational phobias surface in the midteens and sometimes even later. And third, agoraphobia, particularly when severe, can be more debilitating than any specific phobia, even to the point of rendering some people homebound. In fact, medications are generally not even particularly necessary for treatment of specific phobias, but are used widely to relieve agoraphobia. Our discussion will focus on these debilitating conditions that require more complex treatments than specific phobias. If you suffer from a specific phobia, you will find it very easy to transpose the techniques for relieving general situational phobias to your more specific phobia.

Panic and Agoraphobia

We begin our discussion with an example of panic disorder with agoraphobia, the most debilitating subtype of general situational phobia. Laurie could easily identify the creepy feelings that arose at the onset of an episode of agoraphobia. Typically, she would grow apprehensive before or during the drive to the dance studio and, at the same time, become short of breath and dizzy. If she caught it early, she could avert her dizziness by regulating her breathing and reminding herself that she was experiencing nothing more than the physical symptoms of panic.

If Laurie was under a lot of stress or had increased her dizziness by moving the wrong way, most likely the episode would not be preventable. As she and her daughter headed to the car, she would debate if she could make it to the studio and whether the worst of the feelings could be averted by cutting the lesson short and returning home early.

When Laurie decided to go ahead to the studio, she would often wind up regretting it, because she would be in the midst of a full-blown panic attack by the time they got there. She would feel so dizzy and nauseous that she could not even imagine driving home, where she yearned to be. Usually, then, she would tell her daughter that they couldn't stay and call her mother for a ride.

As the case of Laurie illustrates, panic and agoraphobia often go hand in hand. If you suffer from panic, there is a good chance that you are troubled by at least mild agoraphobia because agoraphobia most of all is a fear of panic. Most individuals with panic disorder develop agoraphobia to some degree, varying in severity and associated complications. Only a fraction seek mental health treatment, perhaps because it is not accessible or else because the degree of functional impairment produced by the disorder is mild or transitory. In severe cases, when panic strikes repeatedly and the panicker's resources prove inadequate to restore a sense of security, the circle of safety can constrict so tightly that nowhere but home feels safe. Thus the mantra of some agoraphobics is, "There's no place like home."

Home can be both a special safety zone and a special trap for people with agoraphobia. Consider Casey, who convinced herself that she was unable to leave her house. Her agoraphobia had begun after she broke up with her abusive fiancé, who reminded her of her abusive father. Shortly thereafter, she lost her job and then discovered that she was too anxious and demoralized to seek another. General nervousness dèvolved into wave after wave of panic. After a few weeks, she felt so frightened when she was home alone that even marshaling the resources to send her daughter to school was a challenge.

Sympathetic neighbors brought groceries, toiletries, and other essentials. Six months elapsed, yet Casey had not moved her car from the driveway because she discovered that she would become consumed with panic as soon as she would try to drive to the corner and turn. She felt vulnerable and afraid. She even felt anxious about showering. Her isolation stemmed partially from the growing tide of humiliation that swelled with each effort to enlist others' material or emotional support.

Like Casey, many homebound agoraphobics lack self-confidence and have difficulty internalizing the support of others. They experience their everyday lives as fraught with trauma. The jittery dance that occurs between agoraphobia and panic provides yet another example of the demoralizing tenacity of their problems.

AGORAPHOBIA IS AS MUCH A FEAR OF FEELINGS AS OF SITUATIONS

Realistic fear results from actual safety hazards, like a rickety staircase ready to fall apart or noxious fumes; or perhaps from mortal danger, such as the threat presented by a ferocious dog or violent people bearing weapons. Phobic fears occur in situations that *feel* unsafe, not those that actually *are* unsafe. To a person with agoraphobia, certain settings feel unsafe largely because of the intense feelings of anxiety or panic that seem to develop in them, even though real hazards are limited and mortal danger is absent. Put in cognitive terms, the anxiety reaction—the catastrophic thinking and

Anxiety Disorders May Be Complicated by Underlying Personality Disorders

Anxiety sufferers who are also periodically flooded with intense negative emotional feelings may have a severe personality disorder, such as borderline or dependent personality disorder (BPD or DPD), which substantially affects their treatment and prognosis. Individuals with BPD or DPD have difficulty controlling the intensity of their emotions, soothing themselves, and accepting the reassurance of others once they have undergone emotionally induced physiological arousal. Thus they may have marked difficulty taking the often uncomfortable therapeutic steps that are necessary components of anxiety therapy. Adults with DPD tend to lack self-confidence and need excessive reassurance in order to take initiatives toward functioning more independently. Curative measures may challenge persons with borderline and—to an extent—dependent disorders, so that they are likely to need professional help in working on their anxiety disorders, as well as special, extra gentle and supportive techniques at specific points in treatment.

If your anxiety disorder is complicated by a severe personality disorder, it would be desirable to proceed very gradually through the treatment chapters that follow and to be in concurrent treatment with a mental health professional specializing in anxiety disorders. Anxiolytic medication may be strongly indicated. In some cases, it may even be worthwhile to arrange a special support system in order to jump-start recovery, such as a therapist who makes home visits or someone who accompanies you during real-life exposure.

People with anxiety disorders that are especially severe and tenacious, such as post-traumatic stress disorder, severe agoraphobia, and mixed chronic anxiety and depression—as well as those who have had episodes of intense, prolonged emotional distress lasting for months—should also bear these special considerations in mind.

frightening imagery, *not* the situation itself—is what is feared. If merely *approaching* a setting portends an upcoming panic attack that feels like real fear, it certainly helps explain how a person with a phobia could develop the conviction that the setting is unsafe!

Which came first, the chicken or the egg? When agoraphobia is acute, the anxious person is hard-pressed to know whether to seek relief by trying to avoid settings that provoke anxiety or by finding ways to suppress panicky feelings. Fortunately, practice of the techniques presented in the next chapter will help you to do both. You will learn to cope better with stressors in settings that trigger anxiety, overcome avoidance, and acquire the skills to relieve the unsettling, panicky feelings that emerge in these situations.

Understandably, for an anxiety-sensitive person panic attacks are likely to occur initially in stimulating situations where access to safety and security are limited. The likeliest locales for this devolution from panic to agoraphobia are busy, open places like markets, malls, freeways, department stores, theaters, airplanes, sports arenas, restaurants, crowds, and places of worship.

At the other extreme, but due to the same sense of vulnerability and inaccessibility of security, many people with agoraphobia become uncomfortable at home alone. Their anxiety may be exacerbated if they are caring for young children, and, if married, when their spouses work far away or are traveling. It is not uncommon for females with agoraphobia to feel especially vulnerable when showering. Previously comfortable portions of the environment become charged with the potential for negative arousal, as if high-voltage grids have been secretly installed where the agoraphobic person used to frolic worry-free.

Claustrophobia and Acrophobia

Now let us turn our attention to claustrophobia, the first cousin of agoraphobia. We can learn more about the ways these general situational phobias are related by considering the following examples:

> Ed is anxious whenever he rides the city bus. The more people get on, the staler and deader the air seems to him, and the greater his anxious discomfort. As he feels the "flesh press" close in on him, he inhales the ran-

cid smells of smoke and overheated humans and feels an intense urge to pull the emergency cord, stop the bus, and jump off.

Nadine was bursting with anticipation as she embarked on her first undersea adventure. She donned her face mask, placed the air regulator in her mouth, and jumped into the ocean. As she descended to the lower part of the gorgeous coral reef, she suddenly began to worry that she wasn't getting enough air. She felt the "weight of the water" entombing her and became panic-stricken. She was able to control her frantic ascent only by repeatedly reminding herself that she would die of a pulmonary embolism if she rose faster than her air bubbles.

Raoul was on his honeymoon and had to go to the thirtieth floor with his bride to enter the penthouse suite. He and his new wife were with friends, and Raoul felt foolish using his usual claim of preferring to walk up and "get exercise." He steeled himself for the elevator ride and bit his lip as it ascended. His head began to spin during the brief ascent. As he waited seemingly for an eternity for the door to open, he began believing that he was trapped, and his fears almost instantly turned to panic.

Like people with agoraphobia, these claustrophobic individuals' worlds are full of anxiety-provoking events, situations, and activities that must be endured with great difficulty or else given a wide berth. Consequently, for individuals with both these types of situational phobias, normal functioning is a compromise between accepting markedly restricted liberty by avoiding situations that are routine for others and undergoing substantial emotional pain alone. Almost all agoraphobics are claustrophobic, but not all claustrophobics are agoraphobic.

In fact, claustrophobia stimulates the same kinds of emotional and physical feelings as agoraphobia, but in situations that appear confining or crowded, like cramped, stuffy rooms, often with the appearance of limited air supply. Claustrophobics report feeling surrounded, hemmed in, or trapped. As the examples above suggest, many people with phobias for elevators and public transportation have claustrophobic fears. (In appendix E, detailed information about the operation of elevator safety systems is provided.) Interestingly, other common sites are the "thrones of honor" in dentists' offices and beauticians' salons, the rear seats of two-door cars, center and cramped airplane seats, caves, submarines, and being encased up to the chin inside the long narrow tube of a medical scanning device called an MRI machine.

Similarly, people with height phobia—acrophobia—have phobic feelings when they are in high, apparently precarious places. On high ledges or mountain vistas, Ferris wheels, the upper floors of buildings, or traveling over bridges or on dramatic skyways, they feel intense anxious discomfort, often accompanied by physical symptoms of panic. Riding up and down in a tall building's transparent glass elevator—some of which are actually located on outer walls!—may trigger height phobia, agoraphobia (because of the wide open, unbounded exterior space), and—if the car is crowded—claustrophobia!

Driving phobia and fear of flying are also included in the next chapter's discussion of treatment because they fit our definition of general situational phobias to the tee. Both auto and airplane travel are at least somewhat stressful for both drivers/pilots and passengers. Many people with general situational phobias are phobic for one or both types of travel. Driving phobia and fear of flying have elements of both agoraphobia and claustrophobia. A final general phobia, social phobia, as well as social anxiety or shyness, is covered in two separate chapters.

But Where Do Phobias *Come* From?

Remember Laurie, whose fears prevented her from driving to the dance studio? She was trying hard to confront them, but she wondered why she was still so afraid in spite of her best efforts. Logically, she knew that driving her car on quiet streets a few miles from home wasn't dangerous, so the panic that consumed her made no sense. Laurie remembered studying about classical conditioning in psychology class, but she did not recall ever having frightening experiences with cars, streets, or dance studios.

Classical conditioning only provides explanations for about half of people's phobias, and it did not shed any light on Laurie's. Many people cannot recall anything that might have launched their phobic fears, and may even be afraid of things like wasps that they have never encountered or experiences like air travel although they have never flown.

So how do we explain some phobias?

EVOLUTION

Phobias are *selective,* so fear of heights, snakes, or spiders is relatively common while phobias for plastic or filing cabinets are almost nonexist-

Freeway Phobia, Southern California–Style

Millions of motorists pack the freeways of southern California night and day. Drivers who become too fearful to navigate these mighty rivers of cars may be surprised to realize that tens of thousands of their neighbors share their fears. The power and sheer number of motor vehicles that crowd every roadway mile trigger panic in a multitude of drivers. At the same instant that a bunch of new drivers gear up to cruise the fast lanes, a significant number edgily slide off at nearby exits resigning to forgo the nerve-wracking agony of freeway driving forever.

What do freeway phobic drivers share beside their dread? Triggers of their fears are typically driving in the fast lanes, being passed by fast-moving vehicles, passing big rigs, or traffic jams. Also, most phobic drivers share in *what has not happened to them:* few have actually had life-threatening lapses of control, gone psychotic, or been injured on the road. Nevertheless, they share a fear of madness, bodily injury, loss of control, or death.

What's so dreadful about freeway phobia? Typically, mental confusion and intense anxiety or panic come first. As the anxiety intensifies, it adds to a growing fear that the person's control is evaporating. The feared result? Loss of the ability to steer and a collision with a truck or other car; sudden speeding up instead of braking; or else recklessly slamming on the brakes and being rear-ended. Finally, persons with driving phobias may envision engulfment by urges so strong that they result in an immediate, catastrophic escape from the freeway, wiping out everyone in their path.

How often does this actually occur? Almost never. What usually happens instead? When panicky, don't drivers usually turn into those motorists who travel at 38 mph in the fast lane with their right-turn signals on, looking mortified? We confess that's what *we* do on occasions when we've really gotten petrified because our drives have suddenly turned strange and scary. Unflattering but true . . . is it like that for you?

The most frightening things about episodes of freeway phobia are creations of the phobic's imagination! The last time you had intense anxiety at the wheel and pictured yourself annihilating cars while fleeing the freeway, slamming into trucks, or being maimed, for instance, these things did not happen—nor are they likely to at all. *Intrusive thoughts* like these pop into the minds of 90 percent of us many times a day. On a hot summer Sunday day, after a big breakfast, an intrusive thought of a frosty double chocolate malt might enter your mind; or you might imagine telling your boss who is criticizing you that his mother wears combat boots. Regardless of whether intrusive thoughts please us (like imagining the malted milk), distract us (like the thought of the wise remark to your boss), or terrify us (like the destructive images of the phobia), *they have little or nothing to do with our actual behavior in the situation at hand.*

Freeway phobia can be relieved or cured through self-help, therapy for anxiety disorders, and/or antianxiety medication. To be effective, therapy must relieve the main physical anxiety symptoms (like trembling, trouble breathing, pounding heart, and a sense of unreality) or attacks, train the driver to clear or calm his mind when driving gets nerve-wracking, and help him to plan and implement strategies for regaining control of the road.

ent. Why should the roar of a caged-up lion or the piercing glare of a gorilla in captivity be far more frightening than a giant panda at close proximity? The answer seems to lie in the fact that some fears, and not others, make evolutionary sense. After all, humans survived through the millennia by keeping wary of predators and other powerful aggressors and avoiding positions of vulnerability and helplessness whenever possible—like being surrounded by hostile strangers, alone in the dark, trapped with limited breathing room, or unable to escape to safety.

Psychologist Martin Seligman held that people are *biologically prepared* to neutralize evolutionary justified threats to their survival. Physiological researchers have tentatively confirmed that even people without anxiety problems respond more anxiously to pictures of snakes and spiders than to neutral objects. Once primitive fears are aroused, preparedness is a lightning rod that facilitates swift, virtually automatic avoidance and escape from peril.

Yet biological preparedness seems to be a less than credible explanation for a number of specific phobias, such as those for spiders, insects, and "blood/injury/injections." If specific phobias are the generalized products of fears that helped our ancestors successfully defend against dangerous predators, spiders seem very unlikely candidates when only 0.1 percent of the world's thirty-five thousand identified species can kill a human. Many people are phobic for insects, but probably not because slugs, roaches, and their ilk are deemed serious menaces or sources of contamination. And intuitively we suspect *disgust* more likely than fear is the main emotional response in "body envelope violation" phobias—for the sight of blood, deep injury, or injections.

A weak case has been made for reattribution of the power of disgust to fear-based causes for avoidance, like fear of disease or contamination by rats or bugs. Psychologist Richard McNally has speculated that such claims might be afterthoughts meant to explain away this mysterious yet compelling emotional state. Research indicates that disgust seems to be an emotional response in its own right, rather than just a derivative of fear. Its role in phobic avoidance of spiders and blood/injury/injections seems substantial, and from our clinical experience, we surmise that disgust is also an integral part of the dread of vomiting, a feature often seen in general situational phobias. Disgust may be one of several factors that motivate phobic avoidance, predominating in some phobic reactions and intertwining with or compounding fear in others.

What are the effects of therapy on disgust-based phobias? We agree with McNally: A phobic person's attitudes or beliefs about the things that disgust him are not likely to change, but through exposure-based techniques, like the ones you will encounter in the next chapter, he might be able to train himself to tolerate them more and avoid them less.

SYMBOLISM

According to psychoanalytic or psychodynamic theory, the objects and situations that people with phobias fear symbolize their own dangerous impulses and fantasies. Recall the case of Little Hans, recounted in chapter 1. Freud believed that Hans's fear of horses and being bitten by them actually was symbolic of his fear of retaliation from his father, toward whom he felt aggression because he considered him the sole rival for his mother's love. To further illustrate: height phobia may actually symbolize the fear of falling in the esteem of others. Claustrophobia, the fear of closed places, may represent the fear of being left alone with one's own dangerous impulses and fantasies. And agoraphobia may actually be the fear of helpless exposure and abandonment. In the psychodynamic view, then, phobias speak in a symbolic language about underlying fears and impulses; but little or no evidence supports this point of view.

Catastrophic Thinking

In the midst of fear things are not what they seem. Recognition of this fact is one of the first steps in treating and reverse engineering phobias. When phobic situations or objects are dangerous at all, the danger is by definition exaggerated: It is neither mortal nor imminent. Persons with phobias tend to exaggerate the negative impact of their particular phobic situations. For instance, a motorist who is phobic may imagine that major destruction and personal injury must have resulted from a car accident reported on the traffic report until he hears that it was just a fender bender.

Unfortunately, the *very idea* of being consumed with terror can trigger negative automatic thoughts that cause us to react by recoiling from what is feared. In fact, a critical feature of virtually every phobia is *catastrophic thinking*. When we indulge in catastrophic thinking, we imagine or expect the worst and lose touch with objective reality in the process. We feel certain that our world will be shaken, that we will be unable to cope. And this is the problem that must be corrected.

Anxiety Expectancy

Anxiety expectancy is the apprehension of having an uncomfortable physiological stress reaction. Psychological researchers have found that the stronger the anxiety expectancy, the stronger the avoidance. Ironically, when it is impossible to escape or avoid what is feared, a panic attack is an unwelcome yet likely eventuality. Every attack seems to confirm the dangerous quality of phobic situations, because people with phobias are prone to being very vigilant for evidence that seems to validate their fearfulness. The elevator-phobic person's ears prick up whenever faint noises emanate from an elevator shaft and with each tale of cranky elevator performance. A client whose anxiety was worsened by the 1994 Northridge, California, earthquake recently told one of us that she feels certain buildings in the surrounding San Fernando Valley shaking regularly. She was relieved when she encountered other people with similar experiences, because now she does not feel so alone or strange.

Often the person who is developing an anxiety disorder is unaware of how his catastrophic thinking paves the groundwork for his panic. Panic anxiety may appear seemingly unannounced and unbidden, like the malicious disheartening mischief-maker Pan who would appear from nowhere and pipe his otherworldly tunes in the dark to startle unwitting travelers half to death. The mental trickery that deceives people into exaggerated fear reactions is the very essence of panic and phobias.

So how can this trickery be countered or reversed? Fortunately, with dedicated effort you can reengineer catastrophic thinking about your phobia by assiduously practicing the technique of decatastrophization you first encountered in your reading about panic. We will help you determine the ingredients of your phobia—emotional feelings and physical sensations, frightening thoughts, and impulses to avoid and escape. We will ask you to pose the question to yourself: "What's the worst that can happen?" in order to determine what you are afraid of. We will teach you to estimate the actual likelihood that your fear will become a reality. And finally, we will ask you to consider whether you have the resources to cope with the worst-case scenario in the unlikely event that it occurs, by pondering the question, "So if it happens, what would I do then?"

AVOIDANCE

It makes a great deal of sense to avoid painful situations. After all, since early in childhood we are told not to touch hot objects and to keep our fingers out of electrical sockets, so our natural tendency is to react to painful stimulation with immediate avoidance. In the case of phobias, however, it is vitally important to recognize that any tendency to avoid what you fear, while comforting at the moment, only fuels and maintains that fear. This occurs because as long as you avoid what you fear, you continue to miss the chance to learn that you can be safe in its presence. Your avoidance confirms the anxiety-laden belief that your phobia is stronger than your resolve. We have noticed, for example, that the more our clients avoid elevators and buses, the more likely they are to say to themselves, "I can't go on the elevator," or "I can't ride the bus." This is the way that hopelessness takes a firm hold.

Another interesting aspect of avoidance is that it is difficult, if not impossible, *not* to think about what you fear. Efforts to suppress or avoid thinking anxious thoughts are likely to be unproductive or to backfire. Try this experiment. Do your best not to think about a large dancing bear. In many experiments like this, researchers found that it was difficult for the individuals to suppress such thoughts without them "rebounding," or returning full force, when active attempts to suppress the thoughts ceased.

The difficulty of avoiding thoughts of the dancing bear is likely to be dwarfed by that of avoiding phobic thoughts propelled by fear of death or grievous bodily harm. This assumption was confirmed in a study conducted by Steven Jay Lynn (one of this book's authors) with Robert Kurzhals. This research showed that phobic subjects' thoughts about what they feared were very difficult to suppress for a sustained period of time. This implies that avoidance does not actually succeed in sanitizing our minds of phobic thoughts. The attempt to consciously suppress such thoughts might only make them all the more powerful when they recur, demonstrating the strong hold they have on us. In short, fears only grow stronger as they incubate. By learning to confront, rather than avoid, what you fear, hopelessness gets replaced by the sense of effectiveness.

So now that you know the Draconian penalty of both mental and physical avoidance of what you fear, ask yourself whether you are ready and willing to reverse the process and confront your fears by mastering the step-by-step exposure and cognitive-restructuring techniques we present in the next chapter. If you answer in the affirmative, you will treat your phobia by learning to think realistically during anxious stress reactions, applying this expanded mental capacity to relief of anxious anticipation, and finally, planning and implementing exposure to phobic situations. Good luck!

Chapter Seven

Phobia Therapy

ake the first step in your journey to conquer your phobias by recruiting your valor, a kind of courage defined as "boldness or determination in facing danger." Like the illusory monster in the cave, the
illusion of danger that anxiety produces is every bit as compelling as "real"
danger. Apprehension and dread result from merely thinking about a phobic situation and challenge us to be valorous. Apprehensive thoughts are
catastrophe theories that have the power to frighten even though they do
not correspond with hard facts. Apprehension (also called anticipatory
anxiety) sometimes looms so large that people are deterred from their efforts to confront the monster in the cave—the phobic situation.

Each time Raoul, the highly elevator-phobic newlywed man we met in
chapter 6, drives past an office building, his mind is flooded with apprehension. Raoul feels sorry for himself because he can't attend appointments
and do business in high-rises or go to hotels like everyone else. He glances
at the tall, stately structures with yearning and wishes he could start getting a grip on his phobia; but when he remembers the awful attack he had
during his honeymoon last summer, he looks away and has an urge to
speed up his car. "No way!" he thinks. "The way I am now, I couldn't even
walk into the lobby of that building."

Raoul must learn to think differently about his fears before he can contend with them. He must learn a way to stop confusing his frightening il-

lusions with objective reality. Raoul's apprehension stems from anxious automatic thinking that increases in proportion to his proximity to the situations he fears. Automatic thoughts may take the form of predictions about oneself ("I won't be able to breathe"; "I'm afraid I'm going to throw up"; or "I think I'm going to pass out"); estimations of others' reactions ("They will think I'm a complete wimp"); mental images (such as imagining the expressions of his fellow passengers twisted with contempt); or memories, real or imaginary, of past experiences that triggered seemingly similar distress. For Raoul, as images of possible physical or mental harm arise unbidden from the emotional brain (the part of the mind that generates disturbing emotional feelings), he is flooded with anxiety.

Selecting Targets

In chapter 2, we described anxiety propositions, an important class of automatic thoughts related to apprehension. We defined anxiety propositions as quickly formulated, generally inaccurate descriptions of the apparent connection between "phobic moments"—specific anxiety-provoking events, situations, or activities—and specific feared consequences. Anxiety propositions take the form, "When I *feel* A and *think* B in phobic situation C, I *am afraid that* catastrophe XYZ will result." In the case of Raoul, when he *feels* the potential to panic, and he *thinks* he can't handle the situation when he enters the lobby, he *is afraid* he will have a "whopper of a panic attack."

A good place to start reverse engineering phobias is with examination of anxiety propositions in relation to specific feared situations we refer to as "targets." In order to create a springboard to launch yourself into high-impact recovery, select and prioritize your targets by answering the following questions:

What effect does your phobic condition have on your ability to pursue your important endeavors? Answer specifically.

_____

_____

_____

_____

What phobic situations that have personal importance have you been avoiding completely for a while or else only entering when accompanied by a support person?

_____

_____

_____

_____

What specific situations, events, or activities have you become phobic for that you sorely miss?

_____

_____

_____

_____

Now that you have identified one or more phobic situations that will be your primary targets, identify several of the anxiety propositions that threaten to hold you back from phobic situations. Start filling in worksheet 7.1 by listing your phobic situations in the left-hand column, your feelings and thoughts on the right, and your anxiety propositions in the middle.

Transforming Anxiety Propositions

Successful cognitive restructuring is likely to result in thinking that is both *less anxious and more realistic.* Reverse engineering involves *transforming your anxiety propositions (APs) into realistic propositions(RPs).* Reconsider everything that provokes your anxiety in a phobic situation in order to

Worksheet 7.1
DECONSTRUCTING ANXIETY PROPOSITIONS

Phobic Situation	Anxiety Proposition	Anxious Physical Sensations and Automatic Thoughts
Riding an elevator	I will pass out in a broken elevator and lie unconscious in the unmoving car	Hyperventilation, pounding heart, light-headedness, fear of fainting

provide a basis for formulating a less fearful, more objective way of thinking about it. In doing so you will become more aware of the challenges you face and empowered to tackle the anticipated stressors more effectively.

AP: Susan's phobia is triggered when she takes an air trip. She fears that takeoff will trigger a fatal cardiovascular accident.

RP: Now Susan tries to think of her altered breathing and heart rate during takeoff as anxiety symptoms as well as indicators of her good aerobic capacity, which has been improving ever since she resumed her fitness workouts. By clenching her fists and maintaining slow, regular breathing during takeoff, Susan can keep what remains of her anxious reaction in perspective as the apprehensive prelude to her journey to a desirable destination.

AP: When Marlene feels frightened, self-conscious, and nauseous in front of other people, she fears that she will humiliate herself to the point of being unable to stomach going out in public again.

RP: Marlene recognizes that she has anxiety attacks that include tension and an upset stomach when she feels that she has to perform in front of strangers. She will work on relieving her anxiety as much as she can *before* exposing herself to highly challenging situations where she still runs the risk of becoming very frightened. *During* the challenges, she'll do the mini-practices of SCT, which were introduced in chapter 5, for thirty seconds at a time, tensing and relaxing her muscles and focusing on present-moment sensations. She'll study the social environment as carefully as possible in order to establish that she is not the center of attention, study the physical environment and memorize the locations of the bathrooms, and remind herself that her nausea is an anxiety symptom that rarely turns into a physical problem.

Using worksheet 7.1, you have deconstructed your anxiety propositions into objective—rather than catastrophic—descriptions of your phobic situations. Take the next step: Enter the data from your analysis onto worksheet 7.2 in order to transform your anxiety propositions (APs) into realistic propositions (RPs)—statements of the way you would rather think.

By reversing your anxious thoughts and transforming them into more realistic perceptions, you have begun to restructure your thinking about phobias. If you found it difficult to arrive at realistic propositions, try the technique of *reasoning with yourself.* Discuss the following questions about your anxious thoughts and images with yourself:

- In the past, how often have situations like this come out the way I feared?

- Is this kind of catastrophe something that generally happens in my life? Does it generally happen to other people?

- What's my recent track record with situations like this, and am I starting to improve (or not)?

- If someone who really loves me and has my very best interests at heart were to counsel me about dealing with my fears, what would he or she tell me?

Worksheet 7.2

TRANSFORMING YOUR ANXIETY PROPOSITIONS INTO REALITY PROPOSITIONS

Anxiety Propositions	Physical Anxiety Symptoms	Facts about the Symptoms and SCT Techniques	Anxious Thoughts	Reasoned Challenges to Anxious Thoughts	Realistic Propositions: How Would I *Rather* Think?
I will pass out in a broken elevator and lie unconscious in the unmoving car.	Hyperventilation, pounding heart, light-headedness	Hyperventilation ensures that I'll have plenty of oxygen, and my "pounding heart" circulates it throughout my body; light-headedness results from taking too much carbon dioxide into my body. Slow, regular breathing will relieve my physical anxiety.	Fear that the elevator will break down; fear of fainting	Last time I fainted was ten years ago. The elevator has a very good operating record.	I feel apprehensive and panicky in elevators simply because I've been avoiding them so long, and my anxious mind mistakes these symptoms for real danger. A measure of control will be a big relief, but I'll have to work to achieve it.

Reasoning with Yourself About Air Travel

As of this writing, the tragic aerial suicide attacks on the Pentagon and World Trade Center on September 11, 2001, are painfully fresh in the minds of hundreds of millions worldwide. There is widespread intensification of fear of flying. An anxiety proposition newly installed in many people's minds is that air travel puts them at risk of becoming potential victims of terrorist attacks.

How realistic is this fear? Isn't it reasonable to fear that these tragic events are just the beginning and to avoid unnecessary vulnerability until the threat is better controlled?

But isn't it just as likely that the terrorists chose these measures precisely because they were so awful yet utterly unexpected? Who could have anticipated that terrorists would hijack commercial jetliners, become suicide bombers, and target national landmarks?

Now that the tragedy has occurred, airports and landmarks are being secured and fortified. Like the improbability of lightning striking the same place twice, wouldn't it be really unlikely that terrorist acts, should they occur again, would target the same kinds of vehicles and places a second time?

In addition, Israel, the site of innumerable terrorist assaults in recent years, has always taken the possibility of terrorist acts against airliners very seriously and makes provisions to counteract this potential threat. As a result, El Al, Israel's national airline, has earned the reputation as the world's safest airline. Isn't El Al's outstanding safety record most likely the result of the efforts of a nation targeted for terrorist aggression to make air travel as safe and secure as possible? Might not the determination of the United States to secure its commercial skyways mark the beginning of a long-awaited era of unprecedented air safety?

Some very anxious people who are prone to thinking catastrophically require additional tools. As a result of exaggerating the potential harmfulness of events and situations that trigger anxiety while underrating their own coping abilities, stressful and worrisome situations often seem overwhelming to them. Here are two techniques that psychologists Michelle Craske and David Barlow recommend for combating catastrophic thinking (in chapter 5 we used them for reframing panic as well):

1. Challenging fears by *reestimating* as objectively as possible the probability of being harmed by a really bad outcome of a phobic situation

2. Using *decatastrophization* to correct thoughts about how bad things could get by thinking carefully about one's ability to cope with the very worst of possibilities

REESTIMATING TARGET SITUATIONS

When we are apprehensive about an event or situation, we naturally exaggerate the likelihood that it will come out badly. People will usually dismiss commonplace misgivings as products of the heebie-jeebies. However, an anxious person tends to believe his own skewed, inaccurate odds-making, despite strong evidence to the contrary.

Reestimation helps even the odds and restore realistic thinking. To start reestimation, *rate the strength of your belief that a dreaded event will turn out badly at the moment of your greatest apprehension.* For instance, how likely is panic to occur during ten minutes spent in a busy store during a sale? If you go to the roof of the tallest building in town, how likely are you to fall over the edge? This *anxious probability* should be stated as a *probability percentage*—0 percent if there's no chance of a bad outcome, 50 percent when it seems like a 50-50 proposition, and 100 percent when a catastrophe seems certain. Enter your anxious probability estimations on worksheet 7.3 on the following page. Anchor your "anxious probability estimator" now: Think back on some fears you've relieved or vanquished and rate the anxious probability you experienced when they were at their worst.

Now reestimate the *realistic probability*. Things that provoke a phobic person's anxiety are seldom as dangerous as they seem. Investigate and consider this matter by reasoning with yourself the way you did when transforming your anxiety propositions earlier in this chapter.

Hint: Don't try to act overoptimistic by underestimating the realistic probability of an unpleasant outcome. Just be realistic.

On the worksheet below, rate the anxious probability that the dreaded event will happen and the realistic probability next to it.

As you do this exercise repeatedly you'll notice that the realistic probability that panic symptoms and catastrophic outcomes will occur begin to drop substantially.

Reestimation might seem like an improbable effort to persuade yourself that something that scares you really should not, and you may wonder

Worksheet 7.3
REESTIMATING TARGET SITUATIONS

Automatic Thought	Anxious Probability	Realistic Probability
I can never go to the mall anymore without feeling frightened.	80%	30% (I've quelled most panic attacks lately and have been successfully mini-practicing in crowds and checkout lines.)
I will be really scared to ride the elevator up to the floor of my doctor's office.	95%	50% (I used to be comfortable with the elevators in that building. No panics rated above a 4 this month. I'm getting comfortable practicing stepping into stationary elevators, although I'm still pretty doubtful about riding in one.)

whether it can really help. Actually, reestimation can help you to consolidate your successes in controlling panic by fortifying your reality orientation during exposure practices through replacing catastrophic thinking with a more realistic perspective that is "at odds" with your apprehensions.

Sound psychological research has shown that simply learning to predict the likelihood of panic or anxiety realistically can diminish apprehension and decrease panic. After anticipating an attack that does not occur, the panicker feels less apprehensive for future attacks. When panickers expect physical stress symptoms (such as paniclike feelings after inhaling carbon dioxide–laden air), they tend to react less catastrophically than those who don't expect it. Furthermore, after panickers overestimate the fear they believe they'll feel in a phobic situation, both their expectations of future anxious reactions and the occurrence of panic attacks decrease.

DECATASTROPHIZING PHOBIC SITUATIONS

To implement the powerful cognitive restructuring technique of decatastrophization, start by asking yourself: What is the worst that could happen? *Start small, by determining what specifically you fear during routine episodes of anxiety. Think carefully and spell out the worst-case scenario.*

What would constitute the Full Catastrophe? Be specific and write it out. In the unlikely event that the most dreaded event actually occurred, how would you cope? Wouldn't you be able to endure it? If necessary, then, could you actually cope with the feared event in this way? What would be the worst that could happen *next*? And then? etc., etc., ad nauseum . . . *until you finally arrive at a worst-case scenario that does not make you particularly anxious to contemplate.*

Marlene avoided shopping situations in which she would have to sign her name on a check or charge slip at a checkout counter. When absolutely necessary, she would fill in all but the amount on her check in advance, and risk the trepidation and humiliation she would undergo while completing the process before the eyes of the cashier and the customers waiting behind her in line. The Full Catastrophe she imagined was feeling sudden nausea and an intense, irresistible urge to regurgitate in front of this potential audience of disgusted strangers.

Marlene began her decatastrophization exercise by considering whether she had a history of sudden regurgitation ("No, but . . ."). Next, she thought about the activity level of negative gut feelings she had actually experienced. Did it really threaten to turn into the instant disaster she feared? She realized that even when she had felt very nauseated, she had always had more than enough time to take an antacid pill, eat crackers and drink cool water, or sip some chamomile tea to soothe her stomach.

But what if, *what if,* WHAT IF?? In the very unlikely event that Marlene "totally" lost control, she would forget about her purchases. Most likely she would still have enough time and presence of mind to blunder the few yards through the store exit and lose it away from the public eye. At that instant, she wouldn't care if there were witnesses. Then she'd clean up, maybe drive to a drugstore to pick up an antiemetic medicine, and go home to wash up and change. Would she be able to return to the store to shop and try to pay for her purchase by check or charge card? Probably. How much anxious discomfort would she expect to feel?

Commonly, after people with phobias use decatastrophization and reestimation a time or two to mobilize and "unstick" themselves, their catastrophic expectations for a particular phobic situation become relatively manageable and lose their sway. Similarly, in another strategy of decatastrophizing, recall that psychologist Ronald Rapee advocates approaching automatic anxious thoughts with a more cavalier attitude. He suggests that the phobic ask himself: If the worst actually occurs, so *what?* What would happen then? And how terrible would that be? And then what? In many instances, it becomes apparent that the dreaded outcome is not as terrible as what is feared, that even the worst-case scenario is "survivable."

A sticking point in use of this approach may occur when the worst-case scenario is intolerable even to think about. Despite their growing awareness that their fears are exaggerated and irrational, some who utilize decatastrophization may be unable to shake the conviction that certain death or dismemberment would result from exposure therapy with certain of their phobias. As the following example illustrates, even these catastrophic images may be decatastrophized:

A young woman progressed steadily in overcoming her fear of driving the winding canyon road between her home and the Pacific beaches until she was on the verge of tackling the three-mile-long stretch of cliffs and sheer drop-offs. She came to her therapist, too apprehensive to continue, and, through discussion, realized that she was intimidated by a fear of plummeting to her death.

"If that occurred," the therapist asked, "what's the worst that could happen then?"

After a moment's reflection, she replied, "I don't believe in life after death, so I guess that nothing else would *ever* happen for me again. But my family would suffer so much if I died."

"Would they ever recover and resume living their lives?"

"I'm sure they would, after a period of bereavement."

"Could you please estimate the likelihood that you would so totally lose control of your car on a hairpin turn after all your canyon driving practice and the safe driving that you've done?"

"You know, when you put it that way, it's very low. I guess I should think more about my good track record than about dying!"

"Perhaps if you do more of just that, you would feel an increasing sense of confidence in your driving ability and your anxiety would be more tolerable."

A portion of the individuals who get stopped at this juncture may do best by seeking out formal therapy; another possibility is to take smaller steps using more gradual, less challenging techniques, like reasoning with oneself and reestimation; and a third alternative is to aim for less anxiety-provoking goals.

Think about a couple of your tenacious fears and use them for practice, utilizing the Craske and Barlow–style decatastrophization and Rapee's "So what?" technique to relieve anxiety.

Modifying the way that you think about phobic situations is the first step toward changing. Your emerging ability to cope with frightening thoughts and beliefs will allow you to take the next step of confronting your fears in the target situations you identified at the beginning of the chapter. The mental flexibility you are developing will serve you in good stead throughout the exposure practice sessions we recommend below.

Beginning Exposure Practice

To help envision the process of constructing an initial exposure plan, let's accompany Julia, who is mildly phobic for driving far from her home, shopping, and riding in an elevator (although she has more severe phobic reactions to other situations which probably would not, therefore, belong in her *initial* plan). Hers is Julia's list of phobic situations, and accompanying SUDs ratings, in order from mildly to severely uncomfortable. To refresh your memory, SUDs stands for Subjective Units of Discomfort, where 0 SUDs means that no discomfort is experienced and 10 means that the situation is extremely uncomfortable.

Explaining her ratings, Julia says that when things start turning unpleasant, she would rate her discomfort as a 5. For instance, as she turns into the busy street near the supermarket, she'll probably begin feeling panic symptoms like irregular breathing or a sharp rise in tension, and her SUDs-level will climb to a 5. When she tries to enter the market, her head starts spinning with fears of losing control and not being able to get home—hence, a 6. When she steps into a tall building knowing she must ride an elevator to reach her destination, her discomfort level is a 7.

JULIA'S INITIAL EXPOSURE HIERARCHY

Phobic Situation, Event, or Activity	Maximum Expected SUDs Rating (0–10)
Driving 2½ miles from home to the busy street where the market is located	5½
Shopping at the local supermarket	6
Riding in an elevator	7

VISITING THE SCENE OF THE CRIME

Now that Julia has created her hierarchy, her first step toward exposure therapy is to enlist the help of a support person (see pp. 143–145) and proceed toward her phobic situation until she becomes less anxious. She asks a friend to pick her up, and her friend agrees to follow Julia's lead and accept her limits. She hops in the car, and together they drive toward the supermarket. Partway there, she takes the wheel and drives for a few more blocks with her friend's support, until she starts to get uneasy. Soon she pulls over to the curb or perhaps into a parking lot. She tries to notice her thoughts and feelings and to remain there until her anxiety starts to subside. By visiting the scene of the crime, Julia has tasted the thrills and chills of phobic exposure. That wasn't so bad! Now she develops a plan for beginning exposure practice.

In order to create a challenge without stirring up excessive anxious discomfort, she includes in her plan some features that decrease the difficulty of exposure and others that "sweeten the pot." Initially, she'll go with her cousin, because she feels less anxious when driving with her than by herself. She decides she'll work on getting to the supermarket, since it's a basic and frequent necessity. Also, her new gynecologist isn't far away, and she is really eager to get started with her, so she makes the doctor's office a second destination.

Julia divides both her trips—to the supermarket and the elevator ride up to her doctor's office—into manageable steps, *each of which she plans to practice before proceeding to the next one.* In the hierarchy of goals she creates, each item is likely to produce at least a little more anxiety than the one preceding it.

Julia's Initial Exposure Goals

1. Drive with my cousin to the parking lot of the supermarket.

2. Go into the market with my cousin and buy five things.

3. Go into the market alone at midday and buy five things.

4. Go into the lobby of the building where the gynecologist I like has her office and stand in front of the elevator for five minutes.

5. Get into the elevator while the elevator doors stay open.

6. Ride the elevator up to the doctor's floor, go to her waiting room, and sit for ten minutes.

7. Have a brief consultation with the doctor in her office.

On the worksheet on the following page, Julia identified the specific points or "mileposts" where she believed she would become significantly more anxious when shopping. Then she and her cousin went ahead and practiced exposure therapy by going to the situation and doing what she planned. During the practice, she rated the SUDs she felt at each milepost. As she completed each practice, she planned the next one and continued this process until she achieved her objective during trip 6.

WOW! HOW DID SHE *DO* IT?

As you saw, from the moment Julia created her initial exposure hierarchy until her solo drive away from the supermarket parking lot with her gro-

Julia's Worksheet for Practicing Grocery Shopping

Practice Trips to the Market	Mileposts of Significant Anxiety	SUDs	Max. SUDs
Trip 1	**a.** As soon as it comes into view	2	
	b. I pull into the parking lot	3	
	c. I walk through the entrance	4	4
Trip 2	**a.** Parking at far end of parking lot	2	
	b. Entering the store with my cousin	3	
	c. Walking through the turnstile and staying inside alone for a couple of minutes	5	5
Trip 3	**a.** Entering the store with my cousin	2	
	b. Pushing a shopping basket quickly down one aisle and up another, selecting five items at random, and then leaving the basket and walking out	4	
	c. Accompanying my cousin through the express checkout line as she buys a couple of things	5	5
Trip 4	**a.** Walking through the turnstile with a shopping basket	2	
	b. Pushing the basket up and down two aisles and selecting five items	3	
	c. Meeting my cousin at the express checkout and buying the groceries	4	4
Trip 5	**a.** Taking a basket, selecting five items, and checking them out alone, with my cousin waiting outside	3	
	b. Shopping alone for five items with my cousin waiting in the car on far side of parking lot	4	4
Trip 6	**a.** By myself, shopping for and purchasing five items	2	
	b. Putting items in my car parked near the store	2	
	c. Driving out of the lot to a nearby side street where I left my cousin, sitting on a curb, picking her up, and driving home	3	3

ceries at the end of trip 6, she progressed from an expected discomfort level of 6 to an actual SUDs rating of 3, from suffering a lot of anxious discomfort while grocery shopping to feeling no more than mild anxiety. Julia's tremendous achievement is perfectly normal in the realm of phobia exposure practice!

How could she accomplish all this? First of all, by selecting the local supermarket, Julia chose an *accessible* situation, one that could easily be returned to *repeatedly*. Depending on your phobias, elevators situated in buildings close by, local roadways, freeway entrances or exits, markets, shops, restaurants, or nearby rooftops for height phobia practice may be good starting places for you.

Following her therapist's instructions, Julia returned to the phobic situation three or four times a week so that once she began exposure practice, she could leapfrog each step of progress over the achievements of the previous practice experience. She attempted to *remain at each targeted milestone long enough for her anxiety to peak and then begin to subside.*

By practicing systematically and consistently, Julia created and internalized new emotional memories of her progress in the phobic situation. In addition, by working on regaining her capacity to shop for groceries, she had strong incentives to succeed, because achieving her goal would reward her with her choice of good foods and permit her to recapture an important element of her autonomy.

Julia selected two or three low anxiety-provoking phobic situations from her hierarchy of phobic situations with which to start exposure. Within each situation, she chose activities or events that would provoke a noticeable but manageable amount of discomfort. These are good choices for starting points, according to psychologists Ronald Rapee's and William Sanderson's standard: "situations that clients believe they can encounter if necessary, but would prefer to avoid." In keeping with the principle of *selecting starting points and each succeeding step with both her motivation and her comfort in mind,* Julia decided to use her cousin's support and shop at an hour when the store was not busy. In designing the practices, she varied the length of time she spent in the store and the amount of time by herself.

It's Your Turn

Choose two or three phobic situations that might fit the practice framework we have discussed. The situations should be accessible, involve a noticeable but manageable discomfort level, and give you the prospect of real satisfaction as your reward for mastering them.

Begin with practices you can manage, remembering that "a journey of a thousand miles begins with a single step." You will discover that when anxious feelings occur in small measure they can be quite bearable. Work gently and steadily with your fears, and you will begin to regain a measure of comfort and confidence in situations that you have been avoiding. Remember, the rate of exposure and choice of situations will always be under your control and may be as gradual or swift as you please. Structure your practices so that your discomfort should be limited to a manageable level, taking into consideration the factors listed on page 142. Carefully plan and consistently carry out these initial practices so that you will be able to progress in strides and develop effective ways to master your major challenges.

At the beginning of the chapter you identified some situations in which you have become phobic. Write them in the worksheet that follows, and

A Brief Guide to Exposure Therapy

1. Start with *accessible* situations that you can revisit easily and repeatedly.

2. Start exposure with phobic situations that provoke a noticeable but manageable amount of discomfort that you believe you "can encounter if necessary, but would prefer to avoid."

3. Remain at each targeted milestone long enough for your anxiety to peak and then begin to subside.

4. Return to a practice three or four times a week in order to optimize your progress by creating new emotional memories.

5. In conducting your practices, try to be comfortable but focus on progress. When anxious feelings occur in small measure they can be quite bearable.

next to each, write the *highest* SUDs rating that you would expect to reach—the maximum discomfort—if you were in the situation *today.* Keeping your ratings and your responses to these questions in mind, create an initial exposure hierarchy. List below, *in order from the most approachable to the most unapproachable,* the phobic situations you would like to try to return to and to master.

Worksheet 7.4
INITIAL EXPOSURE HIERARCHY

Phobic Situation, Event, or Activity	Maximum Expected SUDs Rating (0–10)
_____	_____
_____	_____
_____	_____
_____	_____

WHERE SHOULD YOU START YOUR EXPOSURE PRACTICE?

Here are some suggested starting points for exposure therapy.

Table 7.2

STARTING POINTS FOR EXPOSURE PRACTICE

Type of Phobia	Starting Point
Shopping	Corner market Nearby mini-mall Edge of parking lot of nearby maxi-mall
Traveling out of sight of home	Start along the walking trail or bike path just down the hill or around the corner. Drive out of the driveway into the street. Sit in the car, engine off. Sit in the car, engine on. Drive down the block and back.
Aerobic exercise	Walk on a treadmill for a few minutes. Climb a few stairs. Walk around the block at an easy pace.
Elevators	Enter the quiet lobby of a nearby building. Look at an elevator in use from ten feet away. Step inside an open, empty elevator and then step out.
Restaurants	Sit at an outdoor table in a small local café. Accompany a person picking up fast food from a takeout window. Call in for carryout food and pick it up at the counter of a sit-down restaurant.
Driving in traffic	During a quiet time of day, drive along a slightly trafficky stretch of road to a nearby destination where you can get a reward. Visit a friend or buy something you like. Drive an exit or two on the quietest nearby freeway during a low-traffic time.
Air travel	Rent a move like *Fly Away Home*. Write and review a script describing the sounds, sights, smells, thoughts, and feelings you'd experience during a scary part of a flight. Visit an airport and watch planes boarding and taking off.

(continued on next page)

Table 7.2

STARTING POINTS FOR EXPOSURE PRACTICE *(continued)*

Type of Phobia	Starting Point
Ocean cruise	Visit a harbor and watch liners come and go. Get a video from a cruise line and watch the scenes of contented travelers enjoying their trips.
Movie theaters	Go see a couple of engaging movies soon. Be mindful of the "comfort factors" of theater-going—the length of the film, the size of the audience for each show, layout and proximity to exits, number of children, and suspensefulness of the subject matter. Anxious people usually prefer aisle seats to the middle of the row.

SUBDIVIDE PHOBIC SITUATIONS INTO MANAGEABLE STEPS

Effective practice is often the result of breaking up the phobic activity, event, or situation into manageable steps. Work on one step at a time until a tolerable level of comfort is attained. Steps may consist of specific "operations" (like driving down the street as far as a particular store or streetlight and then pulling over to the curb) or of a series of operations (like pulling into the center lane and driving up to a certain point, merging into the next lane over, driving two blocks, and turning right). Another example of a single substantial step in practicing driving might be to go onto a freeway ramp, enter the merge lane, and get off at the first exit. This step would be repeated until it provokes very little anxiety. The next step could be either to stay on the right and proceed for one additional exit or else to move one lane to the left within the first minute or so. The latter step might then be followed by a move back to the exit lane within a mile or so, and then leaving the freeway.

At its most fundamental, this process accords with the Alcoholics Anonymous adage, "One Day at a Time," which may be freely restated as one hour, one minute, one mile, or even one yard, foot, or inch at a time. One of the authors recalls his method of "desensitizing" himself to height phobia: Many

Worksheet 7.5
MY PLANNING AND PRACTICE WORKSHEET

Practice in Phobic Situations	SUDs	First Three Mileposts of Significant Anxiety	Max. SUDs
Example: Ride an elevator six floors up	7	a. Park in the building's parking lot	3
		b. Walk into the lobby with my wife at a quiet time and look at the elevator	4
		c. Stand right in front of the elevator with my wife and imagine entering it	5
My practice 1:			
My practice 2:			
My practice 3:			

times on many days he walked back and forth across safely enclosed bridges that stretched high above the water, until eventually his anxiety dissipated.

READY, SET, GO

Do you feel ready to begin? It's perfectly normal to be apprehensive, to hesitate and think, "What if . . . ?" "What-ifs" are actually anxiety-laden predictions, *theories* about catastrophes that *could* happen. *Your phobic avoidance and the anxious discomfort you feel when you enter phobic situations exist precisely because these fears have not yet been successfully challenged in real life.* As we indicated in our discussion of apprehension, when anxious, we downplay our own ability to cope and exaggerate the risk that something really bad will occur. But things are not what they seem: The risk is generally far less likely and potent than it appears, and you are probably underrating your capability. So go ahead and see what you can accomplish. Fill in the details of your experience on worksheet 7.5 on the previous page.

Visit the outskirts of one or more of the "scenes of the crime"—your phobic siutations—like Julia and her cousin did. Pay a quick visit to dogs or cats at a pet shop if you are phobic for animals. Get someone who isn't afraid of spiders to put one in a jar for your perusal from across the table if you are arachnophobic, or examine vivid pictures of spiders or snakes or bugs—whatever you are phobic for—on the Internet or in nature books. Bring a friend or family member and go to the vicinity of a situation that triggers your anxiety—an elevator, intersection, or shopping mall. Park across the street from the freeway on-ramp and study it. Go just close enough to the phobic situation to remember how it feels and experience a *little* anxiety, perhaps a SUDs level of 2 or 3.

Techniques for Practicing Exposure

Next, start planning your exposure practice workouts. Your workouts should be your own unique combinations of graduated, planned exposure to your choice of anxiety-provoking events, situations, and activities, using applications of select therapeutic techniques such as SCT, challenging anxious thoughts, and reverse engineering anxiety propositions. You probably

What to Say and Do to Prevent Overanxiety at the Starting Gate

- Say to yourself, "I am not my anxiety."
- Only go close enough to the phobic situation to feel a *little* anxiety.
- Remind yourself that what you feel is an exaggerated stress reaction, a little panic. It won't turn into something terrible. Stay in the present.
- When you wander from the present to self-criticism or "what-ifs," return to the present moment by remembering to breathe or tensing and relaxing your muscles.

should plan to intersperse your workouts with ample rewards for success-ful achievement.

Action before feeling is a cardinal rule of behavior change in emotion-ally charged situations where apprehension and anxious thoughts are problems. Plan or schedule a practice. When the times comes, put on your shoes, walk out the door, and head for the practice site. Focus on imple-menting your plan of action *before* you think about your mood or feelings. Try to refrain from asking yourself whether you feel like practicing before doing so, because your feelings actually aren't relevant to the benefit you will derive. Proceed this way every time you work out, and you will be more likely to bypass the anxious inclination to avoid your practice situation.

The three main dimensions of practice are *duration, repetition, and level of anxiety.*

DURATION

Work out for as long as you can with anxiety-provoking material, using cognitive restructuring to cope with anxious thoughts and redefinition and SCT to contend with anxious physical sensations. Try to plan on at least fifteen or twenty minutes in order to gain strength from each practice. Many of the highest-powered, fastest-moving exposure programs utilize forty-five- to ninety-minute sessions.

The consensus of anxiety treatment professionals is that you should *try to continue the workout until your SUDs level has peaked and started to drop.* Leave if and when you have to, of course—if you become too un-comfortable to remain, or if it's no longer feasible to stay, such as when an agitated crowd is clamoring to use the elevator on which you are practicing.

REPETITION

When you enter an exposure workout target situation and have a control-lable, tolerable anxious reaction as expected, plan to return there for mul-tiple practice sessions. *Your goal is to master your anxiety to the point that it does not exceed a SUDs level of 1 or 2 and to be able to repeat this feat at least several times.*

Repetitions of exposure to a specific situation should occur no more than a few days apart, preferably several times a week. If you stop practic-ing in a phobic situation before mastering it, try to resume within a week or two, or else you may slide back a bit. "Spicing up" exposure by working out on two or three different phobic situations is perfectly okay, but remember to devote enough time to each situation and repeat it often enough to cause your anxiety to drop swiftly or even to cease.

LEVEL OF ANXIETY

A number of factors can be varied in order to keep your expected level of discomfort under control during planned exposure workouts:

- Distance from the situation

- Distance from home or safe place

- Are you leaving or returning home? Return home is usually less anxiety-provoking.

- Working alone or with phobia helper

- Time of day

- Number of other people or cars in the situation

- Depth of exposure (e.g., edge of the parking lot vs. fifty yards inside the mall)

Mental Fitness and New Maps of Your Mind

Exposure therapy may seem to resemble a physical fitness regimen, with its emphasis on repetition of specific behaviors and building strength. But it's actually more about *mental fitness:* improving coping skills, restructuring your thinking about anxious situations, reevaluating the realism of the apparent threats, and using your head to modify your physical reactions—in essence, handling anxiety differently and getting mentally stronger. You are rewriting your mental map *while in the situation,* much like mapping out the twists and turns of a canyon as you explore it. Every workout validates the techniques you select for contending with anxiety and strengthens your skills. Each time, you determine anew whether anxiety controls you or you control it.

Between Exposure Workouts

Plan a brief cognitive self-talk before each exposure workout. Review what you plan, as well as relevant conclusions you drew from previous exposures, and state specifically any applicable realistic propositions that you wish to keep in mind. Write up a coping card that includes the main points of emphasis.

We suggest the following considerations in your planning:

- How much anxiety do I want to tolerate in the next practice? The same, more, or less than in the last practice?

- What is a decent-sized step to take in exposure? Would it be preferable to repeat the same step I took last time I was in the situation? In the same way? Should I go deeper into the situation or continue for longer? Or should I try another type of situation?

- Would it be useful to think about the physical symptoms I expect to feel? What techniques might help? What would be the optimal ways to contend with anxious thoughts?

- Are there affirmations, heartening statements, prayers, or insights that I would like to have available to bring to mind during practices?

- What are the addresses of the nearest music store, plant store, art gallery, or ice cream parlor, so I can provide myself with an immediate reward?

Before each exposure workout, vividly envision the phobic situation you plan to work on. Imagine how would it look, smell, taste, and feel. Would you sweat, get short of breath, become tense or nauseous? Then mentally review how you intend to utilize SCT and cognitive restructuring strategies to deal with the anxiety you expect to encounter. Finally, imagine yourself coping with and successfully mastering your fears.

The Support of Others

Every negative emotional state gets more disturbing when compounded by loneliness. A common, often useful practice is to get help from *support persons* during exposure to phobic situations. As Dr. Reid Wilson observes,

As Anxiety Fades Away

After completing exposure therapy to situations that stimulate 5 or 6 SUDs, you may plan exposure therapy with the items you initially rated between 7 (moderately impairing) and 9 (extremely impairing). Once the SUDs levels drop below 2 during several successive exposures to a phobic situation, it is no longer capable of arousing significant apprehension, and the phobic anxiety is said to be "extinguished." Then it's time to tackle the next challenge, and the next, until you are satisfied, or until anxiety fades from every situation.

"the most important role they play is to let you know you are not alone. When you know that someone in the world understands you, then you can feel you have a choice: you don't have to do this by yourself."

Two variables determine the support person's "helpfulness quotient":

1. Can he or she provide *generous* support? The more generous the support, the more exposure practice will increase your sense of accomplishment and the psychological likelihood that you can *internalize* the value of practice experiences.

2. Can the support person assist and encourage you in ways that conform to psychologically sound guidelines and thus can contribute to your progress?

The support of others is generally reassuring, but in order to be part of a program of long-term anxiety relief, it should be a bridge to attainment of greater independence. Thus the "Helper Should Nots" in table 7.3, on the following page, consist largely of ways to minimize pressure, second-guessing, babying, impatience, or irritation at the anxious person during exposure workouts. Abiding by this list, support persons can enhance the efforts of people in progress and may catalyze therapy gains for those who are really stuck.

What would be the ideal support network for a person working on overcoming a phobia? Support persons who are helpful and constructive are validating and valuable, but an "ideal network" might contain a blend of "hard" and "soft" elements. After all, phobias are all about avoidance—desperate, last-ditch defensiveness against fear. Many a phobic has become

Table 7.3

HOW TO BE MOST HELPFUL TO A PERSON WITH A PHOBIA

The Helper Should	The Helper Should Not
• Reassure you that she will be there for support for an agreed-upon period (e.g., until you reach the next stoplight; right up until you get into the elevator)	• Exert verbal pressure that adds to your discomfort
	• Tell you what to do
	• Criticize
• Help discuss and plan the strategy that will be used	• Withdraw assistance in the middle of a practice
• Let you know of any limitations—of time, distance, or situation—that she must impose on a practice	• Act irritated or impatient; she should plan to cope with her own negative feelings without exposing you to them
• Prompt and encourage you in carrying out the strategy, using previously agreed upon language and signs— e.g., thumbs up	• Pressure you to continue further after you let it be known that your limit is reached
• Accept your choices of objectives and strategies as the bottom line	• Discourage you from trying to go a little farther or stay a little longer in an anxiety-provoking situation
• Congratulate you for successes, even when the original plan has been modified or abridged	• Express disappointment or otherwise degrade or minimize your efforts and accomplishments
• Constructively, uncritically discuss shortfalls	• Take credit for your accomplishments

very self-protective and defensive, his confidence in his capacity to cope effectively with stress badly shaken. While a phobic person's angst needs soothing, his capacity to withstand and strategically confront his pain must also be supported.

Unexpected Exposure

Unless you are extremely phobically avoidant, amazingly lucky, or lead a very controlled lifestyle, you are likely to wind up facing some phobic situations by surprise or earlier than planned. You may not feel ready but decide nevertheless to go ahead. Some of the skills you have acquired may help a lot.

Remember about unexpected exposure that *experiencing high anxiety or*

When to Seek Professional Mental Health Help

- If you are immobilized or overwhelmed by your panic or fear

- If your anxiety is too intense for you to attempt self-help for your phobias

- If you have not been able to progress using the strategies in this book, or if you go two steps back for every step forward

- If you are considering treating your condition with psychoactive medication

- If you embark on a course of eliminating your "safety signals" (pp. 153–155) and find that you are feeling too insecure to continue

- If you decide to treat your general situational phobia using either the flooding technique (p. 155) or interoceptive exposure (pp. 155–156)

---

a little panic in a situation where you would expect it seldom sets progress back. Only when a phobic person is forced into a very anxiety-provoking situation *under duress,* or by being otherwise traumatized, is lasting additional anxiety likely to be created. Other than conditions of traumatic coercion, then, "premature exposure" situations are not likely to retard progress. So try to be flexible and consider these events as interesting challenges to your increasing ability to care for yourself when anxious.

Obstacles to Progress in Exposure Therapy

The course of phobia recovery is seldom unobstructed. In this section, we discuss some strategies that may be implemented during exposure for contending with the most commonly encountered obstacles to progress.

POSSIBLE OBSTACLE #1: DISHEARTENING PANIC AND ANXIETY ATTACKS

Are you discouraged by continued panic or anxiety attacks? Many people with specific and social phobias and most with general situational phobias have panic or anxiety attacks. Fear of panic, sometimes referred to as "fear of fear" or "anxiophobia," is an integral part of many people's general situational phobias, so your successes in mastering panic will be likely to take you a long way toward vanquishing phobic anxiety.

For Specific Phobias

If you have specific phobias and your anxiety attacks occur only when you attempt to approach particular phobic objects or situations, they will probably decrease as you practice the treatment strategies described in this chapter. We encourage you to reinvigorate your panic-busting skills by rereading the section titled "Self-Control Relaxation Training" on pages 76–80, so you can better contend with the anxious physical sensations that could emerge as you progress.

For General Situational Phobias

If you suffer from general situational phobias—agoraphobia, claustrophobia, or height phobia—panic is likely to be part of the clinical picture. Review the techniques for gaining control over panicky feelings in chapter 5.

Contending with Anxiety About Physical Sensations

As you start to practice exposure to situations and activities for which you are phobic, you may tend to link the physical anxiety sensations that occur to frightening automatic thoughts such as fear of losing control or going crazy. Start challenging these fears with knowledge. Review the objective cause of each of your anxiety sensations on the "Emergency Response Symptoms" list on pages 83–85 (and see table 7.4 below). Each time the physical sensations occur identify them as "emergency response symptoms" and write them down (see the examples below). Think of the sensations objectively, and utilize self-control relaxation techniques to relieve them. In this way, you can steadily strengthen your credence that physical anxiety symptoms are neither uncontrollable nor lethal.

First Aid for Unexpected Exposure

The most common "panic-busting" technique used by people who have had anxiety therapy is a simple breathing technique—slowing and controlling the rate of breathing.

Table 7.4

OBJECTIFYING ANXIOUS PHYSICAL SENSATIONS

Phobic Situation	Anxious Physical Sensations	Objective Reasons for Sensations
Ms. A is surrounded by semis while driving on the freeway.	Rapid, shallow breathing; altered heart rate	"Panic breathing" results from the tightening of the chest muscles—the extra oxygen that is accumulated and added to the blood gives an edge during a struggle to survive. The heart beats extra forcefully to circulate extra-oxygenated, high-octane blood throughout the body.
Mrs. B tries to take her first antianxiety pill.	Feels like she can't swallow.	When tense and anxious, the muscles around the throat commonly tighten up. Also, rapid, shallow panic breathing creates a tide of moving air that blows the throat dry. This symptom is also experienced as a lump in the throat. The lump is emotional in nature, rather than physical.

Medications and Exposure Therapy

Many general situational phobics take medication either to establish, maintain, or expand their comfort zone. Medications that are effective for relief of panic could also prove to be helpful for limiting phobic fears and the overwhelming anxiety that may hamper some people's ability to engage in effective exposure treatment (see chapter 3). The consensus among researchers and clinicians is that medication is generally *not* indicated for the treatment of specific phobias.

POSSIBLE OBSTACLE #2: APPREHENSION

Exposure can rekindle the apprehensive thoughts and anxious feelings that fueled the avoidance of the phobic situation in the first place. Raoul is learning how to contend with his anticipatory anxiety. He thought about starting to work on his elevator phobia and then let himself register the apprehensive thoughts that stirred in his mind and held him back. In the Phobia Record below, Raoul has written out detailed descriptions of his apprehensions and his plans for coping with them. On the left in part 1 he details the physical anxiety or panic symptoms he would expect to encounter upon taking the first few steps toward riding an elevator, and on the left in part 2 the automatic apprehensive thoughts he is having or expects to have. On the right in each part Raoul has written out the coping techniques and realistic thoughts, respectively, with which he would like to challenge his panic and anxiety.

RAOUL'S PHOBIA RECORD: COPING WITH APPREHENSION ON AN ELEVATOR RIDE

1. Physical Stress Symptoms

Anticipated Symptoms	Coping Techniques
▪ Panic breathing ▪ Trouble concentrating ▪ Rapid heartbeat	▪ Regulate breathing ▪ Explain rapid heart rate as emergency response ▪ Focus on reassuring self-talk

2. Anxious Automatic Thoughts

Automatic Thoughts	Realistic Thoughts
▪ I feel trapped. ▪ I won't be able to handle this. ▪ I won't be able to breathe. ▪ I'll pass out. ▪ Nobody will hear me, no one will help me.	▪ I will step out right after stepping in. ▪ I'll start regulating my breathing before even entering. ▪ I'll only stay until I become a little anxious.

Fill in your own experiences in the Phobia Record on the following page. Imagine or remember yourself approaching your "phobic neighborhood" or in a phobic situation. No matter how outlandish or inexplicable the automatic thoughts that enter your mind when you imagine or visit the situations, write them out here:

Worksheet 7.6

PHOBIA RECORD: COPING WITH *MY* APPREHENSIONS ABOUT THIS SITUATION:

_____

1. Physical Stress Symptoms

Anticipated Physical Symptoms	Coping Techniques

2. Anxious Automatic Thoughts

Automatic Thoughts	Realistic Thoughts

Right before your next practice in this situation, review the coping techniques and realistic thoughts you have written here that you could use to contend with the physical and mental anxiety that may occur. Successful practitioners of exposure therapy find it helpful to *overplan*—that is, to prepare and mentally rehearse ways of coping with more intensely anxious thoughts and feelings than they realistically expect to have. Then, when they are in the practice situation, surprisingly little effort may actually be required to cope, and they are apt to be able to cope with surprise stresses, too. Practice also helps to prevent the return of apprehension; research suggests that the longest-lasting successes are apt to result from *overlearn-*

ing—continuing to practice coping with phobic situations well after the discomfort they produce is negligible.

If your apprehension still renders practice exceedingly foreboding and unmanageable, then "lower the bar" by modifying your practices to lessen the anxiety likely to be produced. Don't enter that building, just drive to the parking lot or circle the block. Instead of sitting down in a busy restaurant, order your food to go and remain near the register, or simply confine your practice to accompanying a friend into the restaurant while he or she orders and pays for the food. Park across from the freeway on-ramp and get comfortable before ever venturing onto the freeway.

POSSIBLE OBSTACLE #3: TOO PETRIFIED TO PROGRESS IN EXPOSURE PRACTICE

Sometimes when people are too petrified to progress, it is because they hold beliefs that are antithetical to therapy. These terrifying beliefs, known as anxiety propositions, are formed when automatic thoughts are welded to alarming physical sensations by the white heat of a highly phobic moment. To the "uninitiated"—those who haven't had panic and phobia treatment—they seem to crop up out of nowhere and can catch them unawares. Yet when expressed at calmer moments, anxiety propositions seem irrational yet rather familiar.

After conquering her fears of grocery shopping, Julia surges toward her next hurdle of entering an elevator, but then grinds to an abrupt halt when she panics the instant she passes through the elevator doors. Aggravated, she calls her cousin to describe her disheartening experience and seek support. As they talk, Julia starts to realize more specifically what she is afraid of—that once the elevator door closes, it will not open again. As she verbalizes those images—indeed, the instant they flash through her mind—she sucks in her breath and starts to hyperventilate. Her ultimate fear is that the elevator will break down, her air supply will be cut off, and she will pass out from lack of oxygen and lie there helpless. On the following page is an analysis of Julia's anxiety proposition, and below it we have left space for you to write out an analysis of yours.

Now, let's follow Julia as she examines the fearful beliefs. She rereads the "Emergency Response Symptoms" list in chapter 5, realizes that her hyperventilation and pounding heart are panic symptoms, and reviews the

Worksheet 7.7
ANALYZING ANXIETY PROPOSITIONS

Phobic Situation	Anxious Physical Sensations and Automatic Thoughts	Anxiety Proposition (Anxious Belief)
Julia enters an elevator and the door closes.	Hyperventilation, pounding heart, fear that the door won't open and of passing out and embarrassing herself	Julia believes she will pass out in a broken elevator and lie unconscious in the unmoving car.

techniques that she could use to control them. After she articulates her operative anxiety proposition—her fearful belief that she would pass out in a broken elevator and lie unconscious in the unmoving car—she reads up on elevator safety in the written materials and Internet printouts she'd been collecting (appendix E of this book contains a highly informative guide to elevator safety features). From her research she learns that elevators are reliable, seldom have breakdowns that go undetected for long, and have plenty of air, because they share in the air supply of the entire building where they are situated.

Julia reassures herself even more by recalling that she's never actually fainted despite recurrent fears that she would. In other words, she *reasons with herself*, noting the highlights of her research on elevator safety and the strongest points made during her discussions with her cousin.

Julia records her conclusions about her anxious thoughts and physical anxiety symptoms in her Phobia Record and reviews it just before embarking on her next practice. In addition, she jots down the points she most wants to remember on a "coping card" that she takes along. On an index card, Julia lists all the data, memory joggers, affirmations, and planned rewards that she finds to be helpful in coping with her fear of elevators.

Here is Julia's coping card:

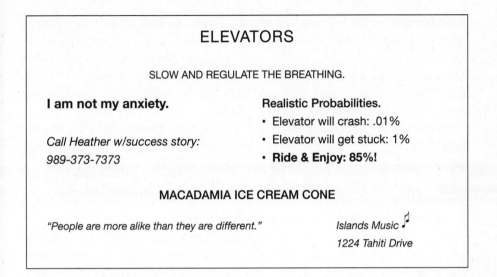

Julia was able to tolerate a full half-minute inside the elevator with the doors open. By reverse engineering her anxiety proposition, she succeeded in jump-starting her practice by regulating her breathing, redefining her other physical panic symptoms, and reasoning with herself. Before setting out on each elevator exposure workout, Julia reviewed the steps to reverse engineer her anxious thoughts and feelings into the realistic propositions that she'd outlined on her Phobia Record. She debriefed herself after each experience and soon discovered that her thinking accorded more and more closely with her realistic propositions.

Decreasing Reliance on Safety Signals

As you learn to cope better with phobic situations and conquer your fears, you may wish to decrease your reliance on *safety signals,* "coping devices" that make anxiety-provoking situations seem more manageable by appearing to reduce threat. Common safety signals include water bottles, extra antianxiety pills, a little food "in case of light-headedness," and the addresses of various nearby emergency rooms.

Safety signals only give the illusion of security, but they appear to "empower" a phobic person as a result of their incidental roles in the less disheartening moments of anxiety episodes. For instance, after a parent gets a little comfort from her baby's smile during an episode of driving phobia, she may bring the child along on every drive. Babies are not actually capable of helping with traffic or apprehension, and phobias are not relievable by even a hundred sweet smiles. Water bottles are also a popular "talisman"; although sipping cool liquid wets the whistle, it does not decrease the high anxiety that dries phobics' mouths.

Nevertheless, safety signals easily get ingrained through their association with security and coping. Despite their illusory nature, they help keep phobics going. *But they also help perpetuate phobias* by hampering the recovering phobic's awareness of her own strengthening capacity to fight her fears without the aid of talismans.

Which safety signals do you use, and when?

Your phobia therapy can include decreasing reliance on safety signals. Leave your lucky charm in the glove compartment when you venture into the mall, or deliberately choose a route that avoids emergency rooms or bathrooms when working on your driving phobia. Since safety signals cover up anxieties instead of building real confidence, anxiety may briefly

Worksheet 7.8
MY SAFETY SIGNALS

Phobic Situation	Safety Signal(s) I Use

become more pronounced without them, but then you will probably rebound to a point of greater confidence and less anxiety. Record in your Phobia Records how your feelings differ without safety signals.

Intentionally Inducing Fears As a Way of Overcoming Them

A faction of anxiety experts maintains that after the phobic person has mastered skills to relieve physical anxiety and panic and cognitive self-therapy to relieve anxious thinking, phobia therapy should include *fear induction techniques*—exposure to deliberately induced, acutely anxiety-provoking stimuli. According to this point of view, these techniques can strengthen the recovering phobic's conviction that his fears are psychological, not caused by actual danger; enhance confidence in his anxiety-busting skills; and more firmly imprint in his mind the processes that enable him to achieve lasting recovery from his phobic disorder.

FLOODING

A behavioral approach to phobia therapy is flooding, which consists of a series of exposures to intensely anxiety-provoking situations, often in rapid succession. Flooding can sometimes result in substantial progress, but the risk is in becoming too uncomfortable, getting discouraged, and weakening one's overall momentum. Flooding should always be done with the support of a professional therapist.

An example of a potentially productive trial of flooding might occur after a person with freeway phobia has had multiple workouts of graduated exposure therapy and has achieved anxiety control in moderately trafficky situations. The flooding option might consist of spending two hours on five consecutive business days in downtown rush-hour traffic in order to extinguish the remaining phobic reactions. Most people favor more gradual exposure, which can achieve just as good results.

INTEROCEPTIVE EXPOSURE

In order to achieve lasting, durable relief from general situational phobias, a number of experts argue for "interoceptive exposure," a program of deliberate induction of the sensations associated with one's anxiety while concurrently training oneself to reframe them as strictly psychological and controllable. We recommend that you enlist the assistance of a professional therapist if you undertake a program of interoceptive exposure.

Simon and Sarah both decided to work on interoceptive exposure. Simon used to have episodes when his heart would pound or he would become short of breath while shopping in mall stores, so he practiced running in place for half a minute before going into the sporting goods store. Sarah, who also suffered from shortness of breath when at the mall, induced her symptoms by entering a mall shop, pulling out a drinking straw, and breathing strongly and quickly through it for between thirty and sixty seconds. Both Simon and Sarah created challenging opportunities to work on their residual fears in formerly phobic situations by *inducing* pounding hearts and shortness of breath and then relieving them through cognitive restructuring.

If you would like to take on this challenge and reap the benefits, here's how.

Ways of Creating Bodily Sensations While Practicing Exposure

- Breathing as slowly as possible for as long as possible (shortness of breath)

- Driving your car with the heater on and windows rolled up (heat)

- Wearing woolen clothes, jackets, or turtlenecks (heat)

- Drinking coffee at a restaurant (racy feelings)

- Carrying a heavy object while walking (racing heart, muscle fatigue)

- Eating pasta or other heavy foods in a restaurant (stomach fullness)

- Walking up flights of stairs in department stores, malls, buildings (racing heart)

- Wearing a backpack while walking (heaviness, fatigue)

- Wearing a tie or scarf when meeting people (tightness around the throat)

- Looking behind you quickly while walking (dizziness, off balance)

Craske & Barlow, 1994

What do you think will happen when you induce the physical sensations that you associate with anxiety-provoking situations? After all, you have worked successfully and extinguished your phobic anxiety in this situation. Discuss with yourself how likely you are to panic. Have you weakened your phobia to the point where panic is probably unlikely to occur? Is your anxiety unlikely to escalate beyond the immediate symptoms that you have deliberately induced?

After Exposure Workouts

Take stock after each exposure workout. Review what you accomplished, how and what you did, thought, and felt. You will often see real progress. Think of the obstacles you encountered as well as your positive accomplishments. Reflect on your experiences and reward your efforts. Debrief on your own, or have a brainstorming session with a support person or, if you are in treatment, with your therapist.

A typical debriefing checklist would include the following:

- How far did I get into the phobic situation?

- How anxious did I get? How panicky?

- What were my anxious thoughts? List them in chronological order.

- What were my physical anxiety symptoms?

- What techniques were helpful with physical symptoms, and how did they help?

- What techniques proved effective in controlling anxious thoughts?

- How did I capitalize on the resources available in the situation to cope effectively?

- In what ways did support people help or hinder my efforts?

Perfectly Panic-Free?

If you are still having difficulty progressing through exposure therapy, consider seeking the help of a mental health professional. But if you have made substantial accomplishments, congratulations! Your determination and the choices you've made have resulted in practices that really count and in real progress.

But if you still feel moments of panic, don't be distressed. A measure of anxiety is unavoidable. Realistically, perfect psychological or pharmaceutical control of anxiety is unattainable. Nature and evolution have configured us with highly functional anxiety systems as a means of effectively dealing with the physical and emotional challenges of life, and people who occasionally overreact to anxiety triggers survive and prosper better than those who are insensitive or tend to ignore them.

Focus on the progress you have made. If you have followed the guidelines in this book, you have likely lessened your anxiety and eased your phobias, enabling you to enjoy yourself and regain some of the freedom your fears had robbed you of.

In the final chapter of the book, you will have the opportunity to study approaches and specific techniques for preventing relapse.

Chapter Eight

Social Anxiety and Phobia

M ost people feel uncomfortable in social or performance situations now and then. If you have ever

- felt socially inept or reached a point where you imagine yourself fleeing from a social situation,

- become unnerved by a deep uneasiness resulting from feeling that other people disapprove of you,

- been too shy or afraid to speak to others let alone to make a toast or a speech, or

- been too bound up with awkwardness to think straight or do anything right,

then you have felt the chilling grip of social anxiety. According to renowned psychoanalyst and biologist Charles Rycroft, most adult anxiety is social anxiety. A certain amount of anxiety can be adaptive in social situations, steering us away from inadvertent lapses of tact, increasing our sensitivity to others, and inhibiting our impulses to commit guilt-producing behaviors and misbehaviors. The opinions of others play a key part in even the most independent and secure person's social sense and values. However, the socially phobic person takes social anxiety a step further by trying to avoid a wide range of interpersonal and performance situations where feelings of embarrassment or humiliation seem likely to occur. What he or she cannot avoid is endured with anxiety discomfort. Here is the formal diagnosis (from the *DSM-IV*) of social phobia, also called social anxiety disorder:

> "[Social phobia is a disorder] characterized by overwhelming anxiety and excessive self-consciousness in everyday social situations. People with social phobia have a persistent, intense, and chronic fear of being watched and judged by others [or losing control in front of them] and of being embarrassed or humiliated by their own actions. The avoidance, anxious anticipation, or distress interferes significantly with the person's normal routine, occupational (academic) functioning, or social activities or relationships, or there is marked distress about having the phobia."

The National Institute of Mental Health estimates that 5.4 million Americans have social phobia. According to a recent summary of research data from the last fifteen years, social phobia occurs during the lifetimes of 13.5 percent of the population, making it one of the most widespread anxiety disorders.

In addition to its high prevalence, social anxiety can be incapacitating. A popular misconception that lasted until the early 1990s held that social fears were usually restricted to dating or public speaking and seldom had enough power to disrupt people's lives. However, severe social phobia impairs sufferers' careers and academic functioning and casts a dark shadow over their personal lives. Despite the fact that their average age is in the early thirties, half of the social phobics surveyed in a major research study had never married, compared to about a third of those with panic disorder and agoraphobia and a sixth of those with general anxiety disorder. There also is a high incidence of alcoholism and depression among social phobics.

Over the past few years, intensive efforts have been made to develop potent treatments of social phobia. Public awareness is growing. Entertainment figures such as Donny Osmond have emerged as spokespeople for social phobia treatment. Celebrities including Sir Laurence Olivier, Barbra Streisand, and Vladimir Horowitz have admitted suffering from stage fright.

But even now, with heightened recognition of the pervasiveness and "costs" of social phobia, only about one person in five seeks professional help. The importance of maintaining a façade of social comfort and conviviality in our society deters people with social fears from admitting or discussing their painful inhibitions. People with the capacity to dominate social and performance situations are usually admired and valued, while those who lack the capacity to hold forth and interact with others tend to be regarded as inept, inferior, and perhaps even worse—ignored.

The Main Problems in Social Phobia

British psychologist Adrian Wells has designated the central features of social phobia as negative self-evaluation and fear of negative evaluation by others. Social phobics' fears of embarrassment or humiliation are triggered in situations where they are likely to be open to scrutiny from others, whether interacting or performing.

Some socially phobic individuals have a narrower range of fears. These specific types of fears are limited to performance of particular actions or activities like writing or signing one's name, eating, drinking, or working in front of others. Stage fright is the most common fear experienced by social phobics. People with performance-type social anxiety and the more "generalized" social phobia—from which about two-thirds of a large clinical sample of social anxiety clients suffer—are concerned that other people will have bad opinions of them. They fear they will be ridiculed or thought to be stupid. Their social misgivings are often independent of their self-esteem, which may be relatively healthy.

The ambiguous nature of many social situations kindles social fears. How are we to interpret teasing, for example? Is it an expression of intimacy and fondness, or thinly veiled dislike or contempt? Edna Foa and her colleagues contend that social phobia is driven by cognitive biases to interpret such neutral or ambiguous social cues as rejecting and hostile. According to psychiatrist Aaron Beck and psychologist Gary Emery, in the presence of others a socially anxious individual believes he is in danger of humiliation and loss of status. When this danger seems imminent, an "anxiety program" is activated: His demeanor turns more submissive and self-effacing as he undergoes physical and mental changes which, in more primitive habitats of humanity's evolutionary past, probably reduced his exposure to real danger. Similarly, psychologists Ronald Rapee's and Richard Heimberg's cognitive-behavioral model holds that the mere presence of an audience constitutes a threat, because socially anxious individuals view themselves as if through the eyes of a critical observer. Some of our anxiety clients have reported that they feel vulnerable and exposed in everyday social situations, almost as if they are made of glass, so transparent that others can see their fears. However, they employ a double standard in interpreting social discomfort: while they are likely to explain away or dismiss other people's blushing, sweating, or shaky hands with non-anxiety interpretations, when *they* are the centers of attention they become intensely critical of their own physical anxiety symptoms and feel that they will inevitably be objects of scrutiny and derision.

Of course, these sorts of negative interpretations intensify the discomfort of people with social anxiety. Members of an audience are perceived as hostile or unfriendly observers who tally one's frailties rather than as friendly, understanding, or empathic. Under these conditions, performance in social or evaluative situations may well falter, engendering negative feedback from others and a heightened perception of one's vulnerability to humiliation and embarrassment.

"Social" Symptoms

Almost as if nature were cruelly compounding their mortification, socially anxious people's anxiety attacks generally include symptoms more visible to others than panic attack symptoms not social in origin. Frequent, strong blushing is a prominent symptom. Primarily automatic and thus relatively difficult to change directly, it's nevertheless helpful to understand the causes of the blush and to discern its purpose. Blushing is a reddening or darkening of the person's face, neck, ears, jaw, and sometimes upper chest resulting from automatic increases in blood flow in certain social situations. Specifically, blushing may occur when people receive *undesired social attention*— even positive regard.

When socially anxious, people often stammer or stutter, hesitate on words, say "um" or "uh," pause unnecessarily, or repeat themselves. Social stresses, such as the presence of authority figures or a large audience or listeners' unfavorable reactions, intensify this "dysfluency" and other social anxiety symptoms. Speech fluency suffers because the speaker is likely to be self-consciously monitoring his own verbal output in a misdirected effort to prevent mistakes, while at the same time getting preoccupied by the threat of disapproval by his audience.

Both unique and generic symptoms are components of social anxiety. While every socially anxious person has physical symptoms, those with performance anxiety have more acute, panic attack–like symptoms that indicate sympathetic nervous system arousal, like rapid heartbeat or a pounding heart, sweating (sometimes profusely), shortness of breath, hot flashes, and tremors.

The physical symptoms of the generalized type of social anxiety disorder are lower key and similar to those of generalized anxiety disorder. In or near social and performance situations, individuals with generalized social anxiety may become tense and unable to relax. Their heart rate and blood pressure are likely to increase a little and stay elevated, with relatively little fluctuation due to variations in stress.

With a focus on possible signs of social rejection as well as the physical anxiety symptoms we described, the socially anxious are prone not only to negatively skewing interpretations of neutral or mildly positive social cues, but also to disregarding or ignoring positive social cues. They minimize the value of their hard-earned social successes and devalue the conversational currency of their diverse interests and life experiences. Thus, under these circumstances, people interpret their interactions on the basis of incomplete, inaccurate, negatively biased information, lending support to their assumptions and underlying beliefs that they are inadequate in social situations. No wonder, then, that social anxiety can lead to intense self-consciousness, avoidance of spontaneous interaction with others, and an escalating spiral of discomfort in social situations.

To illustrate, while Ezra was engaged in a conversation with an attractive female coworker at an office party, she turned briefly away and smiled at someone else. He thought, "I'm boring her," and a three-component "anxiety program" was launched in his mind and body:

1. *Physical and cognitive symptoms*—Ezra felt himself blush, his heart raced, and butterflies swarmed in his stomach as he hyperfocused his attention on them.

2. *Safety behaviors or subtle avoidance*—In order to ease his anxious discomfort, Ezra looked into the distance and avoided eye contact, drifted away to the edge of the group, and let other people do most of the talking.

3. *Shift of attention away from the dynamics of the social situation and toward indications of the dreaded negative evaluation from others*— Ezra scanned each person's face for signs of disapproval like averted gazes, frowns, or yawns. This distraction of his focus diverted his attention from holding a proper conversation and from noticing positive signs of interest from the group.

Ezra's guiding belief in this situation was "no one is interested in me unless they seem to be very interested in me." This bias to interpret other people's nonreaction as disapproval, and his reaction of feeling distracted in the conversations he attempted, led to his withdrawal to the outskirts of the room and mounting anxiety that culminated in an anxiety attack. Ezra was unaware of the fact that it was his fears of social rejection—not actual rejection by others—that impeded his social performance and limited his ability to take control of the way he presented himself in many social situations.

In the next chapter, we will help you augment your understanding of physical anxiety symptoms so you can manage them better. You will have a chance to train your attention so that it can serve you when you socialize and perform, rather than slipping out of your control. You will learn to think differently about the way you function in performance and interaction situations and to evaluate other people's reactions more objectively. We will also guide you in devising experiments to build confidence and try out your enhanced social skills.

The Roots of Social Phobia

As society grows ever more intricate and elaborate, socially adept individuals' capacities for community living must be finely honed. People reach milestones of social functioning when they are very young, but on the other hand many cases of social anxiety develop early in life. Shyness, the earliest form of social anxiety, generally emerges during childhood. As mentioned in chapter 2, psychologist Jerome Kagan found clear signs of a possibly genetic kind of nervousness that becomes the basis for shyness in certain children at the age of sixteen weeks. By about age seven, many of the children who have been impaired by this condition—which he labeled behavioral inhibition—began socializing normally; but the rest continue to be socially anxious or develop phobias that last at least through their late teens.

In their survey of the research literature of childhood social anxiety, social psychologists Mark Leary and Robin Kowalski found that shy and socially anxious children tend to have difficulty with peer relations and seldom talk to adults. They avoid opportunities to socialize and often tend to be lonely. Their misfortunes may redouble when the adults in their lives do not teach them social and performance skills. The most socially anxious children try to avoid school because of their discomfort with interactions with teachers and classmates, and those who regularly avoid school meet the diagnostic criteria for social phobia.

Psychologists Ronald Rapee and William Sanderson summarize the trends of childhood experience and family background of socially phobic people: They recall their parents as overprotective, possibly rejecting, and relatively overcontrolling. Their families are not very sociable. Shy children are likely to be the first born, often have had several serious childhood illnesses, tend to be socially isolated, and may recall specific very humiliating incidents.

How do shy, introverted children, often from uneasy families, develop social anxiety disorder? As discussed above, one cause can be *direct conditioning in the presence of others.* The disorder could develop after a youngster has a spontaneous panic attack in front of others. One of our clients told us of the devastating effects of an experience of shame. He described the onset of his social phobia with this story: "At around eight or nine years of age, I tended to say 'uh' a lot and hesitated when I spoke in class. One of the boys in my class, a notorious bully, would count the number of times I said 'uh' and hit me once for each time I said it. I was already somewhat shy, and this made me fear saying anything in class. This fear generalized to my other classes, and this period in my life was associated with a lot of stuttering and self-consciousness that persists to a lesser extent today."

A second cause is *learning vicariously or by observation* from the examples of others. Children who spend much of their childhood observing their anxious parents acting awkward or being marginalized, or their classmates being mercilessly teased because of shyness, are more likely to develop social anxiety.

The third route to social anxiety is *the provision of anxiety-provoking information or instruction,* such as overemphasis on other people's reactions to a child, especially when coupled with frequent or intense criticism. Vic's problems with social anxiety were in part the product of his parents' ridicule of him combined with their overemphasis on the importance of being perfectly groomed and acting mannerly, because "everyone else's families had more money than they did and sent their children to private schools."

Perhaps much of social phobics' stressful, negative experience could be minimized and even avoided if their anxiety sensitivity and shyness were detected at an early age and, once recognized, treated supportively and therapeutically. For instance, anxiety-prone children could be taught social skills, desirable role behaviors, and other strategies to help compensate for their tendency to get socially uncomfortable. This is a major new direction of social anxiety disorder research.

THE BIOLOGY OF SOCIAL ANXIETY

A number of recent studies of families and twins indicate that social phobia runs in families and can be explained, at least in part, by genetic factors. Although the findings of other genetic studies are as yet inconsistent, like other anxiety disorders a general predisposition for social phobia is quite likely to be transmitted genetically via anxiety sensitivity and behavioral inhibition.

Although stronger evidence suggests that family and childhood history, as well as painful experiences of embarrassment and humiliation, play essential parts, an important focus of study is the biological aspect of social anxiety. Interestingly, socially anxious people and their close relatives "report a higher incidence of hay fever, eczema, stomach cramps, and menstrual problems . . . [as well as] skin and respiratory allergies." There is even a social anxiety hormone: the pituitary gland (the "P" of the HPA axis, the mind-body stress reaction mechanism discussed on p. 49) controls the release of oxytocin, which broadcasts an "all clear" signal when social anxiety is relieved, spreading the physical sense of well-being.

Shy or Socially Phobic?

Because shyness is so integral to social phobia, it is reasonable to ask whether the two states are distinct. At least two out of every five people describe themselves as having a problem with shyness, and twice as many report being shy at some point in their lives. Research has found few if any significant distinctions between shy people and those who receive treatment for social anxiety or phobia. Unless otherwise stated, the information in this chapter about the nature and treatment of social anxiety will apply to the entire spectrum of related problems that ranges from shyness to social phobia to avoidant personality disorder (a diagnosis that signifies an extreme degree of socially anxious discomfort).

Cognitive researchers Lusia Stopa and David M. Clark distinguish between shy and socially phobic people on the basis of their perceptions of others' reactions to them. People in both categories are apprehensive about approaching interpersonal challenges and go through similar sorts of "behavioral freezes," where they hesitate right after entering and nervously check out social scenes. The real difference occurs during tentative social initiatives: the shy person begins to relax if other people respond in accepting ways, but the social phobic does not appear to respond to the reactions of other people, even if they are positive, and may misinterpret ambiguous feedback from others as negative. The socially phobic person's misinterpretation and lack of responsiveness is likely the product of his attention being absorbed by internal negative dialogues.

For instance, Adrienne filters out people's friendly gestures or expressions in every social situation she enters. Instead of taking their warmth to heart, she looks intently for their negative reactions, feels self-conscious, and suspects they can see how nervous she feels.

Neuropsychologist Jeffrey Gray would argue that people like Adrienne should more precisely be called "highly socially anxious" than "socially phobic." High anxiety is "a reaction to a set of stimuli that require entry into a situation, with resulting conflict." Adrienne feels really awful when her fiancé "drags her" to family and social gatherings, but she knows she must go or risk losing out on the relationship. A "true social phobic reaction" would demand avoidance of the situation or departure ASAP. This label fits Vince, who has only been out with his friends four times in the decade since his eighteenth birthday. The first three times he was drunk, and he has been avoiding them at all costs since the one nightmarish occasion five years ago when he went out stone sober.

> ### You Don't Have to Have Social Anxiety Disorder to Be Embarrassed
>
> Like people with social phobia, sufferers from panic disorder (PD) and general situational phobias (GSPs) may anticipate and fear embarrassment or humiliation as a result of their anxiety symptoms. Both these individuals and people with social anxiety disorder may have anxiety or panic attacks when they approach or enter social or performance situations. The big difference between PD, GSP, and social phobia is what captures sufferers' attention. During anxiety episodes, the PD or GSP sufferer is morbidly attentive to physical symptoms of anxiety, but the socially anxious person's thoughts and feelings are far more consumed with doubts about his or her performance or other people's reactions.

Social Components of Other Anxiety Disorders

Social anxiety is an important element of various anxiety disorders, particularly GAD and general situational phobias (especially agoraphobia). Social anxiety appears to be an integral part of general anxiety, since the anxious thinking of people with GAD is often replete with *disturbing mental dialogues and monologues about dreaded interactions with other people.* When phobics are being phobic they suffer from socially inhibiting negative emotional states like embarrassment as a part of their intense discomfort with the environment and often expend considerable energy concealing their anxiety from other people.

People with anxiety disorders often function as ultrasensitive anxiety barometers, divining subtle stressors and threats in apparently neutral situations. They may grow uncomfortable and feel impelled to withdraw from social situations that normally provoke little anxiety in others. For instance, a person with bashful bladder syndrome, or paruresis, a social inhibition anxiety disorder with physical complications, may become incapable of urinating in a public bathroom as soon as anyone else enters. Before people with agoraphobia enter anxiety-provoking situations, they often "map the social topography." By this we mean they become keenly aware of who is nearby and the extent to which they may be relied on for support or ought to be avoided, who may be observing them in the situation, and where security is present or absent.

Social anxiety negatively affects a variety of mental maps of social interactions and situations, as well as all sorts of anxiety conditions. Its effects range from mildly disturbing to terrifying, and "hybrid feelings" are produced that run the gamut from shyness to embarrassment to guilt to humiliation, and shame. Its consequences range from painful emotional distress and alienation to restriction of achievement and pleasure, and its costs include loss of friendship, status, and opportunities. The benefits of relieving social anxiety are profound, and the incentives for overcoming it are tremendous.

Chapter Nine

Treatment of Social Anxiety

We people are highly social, incredibly sensitive to the minutest changes in other people's expressions and the subtlest of their nuances. Even more, we tend to be intensely curious about others' opinions of us and may react vigorously to whatever we discover.

The self-doubts of people with social phobia and their misgivings about other people's attitudes deeply affect their opinions of themselves in the interpersonal world. The tendrils of social anxiety reach far into many lives, dividing people from their friends, family, and associates. Now that your awareness of the causes and constricting effects of social phobia has been heightened, we present techniques and strategies to enable you to relieve social anxiety—to enhance your pleasure of good company and your enjoyment of the appreciation of others.

Recovery rates of up to 75 percent are reported for large samples of clients who complete treatment through clinical programs that combine cognitive therapy training with planned exposure, with a low incidence of relapse after the discontinuation of CBT. The rate of recovery through treatment with proper psychotropic medications is nearly as high; but unless medicine and CBT are combined, over two-thirds of those who complete medication treatment relapse if their medication is discontinued. These improvement rates are generally consistent with our clinical experience.

Successful treatment of social anxiety should provide you with the opportunity to learn to think differently and feel better in social evaluation situations. By learning about social phobia, you've already taken the first step. Treatment begins by learning to understand your anxious physical sensations and recognizing your safety behaviors and the situations that you avoid.

Start Assessing Your Social Anxiety

A. PHYSICAL SYMPTOMS

We suggest you get started by *monitoring the occurrence of your social anxiety in your everyday life.* Jot down the social anxiety physical symptoms you experience in worksheet 9.1 below, and when you notice them happening, fill in the situations in which they occur. Some of the physical reactions you might wish to note include blushing, sweating, palpitations, muscle tension and spasms, diarrhea, dry throat, hot or cold flashes, headaches, trembling, stuttering and speech fluency problems, and crying. Look for most of these symptoms on the "Emergency Response Symptoms" list on pages 83–85, and note the objective causes of each that you suffer.

Next add details—*who* was present, and *what, when,* and *where* the activity, event, or situation was. Start by entering anything that might fit the bill, and then review your worksheet to make sure that every anxiety episode that remains on your list has aspects of social anxiety—fears of being watched or judged, embarrassed, or humiliated.

B. SAFETY BEHAVIORS

Besides physical symptoms, a second, vital means of identifying your episodes of social anxiety is to discern when you are engaging in *safety behaviors* whose intent is to reduce anxiety by avoiding or minimizing exposure to situations that seem threatening. Safety behaviors are a particularly important aspect of social anxiety and a primary focus of treatment. The sense of jeopardy in social or performance situations can be relentless, and in desperate circumstances people resort to wishful, futile measures in order to attenuate their dread and contend with the monster in the cave. On the list below, check off safety behaviors you employ, like trying not to at-

Worksheet 9.1

MY PHYSICAL SYMPTOMS OF SOCIAL ANXIETY

Physical Anxiety Symptoms and Their Objective Causes	Situation: Who, What, When, Where?
Sweating—Activation of the heart and lungs and tensing the muscles for action are hard physical work; the by-product is heat, which makes me sweat. Also, sweating makes the skin slippery, which facilitates escape from an adversary (I wish!). *Dry Throat*—Rapid, shallow panic breathing sets up a tide of moving air that blows the throat dry.	My husband, *his* mother, her dear husband, and their favorite daughter, in their *lovely* home for Sunday brunch. They are *so* condescending.

tract attention, avoiding eye contact, and saying little—all are appeasement responses that we use to divert unwanted attention away from us.

Social Safety Behaviors or Subtle Avoidances

❑ Trying not to attract attention

❑ Avoiding eye contact

❑ Censoring what to say

❑ Sitting at the edge of a room or group

❑ Approaching no one

❑ Letting others do the talking

❑ Always planning what to say

❑ Saying little

❑ Holding cups with both hands

❑ Gripping hands together

❑ Covering face with hair

❑ Wearing extra makeup

❑ Using extra deodorant

❑ Keeping jacket on indoors

❑ Saying little about oneself

❑ Speaking quickly or slowly or softly

❑ Asking questions to avoid self-disclosure

❑ Moving in slow motion

❑ Pretending to study object of distraction

❑ Drinking alcohol

Like safety signals and behaviors in the other anxiety disorders, social safety behaviors are subtle avoidances that only maintain an *illusion* of safety. They may temporarily ease anxiety by blocking some automatic thoughts from consciousness. But as long as the anxiety generated in the situation is stronger than the reassurance provided by safety behavior—as long as the fear overpowers the momentary edge a person can gain by drinking the brandy or striking a demure or strong but silent pose—social anxiety inevitably returns to reinstate the sense of uncontrollability and helplessness.

List your safety behaviors in the left column of worksheet 9.2 that follows describe the situations where they occur in the center column. In the right-hand column, write out the anxious thoughts that go through your mind when you engage in each behavior.

C. OVERT AVOIDANCE

The third component of your social anxiety may be pretty obvious to you. Your "phobic situations" are the ones you avoid, the kinds of situations, events, or activities that your fears really prevent you from getting involved in. Even if you've figured out some ways to compensate, these avoidances nevertheless constrict your ability to enjoy life and liberty.

A classic tale illustrates the limitations of compensating for avoidance. In his 1897 play *Cyrano de Bergerac,* Edmond Rostand dramatized the tragedy of a socially avoidant man. A gallant but ugly seventeenth-century

Worksheet 9.2
MY SAFETY BEHAVIORS

My Safety Behavior	Situation: Who, What, When, Where?	My Anxious Thoughts
Let my hair hang down over my face	Political science class where Dr. Orlee is asking questions for class discussion	I hope he doesn't call on me. I'd be speechless— how humiliating!

French cavalier, satirist, and playwright, Cyrano was enamored of the beautiful Roxane, who in turn had a crush on Christian, Cyrano's handsome but inarticulate acquaintance. Possessed of wonderful eloquence and a remarkably large nose, Cyrano was too shy to proclaim his own love. Instead, he became the ghostwriter for Christian, whose passionate love letters completely stole Roxane's heart, while sadly, Cyrano's love for her remained unrequited.

What situations, events, and activities do you avoid as much as you can because of your social fears?

Think About Your Anxiety: What Are You Afraid Will Happen?

Remember: situations or events themselves do not produce our feelings. Our feelings are the product of our thoughts and interpretations of these situations and events.

Socially anxious feelings are based on our prediction that we will have negative experiences in "social evaluation situations"—situations where other people can observe, interact with, and judge us. In his excellent book

Worksheet 9.3
MY AVOIDANCES

Situations, Events, and Activities That I Try to Avoid	What I Fear Would Happen

Overcoming Shyness and Social Phobia, psychologist Ronald Rapee lists common thoughts and beliefs reported by people with social phobia:

❑ They must think I look really silly.

❑ I am going to blow this.

❑ I look ridiculous.

❑ They are going to laugh at me.

❑ They will realize how incompetent I am.

❑ They won't think very much of me.

❑ Everyone here is better at this than I am.

❑ I won't know what to say.

Sound familiar? Review the anxious thoughts you've recorded in worksheets 9.2 and 9.3—the fears that underlie your safety behaviors and the negative predictions and beliefs with which you warn yourself away from the situations you avoid. In the list above, check off any of the thoughts and beliefs that match what you find in your worksheets.

Be a Personal Scientist: Rethink Your Fears

Rethinking your fears is a good way to determine whether they are truly so scary, in what ways, and to create an opportunity to relieve your anxiety.

1. COLLECT DATA

The first step in learning to think about social fears differently is to state what you are afraid will happen *as precisely as possible.* By doing so, you will make it easier to consider whether your thought or perception is really worth worrying about so much and determine whether it is valid.

In your statements, *be sure to mention your emotional pain.* For instance, the statement "when I try to act friendly, she turns and walks away" is simply a "videotape" of a socially anxious person's uncomfortable experience, devoid of social angst. In contrast, statements like "When I try to act friendly, she immediately gets a cold expression on her face," or ". . . she acts like she thinks I'm stupid," describe *both* the events that occurred *and* your distressing reactions—your thought that she seems unfriendly and your belief that she thinks you look dumb. Or else, you can phrase your anxiety with "I-statements": "When I try to act pleasant, I feel her becoming antagonistic. I feel rejected and ashamed."

It may also be helpful to question yourself as a therapist might when helping you focus on your negative automatic thoughts at anxiety-provoking times. Here are sample questions:

Questions to Help Specify What You Are Afraid Of

1. What negative thoughts went though my mind when I entered the situation?

2. When I noticed myself feeling hot (blushing or starting to shake or stammering, etc.), what thoughts went through my mind?

3. How conspicuous do I think the symptoms are?

4. If people did notice my symptoms what would that mean?

5. How do I think I appeared?

6. If [name a specific significant other person] could have seen me at that time, what would he/she have seen?

7. When I try to conceal my symptoms, what's my impression of how I look to others?

Adapted from Wells, 1997

In the left-hand column of worksheet 9.4 on the following page, list any other negative social events you are worried about, and in the right-hand column, indicate the outcomes of the events that you fear.

2. EVALUATE EVIDENCE FOR ANXIOUS THOUGHTS

Collect and evaluate evidence about your predictions and beliefs, including both *data that supports and disputes them.* Worksheet 9.5 on page 181 will help you to put it all together. Here are some of the best sources to tap:

1. *Consider your personal history* with the situation or activity (e.g., Jess thinks that a woman he wants to get acquainted with seems

Worksheet 9.4
MY FEARED OUTCOMES

Social Anxiety-Provoking Situation	Feared Outcome

very disinterested. If Jess had previous encounters with her, is his current perception of her disinterest consistent or inconsistent with her usual attitude? That is, is she generally quite friendly except for today?)

2. *Gather objective information.* What is the evidence for and against my thought?

3. *Gather the opinions of trusted people.* Ask others questions about the situation, preferably trusted sources. Through discussion with them, learn how their points of view support or dispute your predictions and beliefs.

4. *Consider alternative beliefs.* For instance, since she turned away from Jess and got engaged in animated discussion with Andrew a moment later, maybe she was distracted from Jess because she heard Andrew's familiar voice.

Generating Alternative Beliefs

1. First, specify the anxiety-provoking event precisely and specifically: e.g., *If I start to tremble during a presentation, people will notice my trembling and think that I am strange.*

2. Then, generate alternative beliefs, e.g.:

   - Nobody will notice my trembling.

   - Only a small number of people will notice my trembling.

   - People who notice my trembling will think I am feeling cold.

   - People who notice my trembling will think I am feeling sick.

   - People who notice my trembling will think I am feeling a bit anxious.

   - It is normal to tremble sometimes, so people will think nothing of it if they notice the tremors.

Adapted from Antony & Swinson, 2000

Realistically speaking, how likely is your anxious belief to be the case? How likely is each of the alternative beliefs?

Gather as much information as possible. Fill in the first two columns of worksheet 9.5 below *as soon as you can* after your episodes of social anxiety, because we become conscious of anxious automatic thoughts when our anxiety is provoked, but they fade quickly as our mood dissipates. Since automatic thoughts reflect the deep core beliefs that shape our fears, when we can decipher these shadows of our underlying fears, we can learn to rethink them. The next step is to wrack your brain for challenges to your negative automatic thoughts, and write them into the "Disputing Data" column of worksheet 9.5.

3. RETHINK ANXIOUS THOUGHTS AND BELIEFS

Long accustomed to thinking negatively about social encounters, many socially anxious users of cognitive therapy discover that finding evidence to dispute their negative automatic thoughts is much more difficult than finding evidence to support them. Devote several homework sessions a week to reviewing your records and challenging the evidence for your anxious thoughts. In the example above, Jess felt "shot down" by a woman he approached at a party. He had to think hard before he began to recall data disputing his belief that he appeared stupid and contemptible. Take a look at his results in worksheet 9.5 on the following page.

Fill in the right-hand column with your own alternative beliefs after you have completed the three columns to its left. To do so, brainstorm the thoughts and beliefs that you have come up with and see what believable or convincing alternative beliefs occur to you.

Refine Your Way of Thinking About Social Evaluation Situations

As you embark upon this venture of self-improvement, pay special attention to your self-talk and your social self-image *between practices*. Utilize the opportunity to really change the way you think about and talk with yourself about social evaluation situations.

The old, socially anxious you probably tended to stress the really uncomfortable moments and dwell at length on their bad effects on your self-image. Besides rumination, this process may also have included anticipation and rehearsal of upcoming mortification. Essentially, you probably arranged what amounted to self-image-bashing sessions, periodic exposures to the destructive elements of your social phobia.

The new you will try out techniques and treatments that appear helpful and, as you begin socializing differently, adapt new, less disturbing perspectives. At the risk of being obvious, we advise you not to start challenging your anxious thinking in the middle of a social phobia episode. To do so is like trying to play a violin concerto during a three-alarm fire. During an episode, the anxious output of the socially anxious person's emotional brain provides a lot of disturbing input to his thinking brain, so that realistic, rational perspectives aren't likely to gain a foothold at this point.

Steps to Activate the "New You"
- Between episodes of anxiety, rethink automatic thoughts and restructure your anxious beliefs.

Worksheet 9.5
RETHINKING ANXIOUS BELIEFS

My Anxious Thoughts and Beliefs	Supporting Data	Disputing Data	Alternative Belief
Jess: She thinks I'm stupid. She has contempt for me. I appear stupid and contemptible. I'm inept with women.	Her cold expression; the fact that she walked away; my track record, which indicates I'm inept at talking with women	I talked with three other women at that party. I've been friends with Lisa and Cindy for years. My cousin keeps saying she can fix me up on dates and it will work out. Maybe that's just her general expression or she was nervous herself.	I'm nervous and self-doubting. Maybe I misinterpreted trivial events and convinced myself that I had messed up again. My personality is appealing when I can "promote myself" without extreme self-doubt prevailing.

- Practice applying your new or alternative perspectives during subsequent episodes as "first aid for anxiety."

- Try to label your social anxiety whenever it occurs and challenge your anxious thoughts about your physical symptoms and social evaluation as consistently as possible.

- Replace protracted ruminations about your perceived social failings with structured homework periods.

- Keep track of changes in your subjective level of discomfort during particular social situations as time passes.

- During this period of learning to overcome social anxiety, it's preferable to distract yourself with planned pleasurable activities rather than engage in lengthy periods of self-criticism about your lack of self-confidence.

Address Your Attention Problems

Attention problems are an important part of social anxiety disorder. Research demonstrates that sufferers do not readily learn from positive or neutral social experience because they are unlikely to recognize or believe when they have done something right. Instead, they remain uncomfortably hyperaware of their own fears and experience signs of scrutiny by others as threatening. With their attention biased this way, even friendly, apparently reassuring situations may increase their social anxiety, because the interpersonal contact in itself activates their negative self-evaluations and beliefs about negative evaluations by others.

A powerful way to manage this tidal wave of disconcerting input more effectively is to enhance your faculty for controlling attention. This enhancement will enable you to focus more of your attention on what you are trying to accomplish and shift distractions and self-doubts into the background.

Imagine yourself in the middle of a small group of friendly people seated in someone's den, recounting an enjoyable experience you recently had. As you pause for breath, you meet someone's eyes and immediately become uneasy. Your gaze shifts, but there's nowhere comfortable to look, and you suddenly have an image of how awkward you must appear. You become hot and flustered, start hemming and hawing, and feel too tongue-tied to finish your tale.

Now replay this scene in slow motion and keep track of where your attention went. First you became aware of other people looking at you. As you tried to look away, their gazes seemed to morph into scrutiny, into uncomfortable negative evaluation. When you were finally able to redirect your attention, you became disturbingly self-conscious, caught up in an ascending spiral of nervousness.

Psychologist Ronald Rapee analyzes the tangled mess that results from trying to mentally juggle three tasks at once when social anxiety makes it very difficult to focus at all. The tasks your mind tries to juggle are:

1. Concentrating on how you look and what you are doing in order to make sure you don't look silly.

2. Pondering what the others in the group are thinking, and focusing on making sure that no one appears bored, cynical, or in any way negative.

3. Trying to remember the next part of the story.

It becomes very tough to concentrate on the crucial task of telling the story as well as you can while your attention is pulled in three different directions. In order to do your best in situations like this, you will need to gather all your attention, redirect it toward presenting yourself properly, and avoid getting ensnared by self-consciousness and hyperfocusing on others' reactions.

Would you be willing to practice exercises that will enable you to enhance your attention control so that you can keep much more focused? Rapee observes, "You can think of your attention almost like a muscle in your body. . . . Your ability to concentrate and focus your attention onto particular things . . . becomes weak without regular use. . . . For many of us, before we can learn to focus our attention away from ourselves and others and onto the task at hand, we will need to strengthen [ourselves] by engaging in attentional exercises."

ATTENTION TRAINING I: BREATH COUNTING

The procedure that we recommend to you builds on *breath counting,* a variant of the self-control relaxation (SCT) techniques that were introduced in chapter 5 as part of panic control therapy. (Review the principles of SCT on pp. 76–80.) Start your attention training by setting up a controlled environment for your practices. Shut off your phone, arrange not to be interrupted, choose a comfortable place to sit and practice, and select a convenient time or two each day for about the next ten days to spend ten minutes practicing.

Sit comfortably in a relaxing position with your eyes closed or your gaze lowered. Start breathing slowly and regularly. Don't be concerned with deep breathing or special breathing techniques—just keep it slow and steady.

Start counting your breaths. Count in your mind each time you inhale and mentally say "smooth" every time you exhale. For instance, one (inhale) . . . smooth (exhale) . . . two (inhale) . . . smooth (exhale), etc. Count up to ten and then back down to one in this way, and then up to ten and down to one a second time.

During your breath-counting practices, you'll discover that concentration is a challenge. Thoughts of all sorts, particularly worries, and all kinds of irritating and distracting sensations will come to mind. You must learn to gently move aside those thoughts and feelings that compete for and capture your attention. Label the thoughts "thinking" and put them and the distracting sensations aside—on a shelf, so to speak—and return your mind to awareness of the breathing. Return to the point where you became distracted and pick up about where you left off. The more you practice concentrating, the stronger your ability to focus will grow, the stronger your control of the attentional faculty of your mind.

ATTENTION TRAINING II: ATTENTION WORKOUTS

Once you are consistently able to keep composed and maintain focus on your breathing, in order to build strength and flexibility you should add to the challenge of your practices. Put on music or the TV while you practice breath-counting. Stand, walk around, or even take a slow walk outside.

Just keep your objective in mind: to control the focus of your attention in a gentle, constructive way regardless of what's going on around you. Be creative—try all sorts of combinations of focal activities and varied environments. Count your steps as you go out to your car or bus stop, or as you travel between classrooms at school or offices at work. Count your breaths and synchronize them with your footsteps as you walk. Work steadily on a crossword in a waiting room or maintain your concentration despite the sounds around you while reading articles in waiting room magazines. Do your breathing while you wait for the stoplight to change or during commercial breaks while you're watching TV. Try to keep increasing the length of time you focus your attention.

ATTENTION TRAINING III: APPLIED PRACTICE IN SOCIAL SITUATIONS

If you are ready, now is the time to challenge yourself in social situations. Try to glance into other people's faces at a social gathering, class, or meeting and make active, momentary nonverbal contacts without getting distracted. Listen carefully to people's names and try to keep them in mind for a moment or two. Concentrate on the interests they mention or the ideas they express.

Try, however briefly at first, to focus all your attention on the task at hand in social situations, whether it is conversing with your boss or an acquaintance, asking or answering a question, or providing information. Make an effort to resist checking on how you are doing or trying to evaluate other people's reactions. Try to stay on task. Even if you run out of steam for a moment or two or start becoming anxious, try to refocus your attention on the interactions taking place, or else "go into neutral" for a little while, and just count your breaths and wait.

Focusing on what you are trying to accomplish in a social situation is difficult but worthwhile. You really *are* gaining control and making progress, so keep practicing.

Begin Your Exposure Therapy

The next step in overcoming social anxiety is to combine planned exposure with your cognitive practices. Exposure may be imaginal, or to real-life events or situations. The greatest changes result from real-life exposure. Go at your own pace, but remember: *You have to become anxious to overcome anxiety.*

As promising as the information, techniques, and strategies you've read about may sound, are you feeling pretty stuck? Have you been unable to jump-start your treatment? Sometimes people with social anxiety are so immobilized by *frozen withdrawal* that they find it difficult even to imagine feeling comfortable with other people. The problem may be compounded when they are engulfed in the throes of clinical depression, as well—a combination of maladies for which medication and professional mental health treatment is strongly indicated. Confusion between anxiety disorders and depressive disorders is fed by the common elements of demoralization and apprehension that may be present in both.

Since intensely negative fantasies about imagined social catastrophes probably hold many depressed, avoidant, and highly socially anxious people captive, perhaps *imaginal exposure therapy* can help thaw frozen withdrawal and enable you to start entering real-life social situations.

IMAGINAL EXPOSURE

Imaginal desensitization, or imaginal exposure therapy, like that advocated by psychologist Arnold Lazarus, is a good starting point for overcoming a state of severe avoidance. The assumption underlying this procedure is that "the things we fear in reality, we also fear in imagination"; and the corollary is that "the things we no longer fear in imagination will also not disturb us in the actual situation." Imaginal exposure is also a valuable tool for contending with apprehension prior to entry into *any* anxiety-provoking social evaluation situation.

Ask yourself, "What social situations or interactions do I avoid or get very uncomfortable with due to fear of anxiety?" List and give each situation a maximum anticipated SUDs rating, and then rank the situations by numbering them from 1 to 6 in ascending order of SUDs ratings, from the lowest to highest levels of discomfort.

Worksheet 9.6
HIERARCHY OF FEARED SITUATIONS

Situation	SUDs	Ranking (1–6)

Once you've made your list, begin to desensitize yourself to these situations in your imagination. Practice either breath counting (pp. 183–184) or imagery training (p. 241) regularly for a few days, whichever you prefer, before beginning imaginal exposure practice, so that you can start your exposure practice off by relaxing and focusing deeply. Visualize yourself in the situation you ranked 1, for lowest in discomfort, on your hierarchy. Here's a tip: When we are socially anxious, we see ourselves from an observer's perspective, looking as uneasy and awkward as we believe we do to other people; so imagine how you would appear and feel if a critical, scrutinizing person were observing you.

Imagine the situation as vividly as possible and continue long enough to experience considerable anxiety, at least a SUDs rating of 4. You may find it very helpful to intensify your anxious exposure by writing out a detailed description of the situation and your anxious reaction, reading it onto a recording tape or endless tape loop (available in office supply stores), and playing it back repeatedly during your exposure practice.

Next, mentally switch the scene off. Concentrate on relaxing at least as deeply as you were before starting the exercise. Resume vividly visualizing the anxiety-provoking situation, then switching it off and relaxing deeply. Do so again and again until you no longer feel anxious discomfort during your visualizations. When you reenter the practice situation in real life, you will very likely discover that your anxiety has diminished. If this technique proves helpful, then move on to the next item on your hierarchy.

Once you leap this hurdle, then you can phase in the other, more interactive techniques described in this chapter. Imaginal exposure has beneficial effects in its own right, but may also serve as preparation and rehearsal for real-life exposure. All the varieties of exposure therapy begin with a hierarchy of feared situations.

Rooted as it is in fear shared to an extent by us all, social anxiety often has created enduring, deep patterns in people's lives. Have you already started to feel better in social performance situations? If so, your progress is a tribute to your valor, ingenuity, and determination. Frequently, participation of a mental health professional is a necessity for social phobia treatment to be successful. There are several points in the treatment we describe in this chapter when professional therapy help would be valuable and possibly a necessity.

> ### When to Seek Help from a Mental Health Professional
>
> 1. If you would like to take medication for your social anxiety disorder, or if the medication you receive from your physician is not effective or produces undesirable side effects, arrange medication treatment with a psychiatrist/psychopharmacologist.
>
> 2. Have you been unable to relieve your social anxiety so far using the techniques, or do you feel like you go one step forward and two steps back? If this occurs, we urge you to seek the help of a mental health professional.
>
> 3. Many people prefer the help and security of therapy with a mental health professional during planned exposure practice. The therapist can provide guidance, consultation for resources, and assistance in brainstorming and building realistic self-assurance.
>
> 4. The final, optional techniques in this chapter can be harrowing. Professional support is likely to be desirable when working on discontinuation of safety behaviors that have provided familiar—albeit false—security and conducting "behavioral experiments" to build confidence and flexibility.

Factors That Affect the Difficulty of Exposure

- The presence or absence of authority figures

- The presence or absence of "higher-status" people

- The size of the audience

- The activity level of the audience

- The formality of the situation (e.g., where there is special etiquette or protocol, like at an auction, a formal dance, or toasting the bride and groom at a wedding reception; where everyone is seated and being served; in classes, staff or team meetings, or study groups, where an individual could be called on to speak at any time)

- The accessibility of exits

- The presence or absence of friendly or supportive people

Real-Life Exposure: Individualized Social Exposure Workouts

A lot of the fastest-moving exposure therapy for social anxiety is done in social phobia therapy with a qualified cognitive-behavioral therapist, in groups or individually. Groups afford opportunities to role-play and experiment in front of audience members and to try out social interactions in front of others in a relatively safe environment. Members can report on their thoughts and learn how others perceive them. They have regular opportunities to work on modifying their anxiety reactions so that they accord more and more with reality.

What skills and techniques can you use if you don't have a group available? Plan an individualized program of social exposure workouts.

Choose a situation, event, or activity from the top of your hierarchy to begin with, something tolerably anxiety-provoking, and *make a definite practice date with yourself.* Plan your practice—your exposure workout—for sooner rather than later. If you wish, have a support person accompany you to your first workout in a particular situation. When circumstances permit, remain for a minimum of a few minutes and up to a couple of hours in each situation. *Experience the anxiety,* and you will be relieved to discover that it peaks and then subsides. Schedule at least four practice workouts at specific times over the next two weeks if possible, preferably no more than two or three days apart.

Your exposures should be gradual, or "graduated"—that is, broken down into steps that cause a manageable level of anxiety, each of which should be practiced until your anxiety decreases before going onto the next, more challenging, step.

Robyn played folk guitar but was too shy ever to perform in front of strangers; only her quiet parents and her sister had heard her enthralling melodies. She felt so nervous that she couldn't even bring herself to look people in the eye during conversations. Her heart would pound and she would blush in the proximity of others.

The first two items on Robyn's hierarchy were to make friendly eye contact with all sorts of people and to sit comfortably in the audience of a coffeehouse during a musical performance. These were good choices for her because, despite her real satisfaction with acoustical music and the people who love it, she'd shied away from such situations and interactions for as long as she could remember, fearing she would look weird and people would know how terrified she was. In groups of people, she would cast her gaze downward and bend her head so her long hair covered her face, stay very quiet, and speak in a soft voice only when spoken to.

Let's look more closely at Robyn's objective of being able to sit comfortably in the audience of a coffeehouse during a musical performance. She planned to accomplish her goal through a series of steps over the course of a couple of months:

1. Walking into the coffeehouse for a few minutes in the daytime and making eye contact with several people.

2. Practicing going in and making a purchase, and conversing briefly with the salesperson.

3. Buying a cool drink at the counter and sitting down in the coffeehouse to drink it.

4. Sitting down at the table, ordering a hot drink from the waiter, and drinking it when the place is pretty empty.

5. Doing step 4 when the place is busy.

6. Accompanied by a support person, arriving at the café just before a performance, going in to "look for someone," and standing among the crowd for several minutes (until her anxiety decreases).

7. Doing step 6 solo.

8. Sitting near the exit of a café during a musical performance.

9. Sitting in the middle of a café during a musical performance.

Daily workouts would be ideal, devoted to practice in one or a couple of different situations on your hierarchy, possibly interspersed with opportunistic exposure sessions, discussed next.

REAL-LIFE EXPOSURE: OPPORTUNISTIC EXPOSURE WORKOUTS

Like Robyn, many people with long histories of social inhibition or avoidance may have a limited array of situations where they can practice exposure. Nevertheless, a lot of the opportunities for exposure may arise unexpectedly. Many social situations occur briefly and inconsistently, such as asking for directions and introducing oneself to acquaintances and strangers.

Devoting some of your practice sessions to "opportunistic exposure" can transcend these limitations. During these sessions, a block of time—perhaps an hour—should be devoted to a variety of brief encounters repeated numerous times, rather than trying to adhere rigidly to an exposure hierarchy or practicing prolonged exposures to a single situation. Activities that may be most feasible during opportunistic practices include asking for directions, greeting or smiling at people, signing your name, and interrupting ongoing conversations to comment or ask a question. Practice opportunistic exposures and review your experiences regularly.

Be creative and strategic in planning your practices. Could you transform a community center, coffeehouse, shopping mall, or college campus near you into your social anxiety workshop? Which friends or acquaintances could you accompany to a conference or audit a class session with? Look for food courts to dine at, open houses or orientation sessions to attend, regardless of whether or not you'd be interested in signing up for the program being offered. Why not drop by the vicinity of a nearby business center or office park at around lunchtime and join the milling, nourishment-seeking crowd?

Robyn utilized opportunistic exposure to practice eye contact, first by spending hour-long periods glancing at people's faces and meeting their eyes until doing so produced little anxiety. Then she practiced greeting all sorts of people as she walked near the university around lunchtime, engaging in a moment or two of solid eye contact with everyone who responded positively.

Sample Opportunistic Exposure Plans

1. Make brief eye contact and smile at fifty different people.

2. Greet at least twenty-five people whom you find attractive.

3. Ask twenty people directions to the restroom, the nearest pay phone, the nearest service station, or the nearest Italian, Chinese, Thai, or Mexican restaurant.

4. Introduce yourself to twenty-five people.

5. Purchase numerous small items at different stores. Pay with a check or credit card, so you can practice signing your name in front of other people.

6. Make brief neutral or positive comments to twenty-five different people. For example, remark on the weather, the décor, ambiance, or

efficiency of the staff in the place where you are, or holidays approaching or just past.

Here are a couple of additional, intriguing brief exposure plans:

7. Find out what is fascinating about twenty different people. Do so by watching them carefully, looking at them carefully, and conversing with or about them.

8. Go out and collect rejections. After all, since rejections are what you fear, why not take the bull by the horns and initiate rejecting situations? People who have used this technique often find that they are rejected much less often and more gently than they anticipated.

REVIEW EACH EXPOSURE EXPERIENCE AND CHALLENGE UNREALISTIC THINKING

We recommend that you review each exposure experience. Record just what you did, as well as your thoughts and feelings. Regularly devote time to thinking carefully about what happened so that you can update your perspective on the reality of your social fears. You can accomplish this by selecting techniques from the "Personal Scientist" sections on pages 176–180 (collecting data, evaluating the evidence, and rethinking anxious thoughts and beliefs) and utilizing the advanced techniques described below.

Begin by filling in the first four columns of worksheet 9.7 on the following page.

Review the anxious thoughts that were stirred up during your exposure workout for evidence of unrealistic thinking. The most common "errors of socially anxious thinking" are:

1. *Mind reading* (e.g., He thinks I'm boring.)

2. *Projected self-appraisal,* in which the anxious person assumes that his or her own negative self-impression is also held by others (e.g., I sound really boring to myself, so *they* must think I'm boring. My ears always look too large, so *they* must be fixating on my overlarge ears.)

3. *Personalization* (e.g., They're not talking to me, so I must have said something wrong.)

4. *Fortune-telling/catastrophizing* (e.g., If I'm asked to sign my name, I'll be unable to write.)

Worksheet 9.7
EXPOSURE WORKOUT WORKSHEET

Situation	Highest Anxiety Level (0–10 SUDs)	Physical Anxiety Symptoms	Anxious Thoughts	What Would I *Rather* Think?
Robyn's step 5: Drinking coffee in a busy coffeehouse	6	Blushed when the waiter approached to take her order. Her heart was pounding.	I must look incredibly weird. Everybody can tell how nervous I am.	Probably nobody or hardly anybody notices my uneasiness. I'm going to calm myself, drink my coffee slowly, and savor every sip.

Once you have identified those of your unrealistic thoughts that fall into these categories, you can learn to challenge them in straightforward, specific ways:

1. *Mind reading.* Do you really believe you can read minds? Can you often read the total cost of your purchase from the checker's mind in a store or a pet's name from its master's mind? Can you usually tell when people are thinking about their friendly or generous feelings toward you? If you answered these questions in the negative, perhaps you are applying a different standard to yourself in such neutral and positive situations than you do when you fear negative evaluations. Recall that a tendency to believe that others are thinking badly of you is characteristic of social anxiety.

2. *Projected self-appraisal.* Where is the specific evidence that *they* are negatively evaluating you the same way *you* negatively evaluate you? You ought to be suspicious at this juncture, since research has shown that the self-evaluations of people who are socially anxious usually take the form of the negative evaluations that they believe other people make of them. If you're still in doubt, ask a significant other person whom you believe is objective what evidence he or she sees to support your theory. In the example above, Robyn recognized that she was projecting her self-appraisal when she thought that everyone noticed her nervousness. She corrected her anxious thought and arrived at a more realistic alternative.

3. *Personalization.* As much as you may feel like a magnet for negative attention in social evaluation situations, realistically you seldom have a major part in other people's negative expressions and disregard of you. The fact that they aren't talking to you may be for any of a multitude of reasons that involve you little or not at all. The alternative, more realistic ways to explain the anxious belief, "They're not talking to me, so I must have said something wrong" include:

- They don't know how to reply to what I said.
- They think I look uneasy and don't want to intrude.
- They are acting just as I am acting, since *I* am not talking to *them*.
- They don't notice that I am inviting their conversation and so think nothing of it.
- They can't think of anything to add to what I said.
- They have their own agendas.

4. *Fortune-telling/catastrophizing.* How good are you at predicting the future? Test your skill: Pick the next winning lottery numbers or predict what color cars you will see first the next ten times you turn a corner. By how much do your skills as a fortune-teller exceed chance? If you discover that indeed you have *not* found your calling, when you commit the fortune-telling error, an alternative thought to write in the right-hand column of worksheet 9.7 is "I'm not a fortune-teller."

Catastrophizing is a fundamental error of anxious thinking in which we exaggerate how negative an outcome will result or has resulted from us entering an anxiety-provoking situation. The catastrophic images that fill the anxious person's mind are the direct consequence of her automatic thoughts when she is negatively aroused by anxiety. Recall from chapter 5 that catastrophic thoughts are the cognitive portion of the fight-or-flight response to immediate, mortal danger whose function is to prod the thinker into immediately fleeing the situation for her life.

But situations that provoke social anxiety, as exceedingly uncomfortable as they get, are not really immediately, mortally dangerous. Catastrophic thoughts that occur in the context of exposure workouts should be recognized as no more than *theories about a possible worst-case scenario.* When you revisit them during reviews of your practice, reestimate the likelihood that a catastrophe has actually occurred or is awaiting you, and then pose to yourself the fundamental question about your fears: "SO WHAT?"

- "People did not approve of how I was dressed." . . . "Not everybody has to like me or give their approval."

- "I stuttered and sweated and felt like I came across as really dumb." . . . "Probably hardly anybody noticed, and even if they did, what difference does it make?"

- "I told him that he looked nice and got this disgusted look back." . . . "I don't have to please everybody or get a pleasant reaction from him in order to validate myself socially."

- "Everybody noticed my stammer." . . . "If I hesitate when I speak, it doesn't mean I'm completely discounted. I'm more than my stammer."

When Robyn, through real-life exposure, was able to spend an hour listening to a talented local guitarist at the café, she didn't feel nearly as uneasy as she had feared. As her anxiety climbed to a mildly uncomfortable maximum, she realized she'd been absorbed in the performance with her head raised, her face unshielded by the curtain of her hair. Slowly she looked around. She noticed other people's expressions and a few glances in her direction. Suddenly she felt exposed, her heart aflutter.

Then she got a grip on herself. She refocused her attention, took a couple of slow breaths. "People probably aren't busy noticing how anxious I look," she thought, "and if they are, so *what?*" A few moments later, she was grooving on the music again and had all but forgotten her anxiety.

COMPLETE THE EMOTIONAL RELIEF PROCESS

Challenge your anxious thoughts and negative appraisals of your anxious behavior with others as consistently as possible after exposure workouts. *You will probably notice that your anxiety about social evaluations decreases* during the process of your reviews and after most experiments. In order to recycle this emotional relief into your interactions and performance situations, take a couple of additional steps:

Table 9.1
COUNTERING RIGID RULES WITH BEHAVIORAL EXPERIMENTS

Rigid Rule to Counter	Behavioral Experiments
I must always fit in.	Disagreeing with people
	Making complaints
I must not inconvenience anyone.	Asking favors
I should always behave properly.	Deliberately making mistakes
	Trying on ten pairs of shoes and not buying any
I mustn't draw attention to myself.	Talking in a loud voice

Adapted from Wells, 1997

1. Whenever you arrive at a rational, alternative perspective on your social anxiety that fits well and works for you, highlight it on your worksheet.

2. Write out this "coping thought" on a coping card that you label at the top with the type of situation where it should prove most useful—e.g., "making a date," "talking to my boss," "sitting in economics class," "dinner at Heather's parents' house."

3. Try to make sure you revisit this situation, coping card in hand, for more exposure workouts. Failing this, practice exposure in other situations that stimulate similar physical symptoms of anxiety and similar anxious thoughts.

OPTIONAL EXPOSURE WORKOUTS

Behavioral Experiments

One benefit of doing things perfectly is that you can expect never to be criticized for doing things wrong. But is this realistic? Many socially anxious thoughts contain unrealistic propositions about the importance of avoiding criticism by striving for perfection, and "playing it safe" by following rigid, narrow rules of behavior in social contexts. These center on the expectation that humiliation, embarrassment, or outright rejection will be the result of a less than flawless or exceptional performance.

Rigid rules (also known as *compulsive rules*) are reflected in assumptions such as "I mustn't draw attention to myself," "I must always fit in," "I must not inconvenience anyone," and "I should always behave properly." Psychologist Adrian Wells suggests use of *behavioral experiments* to help widen those narrow safety zones. These experiments involve selecting anxiety-provoking actions to take that will test compulsive rules. Table 9.1 contains examples.

Our clients report that these experiments are especially effective in the company of a support person who can help them arrive at an objective review of their experiences. After each behavioral experiment, fill out an Exposure Workout Worksheet like the one on page 193.

Discontinuation of Safety Behaviors

During exposure workouts, eliminate safety behaviors, both the positive ones like frequent apologizing and smiling nervously, and negative ones like hiding behind your long hair, avoiding eye contact, or hanging near the edge of the group. That way you can learn that the feared outcomes your safety behaviors "insure" you against don't actually occur, or only occur to a lesser degree or in a more manageable fashion.

Here are some examples of socially anxious men and women's reviews of their successful experiments in discontinuing safety behaviors:

- Even though I wore a thin, cotton shirt on a hot day, the other person did not comment on my sweating.

- I resisted gripping my hands together. Even though I felt a tremor it seemed hardly noticeable to others.

- I stayed right in the middle of the crowd and felt no more anxious than I would on the outskirts of the room.

This kind of practice will enable you to orient your attention away from yourself and toward the people around you so that you can gather information that disconfirms your fears. Successfully resisting your safety behaviors in social evaluation situations can significantly boost your self-confidence, as well. One caveat: Since safety behaviors are often such familiar devices for warding off fear, you may prefer to be in treatment with a mental health professional upon whom you can rely while working on forgoing the false sense of security that your safety behaviors maintain.

Symptom Exaggeration

Psychologist Michelle Craske sometimes encourages her clients to work on extinguishing safety behaviors by *deliberately trying to exaggerate their symptoms.* For instance, a man who wears absorbent clothes to soak up his excessive sweat might be encouraged to wear an extra-warm shirt in order to sweat even more. A young woman who feels awkward at social gatherings and tends to speak haltingly might deliberately drop a fork, a knife, and then her purse, and later speak for a few moments with intentionally prolonged pauses.

Craske's socially anxious clients usually discover that despite their strenuous efforts to worsen their symptoms, they actually feel *less* conspicuous and awkward than expected, because anxiety colored their expectations. If you can successfully utilize the symptom exaggeration technique, modify negative impressions of yourself as consistently as possible during emotional processing. Whenever you notice those familiar distorted thoughts putting yourself down, correct them. For instance, it might be appropriate to say, "My symptoms feel worse than they look"; "I look calm even when I feel anxious"; or "I know I look nice no matter what other people say." Inscribe your realistic self-impressions on coping cards that you bring with you into every situation where similar anxiety could be activated.

Bashful Bladder Syndrome

An estimated 7 percent of the population has an embarrassing subtype of social anxiety known as bashful bladder syndrome (BBS). Sufferers from BBS—also called shy bladder syndrome, ballpark syndrome, or paruresis—are restricted in their ability to urinate in the proximity of other people, in public restrooms, or, in severe cases, anywhere away from home.

Could Public Speaking Fear Be Treated As a "Simple" Social Phobia?

Eighty percent of individuals who are afraid of public speaking report feeling fearful of their physical symptoms of arousal. Craske speculates whether effective treatment might consist of education about the actual causes of the bodily symptoms combined with interoceptive exposure therapy (pp. 155–156). The first phase of this treatment for a person who suffers, say, from rapid heartbeat, sweating, and tremors would be to look these symptoms up on the "Emergency Response Symptoms" list (pp. 83–86) and learn their objective causes. In each performance situation where they occur, she would try to label them as anxiety and redefine them.

The second phase would consist of interoceptive exposure, beginning with practice in deliberately inducing these symptoms (see above). For instance, the person could induce rapid heartbeat and sweating by running in place while holding a heavy box in a warm room, or by exercising in a bathroom immediately after someone has showered. She could produce tremors by straightening and stiffening the arms while holding weights tightly in her hands. She would sustain each symptom until she gets anxious and then relieve them using psychological techniques like SCT and self-talk. Techniques such as these for creating physical arousal should only be used with your physician's approval.

About nine out of ten paruretics (pare-yoo-*ret*-iks) are male, which really is not surprising. In public places, young boys and girls are usually "chaperoned" to the bathroom by parents—most often mothers—so that they typically wind up toileting in a stall of the ladies' room. Things suddenly change when they turn seven or eight, because by then they are expected to use restrooms independently. Unchaperoned boys are no longer welcome in ladies' rooms, so they often wind up alone in unfamiliar men's rooms for the first time in their young lives. Males are relatively "exposed" and can feel vulnerable and unprotected while using urinals because in the United States most have insubstantial partitions or else are open-trough urinals, such as those at ball parks and many gyms and schools.

People with BBS react as if an adversary is invading their personal space in public restrooms when other people are nearby, waiting outside the restroom door, or even just audible in their vicinity. Sometimes a good-natured remark like "Hurry up, can't you?" is all it takes. In their very informative book, *Shy Bladder Syndrome,* S. Soifer, G. D. Zgourides, J. Himle, and N. L. Pickering list the most common triggers of bashful bladder as "anxiety, anger, sensitivity to scrutiny and criticism, proximity to others, invasion of 'personal space,' presence of strangers, lack of visual or auditory privacy, lack of suitable partitioning, and sensitivity to odors and noises."

When we are stressed, the body's sympathetic nervous system reaction can automatically inhibit urination by relaxing the muscles under the bladder and tightening the internal and external urethral sphincters. These two valvelike muscles open and close the urinary passages, ordinarily with little effort on our parts, when we are functioning normally. The stress response of a person with BBS locks one or both sphincters in the closed position and may defy vigorous efforts to open them.

Once physical causes are ruled out, a BBS sufferer should consider self-help or therapy treatment with graduated exposure. Soifer and his coauthors advocate scheduling hour-long sessions in public restrooms as often as possible, but at least once a week. Before the sessions, it's best to load up on fluids in order to urinate as often as possible. This in itself is a "behavioral experiment," since most paruretics engage in a safety behavior of limiting or avoiding fluid consumption before going out in public.

The paruretic should provoke anxiety by "doing what he fears"— choosing public restrooms and perhaps bringing along a practice partner who will stand at a distance that he specifies while he attempts to urinate. Factors likely to affect anxiety include:

- Number of people nearby

- Whether or not the restroom door and stall doors are lockable and whether or not they are ajar

- Amount of adjacent public traffic (e.g., an outhouse in a national forest versus a public restroom in the lobby of the Empire State Building)

- Number of urinals and stalls, and the extent to which people are waiting or lined up

- Noisiness of the other patrons and whether or not they are talking to the paruretic

- Time pressure

Two successful practices of a few seconds' duration represent a success, after which the person should move on to a somewhat more anxiety-provoking challenge. A different restroom might be in order or the partner might move somewhat closer. The partner may stand just outside the restroom, just inside, right next to the stall, or at a nearby urinal. He may remain silent, chatter away, or even make annoying remarks.

Since use of a partner in behavioral strategies might be an uneasy or unavailable expedient, other techniques might prove more feasible or effective. Cue-controlled relaxation, arriving at alternatives to anxious beliefs, and cognitive restructuring of catastrophic thoughts (the "So what? technique) may be used to treat BBS. For instance, an alternative thought to "It would be terrible if someone came in while I was trying to use the restroom" could be "Even if I am distracted by an interruption, I can refocus on my practice in a few moments." A challenge to "I concentrated hard and had almost succeeded when those loudmouths came in and ruined my practice!" might be "I concentrated hard and was nearly ready to go, but then people's loud voices broke my concentration. Frustrating . . . but so what? It's quiet enough to resume my practice!" A paradoxical technique may prove to be effective. Repeatedly load up on fluids and then just stand there in a public restroom for an indefinitely long time; eventually you're likely to say, "What the heck?" and urinate. In the clinical trials reported by Soifer et al., the condition of 75 to 80 percent of people with BBS who completed between eight and twelve sessions of graduated exposure therapy using partners was much to very much improved.

> ### An Innovative, Solo Course of Graduated Exposure to BBS
>
> Armando decided to utilize graduated exposure to overcome his moderately severe case of BBS, but he didn't have a partner to practice with. So he would imagine somebody standing close by when he practiced or else he would work in areas where people would pass every few minutes. Within a few weeks, he made a lot of progress and then hit a plateau, so he decided to "live better electronically." He persuaded a friend to sit in a nearby Starbuck's with a walkie-talkie on "receive," listening to Armando while he practiced. Armando set his walkie-talkie to "transmit" and left the microphone open during practices, so that his friend could hear *every sound he made*. It was a lot like having a partner right there in person!
>
> His second bright idea came to him during a raucous Superbowl party when he realized that his buddies sounded like a lavatory full of rowdy football fans. He tape-recorded them on the spot, and found that when he loudly played back parts of the recording through an earphone while trying to urinate, he felt almost like he was learning to cope with the restroom of an actual sporting arena.

Medication Treatments

ANTIANXIETY/ANTIDEPRESSANT DRUGS FOR SOCIAL ANXIETY

A quirky family of antidepressants, the nonreversible monoamine oxidase inhibitors (MAOIs), the most popular of which is Nardil (phenelzine), are the most effective medications for social phobia, but have considerable side effects and severe drug-drug and drug-food interactions if pharmaceutical precautions and dietary restrictions are not followed.

The effectiveness of several SSRI (selective serotonin reuptake inhibitor) medications, which we discussed in chapter 3, runs a close second to the MAOIs, but with far fewer restrictions and much less severe side effects. Paxil has been widely publicized because it has the distinction of being the first medicine in the United States approved for treatment of social anxiety. Psychopharmacological research has also demonstrated the efficacy of Luvox (fluvoxamine), Zoloft (sertraline), Prozac (fluoxetine), Effexor (venlafaxine), and Celexa (citalopram).

On the other hand, several other popular antidepressants are *not* effective. Tricyclics (TCAs) such as Pamelor (nortriptyline) do not help social phobics, nor does the powerful anti-OCD drug Anafranil (clomipramine), presumably because both increase the level of norepinephrine in the brain, which does not appear to be therapeutic for social phobia. Wellbutrin (buproprion) is another popular antidepressant which has been shown by research not to be particularly helpful for relief of social anxiety. The antidepressants that *are* effective for social phobia generally reduce the levels of brain dopamine—the general arousal-producing neurotransmitter.

HIGH-POTENCY BENZODIAZEPINES

Recent research has shown the BZD Klonopin (clonazepam) to be as effective as cognitive-behavioral group therapy for treatment of generalized social phobia, with both treatments producing improvement in over 70 percent of the clients. On the other hand, evidence demonstrating effectiveness of the very popular BZD Xanax (alprazolam) is slim. In fact, one recent study showed it to be little more beneficial for social anxiety than sugar pills. The likelihood of relapse is much greater after discontinuation of medication treatment, particularly with the benzodiazepines, than after cognitive or behavior therapy.

NEURONTIN

Neurontin (gabapentin), an anticonvulsant medication, has been used successfully for a spectrum of psychiatric disorders over the past several years. Although the action of Neurontin is not fully understood, research indicates that it has proven effective as treatment for as many as 32 percent of social anxiety clients to whom it is administered. Neurontin appears to help augment the presence of GABA, a neurotransmitter that calms overexcitability, in the anxiety centers of the brain.

BETA-BLOCKERS

Beta-blockers are a popular treatment of stage fright or performance anxiety. A survey of over two thousand professional musicians found that 27 percent had used beta-blockers to relieve their stage fright. John Greist, M.D., reports that 15 percent of the speakers at the 1983 Conference of the American Cardiology Association took beta-blockers to relieve their anxi-

> ### If You Are Prescribed an MAOI . . .
>
> Talk to your physician and follow the tyramine-restricted diet *religiously*. The most commonly consumed foods to be avoided include aged cheeses, American and Gouda cheeses, sour cream, yogurt, ale, draft beer, many wines, distilled spirits, sausage and lunch meat, salted, dry fish, liver, caffeine in coffee, tea, or sodas, chocolate, soy sauce, overripe avocados, bananas, eggplant, soybean products, spinach, tofu, and tomatoes. Also, make sure you haven't had Prozac (fluoxetine) in your body for at least two weeks before starting to take an MAOI.

ety. Inderal (propanolol) and Tenormin (atenolol) are used the most often for this purpose. They are widely available from physicians, comparably effective, and studies show that many who use them for stage fright do so without a prescription.

Why should medicines that regulate the human heartbeat be so widely utilized for anxiety reduction? Beta-blockers block the "peripheral autonomic response," limiting anxiety symptoms like tremulousness and increased heart rate in performance situations. With these physical anxiety symptoms relatively in check, the person is more likely to perform successfully because he feels more in control of himself.

Working predominantly in the body rather than the brain, most beta-blockers are not psychoactive to the extent that most anxiolytic medications are. In this respect, we think that when beta-blockers work, they fulfill people's fantasies of controlling their anxiety symptoms without tampering with their minds. Nevertheless, beta-blockers are far from harmless. In fact, you should be aware that some people report that they feel depressed after they take a course of beta-blockers. However, when prescribed by a physician and taken only as needed, many people with episodes of performance anxiety (but not general social phobia) are likely to benefit from beta-blockers.

An important consideration of the role of medications in cognitive-behavioral therapy (CBT) is the inadvisability of taking benzodiazepines, beta-blockers, alcohol, or marijuana specifically to ease possible anxious discomfort *just before or during practice sessions*, because the effectiveness of the CBT will be reduced.

Chapter Ten

Dismantle Generalized Anxiety Disorder and Stop Worrying Yourself Sick

How much do you worry? Do you sometimes feel consumed by worries, your sense of well-being virtually swallowed up whole? How often do you have experiences like this one?

A concern or problem crosses your mind; the topic is:

- one of the regular daily hassles;
- a problem with finances, work, or school; or
- concern about your health or your family's or friends'.

You start to worry and grow noticeably apprehensive. Despite efforts to shift your mind elsewhere, your uneasiness escalates. Before you know it, your mood has changed so that your anxious negativity seems to affect everything and everyone around you. Perhaps you also begin to experience your anxiety physically, tensing up and even undergoing some panic symptoms.

If this experience seems familiar, then you may be among the millions of men and women who have had a taste of GAD—generalized anxiety disorder. Worry that is difficult to control is a common occurrence, but people with GAD report that they worry for an average of 60 percent of each day, compared to 18 percent for the rest of the general population. GAD is nearly synonymous with anxiety, and experts believe it may be the core anxiety disorder out of which the others develop. The other main criteria for the full diagnosis of GAD are symptoms of physical tension—a "keyed-up" or restless feeling, easy fatigue, muscle tension, difficulty concentrating, irritability, or sleep disturbance—and "the anxiety, worry, or physical symptoms cause clinically significant distress or impairment in social, occupational, or other important areas of functioning."

A couple of million people in the United States have GAD as their primary anxiety problem, while for many others it is secondary to another anxiety disorder, either in a relatively mild form or lurking in the background. About 9.2 million people nationwide fully meet the diagnostic criteria for GAD as their primary or secondary psychiatric diagnosis. GAD coexists with other anxiety disorders so often that the average sufferer has 1.5 coexisting disorders—especially panic disorder, specific phobias, or social anxiety disorder.

Even if you don't fully meet the diagnostic criteria, perhaps your worries are disturbing or occur all too often. How do overworriers and people with GAD worry differently from the general population? How come they wind up relinquishing so much of their power to anxiety? Psychologist Michelle Craske has identified two characteristic "tricks of thinking" that play a major role in the points of view of people with GAD:

- A tendency to believe that negative events are meaningful and beyond one's coping ability

- A belief that worry prevents future negative events

Perhaps these two tricks of thought seem familiar. They embody the dread, misgivings, and pessimism that touch us all from time to time. This type of thinking is likely to slip in after misfortunes occur in our lives. One-third of those suffering from GAD develop the disorder subsequent to a significant stressful event—like marriage, illness, or the death of a significant other—or else as a result of lifestyle changes, such as completion of school and embarking upon a career, becoming a parent, or experiencing empty nest syndrome.

Many whose lives are filled with tension and unhealthy worry are serious men and women who are often quite productive and successful. The case of Seth illustrates adult-onset GAD. An industrious twenty-three-year-old man from a town of twenty thousand, Seth was well qualified for his first big city job as an urban planner in Chicago. His new employer rec-

Anxiety and Depression

A tendency to react to stressful life events with gloom and doom is reminiscent of both anxiety and depression. Depression and GAD are often confused, but although depression is mixed into many anxiety disorders, it is a very different condition. Psychologist David Barlow observes, "almost all depressed patients are anxious, but not all anxious patients are depressed." According to Barlow, anxiety implies an effort to cope with difficult situations, while depression is characterized by behavioral retardation and an associated *lack of arousal* (italics ours).

ognized Seth's naïveté in business matters and assumed a paternal pose. He urged Seth to hire on as an independent contractor and underscored the benefits of higher take-home income if he paid the income tax "later—after you've gotten the Mercedes, the wardrobe, and the condo that will distinguish you as a true professional."

By the time three years had elapsed, Seth discovered that his boss's advice was self-serving, and as a result he was in "Stress City." He (and the mortgage company) owned the condo, but he owed the IRS back income taxes and was up to his eyebrows in interest charges and penalties. He cut a deal with the taxman, but wound up paying dearly for his misjudgment with more than his money. Seth became irritable and developed difficulty sleeping and the habit of worrying a great deal about his financial obligations—the threat of having his car repossessed, all his credit card debts, and the challenges of keeping out of further financial trouble.

Two-thirds of GAD sufferers, including most of those whose conditions are relatively severe, have struggled with tension and excessive worry through most of their lives. For Stephen, a nineteen-year-old student, worry was a constant companion for as far back as he could remember. Until his family sent him to live with relatives in Pennsylvania when he was fourteen, he was raised by his politically active parents in a region of the Balkans where international conflicts were mounting and "ethnic cleansing" was occurring. He tended to develop tension headaches whenever stress mounted and would worry himself sick writing papers and preparing for tests despite his superior academic standing.

> ### Irritability vs. Worry: Is Anger or Anxiety the Main Problem?
>
> An overworrier's mounting irritability or temper may be the first sign of rising stress. Manifestations of low-key anger can be confusing, because they occur even when one's thoughts are primarily anxious. Anger and anxiety have three features in common: both involve disturbed facial expressions and defensive posturing and gesturing; both include uncomfortable physical tension; and in both, the mind urgently quests for causes of the distress.
>
> So how can we figure out what's what? Quite different mental themes run through the minds of anxious and primarily angry people. When anger is the main problem, the person typically is thinking about feeling hurt, feeling deliberately harmed by others, and blaming. However, when anxiety is the core concern, the prevailing thoughts concern uncontrollability, feeling overwhelmed, and the dire consequences that are dreaded.

What *Is* Worry?

Worry can help us adapt to the world. It chains together thoughts whose primary function is to enable us to consider and evaluate the possible outcomes of our plans, one or more of which could be negative, in light of the present situation and relevant past experiences. We size up a problematic situation, reflect on what we know about seemingly similar situations, and "worry it" by conducting "mental conversations" or "tape editing sessions."

The "mental symposia" that make up worry are largely conducted between the hippocampus, where emotional and long-term memories can be accessed in the brain, and the frontal lobes, where efforts to cope with challenging or anxiety-provoking situations are planned and executed. This activation is predominantly verbal rather than visual. The desired outcome of worry is to hammer out a point of view or a plan that makes sense of the problem or resolves it.

A basic function of worry is to reduce acutely uncomfortable feelings like fear and anger by inhibiting emotional processing of them so they seem less overwhelming. "Inhibition of emotional processing" connotes doing or thinking something to prevent experiencing emotions intensely or deeply. Common examples are preventing oneself from crying or laughing out loud.

Worry is a powerful force that discourages us from getting preoccupied with disturbing images and impulses. Its effects diminish or even prevent strong, troubling emotional reactions like panic or fear paralysis, terrifying nightmares, and other gross disruptions of functioning due to emotional distress. When it isn't too excessive, this reduction of discomfort permits us to contend with considerable stress, keep functioning, and solve problems effectively.

As psychologist Michelle Craske has observed, "worry contrasts with fear and competes with fear." That is, as a result of healthy worry, a disturbing concern or an unmanageable problem may seem manageable. While problem-solving, organizing, and planning may seem to be drudgery or fussiness and not particularly positive, they empower a person to cope effectively with frightening situations while creating only negligible emotional stress.

HEALTHY WORRY VS. UNHEALTHY WORRY

Worry can be healthy or unhealthy. In the midst of stressful situations, we may experience sizeable doses of healthy worry as a form of stimulation. We've all had that sense of "edge"—the keen nervous excitement that heightens the senses and accelerates the thinking so we can do our best. A measure of "edge" enhances performance, but excessive anxiety hampers this powerful process. Too much internalized anxiety or external stress overwhelms the capacity to think clearly enough to coordinate mind and body effectively, and consequently productivity drops.

But, as table 10.1 illustrates, even unhealthy worry serves a purpose; it can be very disturbing, but it keeps us from becoming petrified by fear.

Although the thoughts in column C are really disturbing, wouldn't these "unhealthy worries" be more bearable than the full-strength catastrophic reactions of column B? When a situation produces fear or anger, very commonly glimpses of despair or flashes of terror or hatred like those in column B are experienced. But these automatic, intensely emotional reactions seldom persist; instead, they morph into more diluted states like worry, regret, or guilt. A person *without* an anxiety disorder is likelier to worry more healthily, with thoughts like those in column D, while someone with GAD may have more disturbing worries like the ones listed in

Table 10.1

EMOTIONAL PROCESSING OF FEAR AND ANGER, INHIBITED BY WORRY

A. Situations	B. Most Intense Reaction	C. Unhealthy Worry	D. Healthy Worry
My husband drives way too fast and wildly, and he is driving us through pouring rain to Aunt Sally's for the holiday.	He's going to get us all killed. I'm going to grab the keys and jump out of the car.	Every time he tailgates another car or curses a driver, I'm afraid his next move will be his last. I get so nervous I'm afraid I'll have a heart attack.	The way he drives, it's a good thing I don't have heart problems. I'll put on good music and talk with the kids. If they or I get too uncomfortable, I'll politely but firmly ask him to slow down for my sake.
The guy my sister is going out with looks really dangerous.	He will harm her. I should hit him over the head with that heavy ashtray and then call the police.	I hope my sister doesn't get hurt or threatened. That guy reminds me of a gangster. I should find out where they are going. I will worry ceaselessly until she's home again.	I'll chat with the guy and check him out. I'll take down his license number. I'll ask my sister to call and check in with me during the date. Maybe she'll have a nice time. She really has the right to make her own decisions.
My vision is blurred. I see little specks floating around. I have never seen an eye doctor.	I'm afraid I'm going blind. I'm going to call 911.	This is my punishment for years of neglecting my eyes. What if those specks are minute nicks in the surfaces of my eyes? I bet I will never see clearly again.	I'll arrange to see an eye doctor. Maybe I need glasses. Someone I told about the specks mentioned something about "floaters" and said they are common.

column C. A study by Butler and Mathews found that people with generalized anxiety exaggerate the likelihood that they will suffer from negative events and convince themselves that their misfortunes will be worse than most people's. Of course, once you recover from GAD or a state of "worrywarthood," your rewards are likely to include a shift of your thinking to a preponderance of column D–type worries.

When Good Worry Turns Bad

When worry turns unhealthy and maladaptive, the fear that underlies and powers it begins to break through. Frightening thoughts and images start emerging into consciousness, impairing objectivity and clarity of mind. Once triggered, unhealthy worry persists too long, is too constant, and may continue long after the problem has been solved or the matter thoroughly considered. An unhealthy worrier's high degree of anxiety sensitivity often makes him uneasy even though he may not be aware of the origin of the sense of threat, and his anxious distress can increase until it becomes difficult to stand. When worry starts controlling us more than we're controlling it, it has become a consuming mental habit.

Three disturbing thought patterns—apprehension, rumination, and obsession—typically constitute unhealthy worry. We have frequently talked about *apprehension* in this book, and here we will define it as vigilance and mental preparation for an apparently approaching threat. *Rumination* is a thought process characterized by the excessive self-focused attention that frequently is a part of both anxiety and depression. Psychologist Thomas Borkovec labels it "If only . . ." thinking, which is often characteristic of disheartening mental reviews of unsuccessful or unpleasant encounters. For instance, Cindy tends to ruminate, "If only I could persuade my frail mother to stop smoking, she would be healthier. It's my fault she smokes." Randy gets painfully shy whenever he goes out on dates, and afterward he reflects ruefully, "If only I weren't so awkward on a date, I would have someone to love." Rumination prolongs and presumably may intensify and thus worsen anxious moods.

Obsession is anxiety-laden, persistent, and intrusive. However, unlike apprehensions and ruminations, which reflect basically realistic but excessive preoccupation with everyday problems, *obsessions are not realistic and seem to the individual to be inappropriate.* The content of obsessions frequently includes "unacceptable" thoughts about such topics as contamination, sex, aggression, or religion. A person typically will make more vigorous attempts to suppress obsessive thoughts than she does other worries, with minimal success. The uncontrollability of obsessions and the disturbing nature of their content require the use of different cognitive and behavioral techniques in order to master them. Chapters 12 and 13 are devoted to understanding and treating obsessive and intrusive thoughts and compulsive, ritualistic behaviors.

In the chart on the following page, we compare the processes of healthy and unhealthy worry.

A comparison of the types of worry in columns A and B yields several points. First, recall that worry is a thought process that helps people adapt to the world by enabling consideration and evaluation of the possible outcomes of our plans. All the mental processes in column A are familiar and adaptive ways of thinking. The column A styles help us solve problems and turn plans into realities.

The column B thinking styles darkly mirror the column A styles, somewhat in the way that Robert Louis Stevenson's Mr. Hyde was grimly reminiscent of the thoughtful, astute Dr. Jekyll. The differences between them are due to anxiety that infuses the thinker with dread, inhibits him, even freezes him in his tracks and leaves him quaking in his boots. As men or women succeed in overcoming generalized anxiety, their worrying styles can slip loose of the grip of automatic anxious thoughts of column B and become more objective, productive column A worries.

ACTING NERVOUS: THE HIGH PRICE OF COPING

Overreacting and catastrophic thinking are only two of the unproductive ways overanxious people react to everyday stresses. Other anxiety-laden coping strategies may be used as well.

Safety checks are a kind of coping device commonly utilized by people with GAD. They resemble the safety signals and behaviors that were discussed with relation to phobias and social anxiety. These safety signals are behaviors that have ingrained associations with security and coping, such as making sure to carry a water bottle or a few extra Xanax pills everywhere "just in case." Similarly, safety *checks* give anxious people transitory relief from stress and make anxiety-provoking situations seem more manageable; but their drawback is that they also nourish an anxiety disorder. In an effort to limit their anxiety, people with unhealthy worries may

Table 10.2

PROCESSES OF HEALTHY AND UNHEALTHY WORRY

A. Healthy Worry	B. Unhealthy Worry
Mental Notebook and Planner Review of important aspects of a situation and planning coping strategies. An example is planning what price you are willing to pay for a car and the ways you will respond to the salesperson's pitches regarding accessories, choice of models, financing, and trade-in.	*Apprehension* Thinking with mounting anxiety about approach, entry to, or participation in a situation—e.g., "What if I arrive late and everyone in the group turns to stare at me and sees how nervous I am? Then they'll go around with introductions, and I'll be too tongue-tied to say a word. How embarrassing!"
Rehearsal Constructive repetition or review in order to augment learning, such as getting ready for a test or presentation by going over the main points you have selected.	*Rumination* Anxiety- or depression-provoking repetition or review of unnerving or disturbing aspects of a past event—e.g., "If only I hadn't gotten mad and said what I did when he made that remark! I don't know if he really meant it, but it really bothered me. . . ."
Problem-Solving Considering, evaluating, and arriving at effective ways of understanding and resolving problems—e.g., teaming up with neighbors to discuss the best way to get better street lighting on the block.	*Obsession* Persistence of ideas, thoughts, impulses, or images that are experienced as intrusive and inappropriate and that cause marked anxiety or distress—e.g., impairment of your concentration due to your preoccupation with a physical feature you find grotesque in a person you are introduced to.

check on their loved ones' safety by phoning them regularly and often to assuage their own worry, or by regularly reading the obituary columns of newspapers out of a displaced fear for their mortality.

Both safety checks and other safety behaviors and signals have similarities to compulsive behaviors (covered in chapters 12 and 13). Like compulsions, they are detours from the path of progress in order to avoid the legendary "monster in the cave" and involve avoidance behaviors that seem ineffectual as coping techniques even as we perform them. But in a subtle way, *safety checks and compulsions give temporary relief from intense anxiety while actually fueling fears and worries.*

For instance, Lily feels nervous whenever she *doesn't* wipe the serving spoon's handle before she dishes out her portion of carrots, because her excessive cleaning behavior *maintains and heightens* her fear of contamination. After Harry became disabled, he felt reassured when his wife would phone in every hour while she was out running errands, but his anxiety would shoot sky high if her calls were delayed even by a few minutes. In chapter 11, the methods you will learn for controlling safety signals by reverse engineering are likely to decrease and dissipate your anxiety. These behavioral techniques resemble those described in chapter 13 for overcoming compulsions, since these two types of behavior maintain anxiety in similar fashions.

ANXIOUS MIND, ANXIOUS BODY

Let's take a look at what takes place in the body of a person who feels consumed with unhealthy worry. Muscle tension, elevated heart rate and blood pressure, changes in the way the stomach works, and mental confusion are all characteristic of an anxious physical reaction. Scientists believe that when a person is overly stressed or generally anxious:

- It is as if her parasympathetic nervous system is impaired and "refuses" to cooperate by shutting down the negative arousal.

- Rest and relaxation get difficult and elusive.

- A biochemical called CGRP is overproduced and "gunks up" specialized cells whose job is to capture infectious agents and deliver them to the immune system to be neutralized. As a result, the immune system is partially impaired, and an overstressed person becomes more susceptible to infection.

Often when we suddenly get anxious, we find we can't think straight. That's because, at that moment, the locus ceruleus has discharged the neurotransmitter norepinephrine (NE)—basically, fear-type adrenaline—into the cerebral cortex. As a result, we feel fear. The NE throws the doors to our senses so wide open that we can detect hints of danger from any immediate source. Concurrently, we are flooded with input that overwhelms our capacity for critical thinking so we cannot distinguish useful from useless data.

The locus ceruleus concurrently activates a biochemical hyperlink to the vagus nerve and as a result the anxious person's heart rate and blood pressure stay elevated while his digestive operations virtually shut down. Once closed, these "switches" that trigger changes in bodily state are slow to reopen. Cardiovascular tone remains high and normal digestion is not restored for hours.

A chronically irritable or nervous stomach is a widespread problem especially pronounced among sufferers of GAD. For many of them, a nervous, queasy, or nauseous feeling in the stomach can become an anxiety trigger in its own right. A recent study surveyed a thousand new outpatients who sought treatment for gastrointestinal complaints at Cornell University Medical Center in New York City. They were administered a diagnostic test for anxiety disorders along with the paperwork they completed during their first visit. Talk about validation of the gut feelings of fear! One-third of the subjects were determined to be suffering from coexisting anxiety disorders.

Table 10.3 summarizes the bodily effects that occur during different states of anxiety and panic.

An Adaptation to Stress That Backfires

The chronic anxiety state of GAD may be the result of prolonged exposure to a high level of stress during part or all of one's youth, so that worry gets established as a mental habit for dealing with stress, frustration, and dissatisfaction. The more habitually an individual responds to stress by worrying, the wider the range of situations that become associated with negative, anxious feelings. Ultimately, worrying can spread and intensify until it becomes very negative, darkens emotional life, and impairs coping ability. After serving as an adaptive and useful reaction to one set of circumstances like growing up in a dangerous setting or surviving a natural disaster, worry can become a pervasive negative mood and an overreaction if it generalizes to everyday situations where survival isn't an issue.

Those most likely to have problems have histories of unpredictable bad experiences while growing up that seemingly could not have been con-

Table 10.3

SOMATIC EFFECTS OF HEALTHY AND UNHEALTHY ANXIETY AND PANIC EPISODES

	Healthy Worry	Unhealthy Anxiety	Panic or Fear
Frequency and Duration	18% of wakeful time—episodes lasting minutes to days	With GAD, 60% of waking time—episodes last minutes to days	4 to 25 minutes for panic; no effective limit for fear
Central Nervous System	Activated at the onset, deactivated when threat is over	Activated at the onset, not fully deactivated afterward	Swiftly activated
Behavior Mechanism	Activated, preparing for danger	Inhibited, safety checking, freezing	Escape or avoidance
Cardiovascular System	Elevated heart rate and blood pressure during episode	Chronically elevated heart rate and blood pressure	Up to 180% of normal heart rate and blood pressure during episode
Gastrointestinal System	Digestion quits during episode	Digestion quits and is slow to be restored	Digestion quits during episode, possibly accompanied by hyperacidity, nausea, or urgency for elimination
Sleep	Interrupted during episode	Possibility of chronic impairment	Interrupted during episode, heavy afterward

trolled or prevented. These men and women understandably feel perpetually unsafe—haunted by a sense of threat, constantly on guard and anxious.

BEING A PARENTAL CHILD

Parental children, "appointed" by their busy, ill, overworked, or overstressed parents to function as junior parents, generally assume responsibility for their younger or less reliable siblings. Parental children may receive their appointments as early as age eight, and their duties may continue into adulthood. They may bear most or all of the stress and frustration of parenting, combined with a scant measure of love and satisfaction. Their family relationships are fraught with seriousness and responsibility and short on fun and play. They largely fulfill their "job descriptions" by worrying to an unhealthy extent, since they are mandated to deal with adult-sized stressors at an age when they have only child-sized emotional resources.

ENDURING A TRAUMATIC UPBRINGING

Traumatic upbringings can create long-term anxiety, and survivors may develop GAD or post-traumatic stress disorder. External trauma results whenever children are raised in war zones and also is likely when they are raised in communities or neighborhoods where crime is rampant or street gangs hold sway. A client born and raised in the Mideast recounted a bomb exploding a few yards from her bedroom and recalled her anxiety when hearing the whistling sounds the bombs made as they dropped toward their targets. She was consumed with worry about her own children's safety. Another chronically anxious client recounted the destruction of all that was familiar when the Nazi army invaded her town in the Netherlands in 1940.

Internal traumas include terrible personal losses, victimization by abuse, neglect, or molestation, as well as growing up in homes where parents are violent, alcoholic, or drug abusing. Even years after the traumatic situation has ended, these people find themselves reacting in very uncomfortable ways to anything vaguely reminiscent of their earlier feelings of loss, lack of control, or victimization. The anxiety of a client who lost a parent in a flying accident when she was a child resurfaced, along with that of a multitude of other Americans, after the explosions of the World Trade Center in 2001.

Treatment of Anxious Thinking

Unhealthy worry and chronic anxiety respond well to cognitive-behavior therapy that facilitates modification of anxious thinking. An anxious person does not have to be able to suspend doubting and incessant worrying in order to start improving. He can learn to watch himself worry while utilizing the simple new tools and techniques he acquires to decrease the power of worry over his mental and emotional life.

Many people who complete psychotherapy for GAD undergo striking changes:

- Time spent worrying typically drops by about one-third, from an average of 60 percent of the day to an average of 40 percent.

- The number of coexisting anxiety diagnoses that people with GAD suffer from drops sharply when they are treated. This reduction seems to lend validation to the integral role that anxious thinking can play in the maintenance of all sorts of anxiety disorders.

Once treatment helps the worrier to steer or stem the flood of catastrophic thoughts, the triggering problem or event can be more effectively explored from different, more objective, realistic perspectives and resolved. Treatment can substantially relieve the anxiety of a person with GAD, improve his ability to deal with frightening situations, brighten his outlook, and restore his "edge."

Chapter Eleven

Relieving Worry
and Generalized Anxiety

When worry has too much control over us, it seems like it can pop up nearly anywhere and lodge uncomfortably in our spirits. At such times, once we begin feeling anxious or worrying about one thing, the next thought will most likely be anxious, too. Similarly, when an anxious mood takes hold, all too often we find that we have resolved one stressful situation only to have another ruffle our composure all over again. An anxiety reaction or bout of worry can ensnare us without our knowledge. Unhealthy worry can take hold of our lives and overshadow our sense of well-being. It can render us too nervous or pressured to relax.

Sometimes our anxiety is spread so widely throughout our day-to-day situations that we don't fathom its presence or extent until other people point it out. Have people remarked to you, "I don't know how you do it! You never seem to let up"? Perhaps you have a lot of trouble taking vacations. Do people observe that you seem stressed out or wonder out loud if you ever relax? Do you feel somehow irresponsible when you're *not* trying to solve some problem—regardless of whether it's yours or someone else's?

If you have answered these questions in the affirmative, or if you have already assessed the fact that you are overly anxious or worry to an unhealthy extent, you may be suffering from generalized anxiety. Why not commit yourself to getting the jump on unhealthy worry?

Practicing Early Worry Detection

Start by learning to catch anxiety early. Unhealthy worry may be discerned by its palpable negative charge and sense of uncontrollability. Through use of *early worry detection,* you can heighten your awareness of the physical, cognitive, and behavioral indicators that anxiety has crept in and establish a framework for checking anxiety regularly.

Checklist: My Physical Indicators of Anxiety

❑ Tightness in neck and/or shoulders

❑ Tension headache

❑ Sweating

❑ Frequent urination or bowel movements

❑ Queasy, crampy, or nauseous stomach

❑ Breathing fast

❑ Difficulty catching breath

My own additions:

❑ _____

❑ _____

❑ _____

❑ Restless or impaired sleep

❑ Dry mouth

❑ Jumpiness

❑ Clumsiness due to inattention

❑ Pressured feeling

❑ Knot in the stomach

❑ Tight, achy muscles

❑ _____

❑ _____

❑ _____

Anxious thoughts often arise as we try to plan to cope with a disturbing problem or anticipate a challenge. The object of our consideration may be a commonplace matter involving work or school, family or friends, finance, health, or daily responsibilities. Nevertheless, before we know it our thinking shifts into disturbingly morbid directions. At other times, automatic, fear-tinged thoughts drift into consciousness seemingly from the nether regions of our emotional brains.

Checklist: My Typical Anxious Thoughts

- ❑ I'll be late.
- ❑ I won't measure up.
- ❑ This is more trouble than it's worth.
- ❑ _____ is upset with me.
- ❑ _____ doesn't like me.
- ❑ This is more than I can manage.
- ❑ I won't/don't have enough time.
- ❑ I can't/won't be able to afford this.
- ❑ This seems unsafe.
- ❑ Where *is* he/she?
- ❑ I'm responsible for this tangled mess.
- ❑ I can't straighten this out.
- ❑ I'm afraid that _____.
- ❑ What if _____?
- ❑ _____
- ❑ _____

- ❑ I can't get the help or support I need.
- ❑ I'm too stressed out to handle this.
- ❑ Too many things going on at once—I'm bound to mess up.
- ❑ I can't do this without help, and there isn't any (or not enough).
- ❑ This is going to blow up in my face.
- ❑ This is turning into a nightmare.
- ❑ I bet I look awful.
- ❑ I don't think I am competent.
- ❑ I can't work quickly enough.

Checklist: My Anxious Habits

- ❑ Fidgeting
- ❑ Tapping my feet
- ❑ Drumming my fingers
- ❑ Rubbing my hands
- ❑ Rubbing my face
- ❑ Snacking
- ❑ Biting my nails
- ❑ Clearing my throat
- ❑ Licking my lips

- ❑ Stammering
- ❑ Stuttering
- ❑ Chewing my lips
- ❑ Facial tics
- ❑ Vocal tics
- ❑ Adjusting my clothes
- ❑ Talking to myself

- ❑ Nervous smiling
- ❑ Talking too much
- ❑ Nodding my head
- ❑ Grinding my teeth
- ❑ Coughing
- ❑ Sighing
- ❑ Interrupting

- ❑ Finishing people's sentences for them
- ❑ Smoking cigarettes
- ❑ Drinking alcoholic beverages
- ❑ Twisting my hair
- ❑ Picking my skin

My own additions:

- ❑ _____
- ❑ _____
- ❑ _____

Use these inventories to help you detect worry early. Notice when the behaviors you are engaging in are typical of when you are nervous. Note when you are thinking the kinds of thoughts that get you anxious. See how early you can detect the physical sensations of anxiety. Once you've begun to master early worry detection, challenge yourself to notice your worries even earlier.

Sometimes "free-form" worry detection—noticing worry early just because you've decided that you will—is successful, but a structured approach is likely to be more effective. Among the strategies for monitoring suggested by psychologist Thomas Borkovec is to *notice whether you are anxious every time you go through a doorway.* This process might consist of using every pass-through as a cue to ask yourself whether or not you're anxious and replying yes or no. If yes, then ask yourself: "What about?" and see what comes up. Why not try out this technique with the very next doorway you go through?

Two other methods of structuring early worry detection are:

- Trying to notice nervous behaviors, like fidgeting and foot tapping, or whatever is typical of you, as soon as possible after you start them

- Using "stickies" (colored Post-it Notes with adhesive backings) placed in prominent, easily noticeable locations

Each time you detect your nervous behavior, or rest your eyes on a Post-it, ask yourself whether you're worried or anxious, and, if so, about what. Alter the locations of the stickies often enough to keep these reminders effective.

We ask our clients to keep a Worry Record. Try it. Get a notebook and rule it to make charts for recording your worries. Write them out in narrative form or use the sample form on the following page. There is an extra copy included in appendix A.

By simply catching your worries early and making note of them, you begin to alter the worry process. *Spell them out as precisely as possible.* This kind of systematic thinking will heighten your awareness of the situations, thoughts, and behaviors that lead you to become anxious. In addition, you will begin to discover the therapeutic value of being objective or scientific about your anxiety.

Zinbarg, Craske, and Barlow identify a number of key processes that maintain anxiety: confused and unsystematic thinking, excessive focus on anxiety-producing matters and fearing the worst, chaining of worried thoughts together, automatic thinking, safety checking, and subtle avoidance. Fortunately, each of the maintaining factors that we discuss below can be changed and the vicious cycle of anxiety broken.

Uncoupling the Train of Worrisome Thoughts

Do you become suddenly nervous and flooded with worries? Worries typically include overgeneralized, tangled messes of interrelated concerns. These "mental disaster zones" consist of clusters of worries produced when the person encounters stress and frustration while in a negative, nervous frame of mind. During an anxious mood, a person's train of thought travels in a negative, nervous direction. Each thought is likely to be related in some way to the one preceding it, resulting in a chain of interrelated, interlocking negative thoughts.

Worksheet 11.1
WORRY RECORD

Situation: Who, What, When, Where?	Worry Topic and Specific Worrisome Thought	Anxious Behaviors	SUDs (0–10)	Actual Outcome
In the waiting room of the medical clinic, a guy reminds me of my cousin Sid.	With his incessant headaches I wonder if Sid has a brain tumor. Shannon's Uncle Pen died of a brain tumor.	Licking my lips, fidgeting	3	Sid's doctor tries him on a new migraine pill and his headaches get completely controlled.

By learning to tease apart worry clusters and separate them into their components, you can identify and deal effectively with the actual causes of anxious distress. One secret of success in untangling worries is to conceive of them as *chains of thought* or *trains of thought*. We will use these metaphors interchangeably. The first link in the chain is an *automatic thought* (AT) that literally pops or slips right into our heads when we get anxious. Early worry detection can enable us to register the anxiety right after the AT is triggered. We have choices about subsequent thoughts: By learning to "steer the trains of thought," we can control their direction and that of our minds.

First, we'll learn to uncouple worrisome trains of thought. Choose a recent worrisome experience, write your thoughts about it out completely, and give each thought a SUDs rating according to the degree of anxiety you felt. See how many of these worrisome automatic thoughts that make up the train or tangle you can distinguish, and write them down below.

Write out your tangled worry:

List the thoughts that make up the tangle (give each a SUDs rating):

1.

2.

3.

4.

5.

6.

Now, fill in the following diagram. Put your initial anxious automatic thought (AT) inside the train car furthest to the left. Then, following the arrows to the right, write a phrase that describes the topic of each of the worries in a different car.

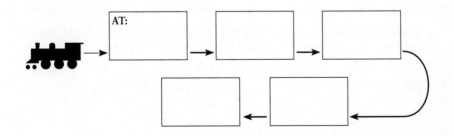

To illustrate, Tasha became apprehensive while waiting for her fourteen-year-old daughter, Tia, to call from the friend's home where she was visiting during spring vacation. Tasha decided to study her anxious thinking and discovered that she had intertwined several worries:

1. A fear that Tia was not being truthful about what she was *really* doing

2. A concern that she was losing control of her daughter

3. Fears that Tia would prefer her friend's family to her own

Once Tasha unjumbled her worries, she was able to evaluate each one separately and felt much better. Here is an illustration of Tasha's chain of thought. Although the first link in her chain is an automatic thought (AT), as we discover below Tasha has learned to exercise choice about subsequent links of the chain.

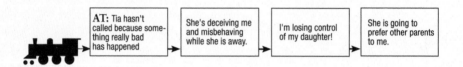

EXAMINING THE EVIDENCE

Now that we've learned to analyze our tangles and distinguish the worries that constitute them, let's learn to *rethink them* by examining the evidence. After expressing each worry as clearly as possible, weigh the evidence of its accuracy or inaccuracy by answering the following three questions:

1. *Past Experience*—How often has this occurred in the past?

2. *General Rules*—Does what I am worried about usually happen?

3. *Alternative Explanations*—What other explanations are there?

Then come up with a preferable way to think about each of your concerns.

Do you think it's useful to examine the evidence for your anxious thoughts? Keep practicing this technique by utilizing it whenever you review worries that you have noted in your Worry Record.

Table 11.1

TASHA EXAMINES THE EVIDENCE FOR HER WORRIES

Worry	Past Experience	General Rules	Alternate Explanations	How Would I *Rather* Think?
1. Fear that her daughter wasn't telling her what she *really* was doing	Tia has rarely gotten in trouble at friends' houses.	Tia is nearly always truthful.	She hasn't called because they're at a show or somewhere with limited access to a phone.	She is enjoying herself in a responsible way. It just feels strange not to hear from her, but there is no sign that anything is wrong.
2. Concern that she was losing control of her daughter	Tia checks in whenever she's been asked to. Sometimes she even calls just in case I might worry.	Tia's behavior generally indicates that she accepts my parental authority willingly.	At friends' houses, Tia is probably following her friends' parents' rules.	There's no reason to presume that I'm losing control.
3. Worry that her daughter could enjoy her friend's family more than she enjoys her own	Tia likes a lot of her friends' families but occasionally does not. She introduces her friends to us and participates in a lot of family activities with us.	Tia exercises flexible social judgment in her attitude toward her friends' families and generally acts positive with her own family.	No evidence that she prefers friends' families.	Tia is probably enjoying herself with her friend and her family, illustrating that "variety is the spice of life."

Reducing Anxiety by Careful Thinking—As Easy As ABC

When psychologists discuss anxiety with their colleagues, they may describe it in terms of "activity, valence, and controllability." *Activity* refers to the swiftness or aggressiveness with which the anxiety develops, ranging, for example, from the gradual realization that you are in the wrong career to a swift, catastrophic reaction to an earthquake. Valence is the negative charge—or *badness*—of the anxious reaction. The badness of your anxious distress when your car won't work because it needs gas when another working vehicle is on hand is far less than that of someone learning that he has fast-growing cancer. The angst experienced upon learning about such a terrible illness is much less *controllable* than the frustration, say, of hunting for a different plumber to repair a dripping pipe than the one you've been using; the plumber problem is of course far more easily controllable if you work at it.

We abbreviate these dimensions as *A = activity; B = badness; C = controllability*. This morning, when Jane saw a baby spider crawling up the bathroom wall, she performed an ABC analysis on the thought "that spider could bite me and make me sick!" as follows:

A: It was moving steadily but not quickly, maybe a few inches a minute.
B: It was only a wee baby, so small that its biter—if it even has one!—would be very tiny.
C: Should Spidey somehow actually become a threat, there are plenty of ways to handle it, such as wiping away its web, picking it up on a matchbook and carrying it outside, or squashing it.

An example of the application of ABC analysis to a worrisome situation is your distressing concern that you will lose custody of your child as a result of tomorrow's child custody hearing involving your contentious, estranged spouse:

A: Since I have been doing a good job taking care of my son and sharing custody, it's unlikely that the judge will order any sudden change in the custody arrangements.
B: There is no black or white in this custody situation, so even if the court changes its custody ruling, there's no chance that either my ex or I will suddenly become "the white knight parent" or "the outcast parent."
C: I have a good lawyer and so does he, and I can make a good case for re-

taining full custody of our child. Even if tomorrow's hearing turns out badly, I may still be able to regain control by applying for another hearing.

ABC analysis is both a *cognitive reframing (or rethinking) technique,* because it enables the worrier to arrive at different thoughts about the situation, and an *exposure therapy technique,* because it provides an opportunity to relieve anxiety by thinking at length about a worry and correcting errors of fact and perspective.

Correcting Thinking Errors

Five kinds of anxious thinking are prevalent in unhealthy worry and chronic or generalized anxiety. Examine your Worry Records and learn to recognize the kinds of anxious thinking you do.

Kinds of Anxious Thinking Prevalent in GAD

1. *Filtering* is a kind of tunnel vision. The anxious thinker focuses on one aspect of a situation to the exclusion of everything else—such as Tiffany remembering a week as horrible despite at least one good day, or the vacation she and Keith took last summer as a disaster despite a number of enjoyable times.

2. *Black and white thinking* refers to thinking about things in "all or nothing" terms instead of on a spectrum. Pete personified this problem. He would think, "If I'm not perfect, then I'm a total loss." He was very anxious throughout the time he was interviewing for a computer programming job, because while "psyching himself" he would "stress himself out" with self-talk like, "If I get anxious at all during the interview, I won't have a chance to get the job."

3. *Overgeneralizations* are conclusions drawn on the basis of a single incident or piece of evidence. Susan overgeneralized by interpreting her sister-in-law's negative comments during a phone call as indication of a family feud, despite the fact that their relationship was generally good.

4. *"Shoulding"* is rigid thinking about "right" and "wrong" thoughts or behaviors. "Should" statements result in judgmental self-talk and considering oneself and other people bad or defective. Jake would

often get uneasy in social situations when he got wrapped up in shoulding, such as "he shouldn't be so crude in front of me!" or "I shouldn't be so jumpy!"

5. *Personalization* is the tendency to relate everything to the self, compare oneself to others, and downgrade one's self-worth. While personalizing, every experience, conversation, or glance can become an indicator of one's lack of value or personal unworthiness.

After you identify the types of anxious thinking you engage in, correct them. Write out straight, realistic thoughts to challenge or replace the overanxious misinterpretations. The correction of thinking errors is illustrated in table 11.3 on page 232.

Replacing Agonizing with Action

Once you learn to recognize and contend with thinking errors and tangles of confusing worries, you can determine what is on your mind and deal with it. Often you will discover that there is a decision to be made. Instead of agonizing, you can utilize brainstorming or other problem-solving techniques to consider choices on the basis of their merits, select the best one, and develop an action plan for carrying it out. By doing so, you replace agonizing with action.

THOUGHT STOPPING

Thought stopping is a simple, sometimes quite effective way of taking action to relieve anxious thinking. Our sense of positive control appears to be enhanced when we can use it to stop, interrupt, or refocus our thoughts onto matters of our choosing. Thought stopping consists of the following steps:

A Case of Anxiety-Building by Personalization

A manager comments during a staff meeting, "I've got a surprise in store for those of you who think that just because we provide you with nice, new computers, you're free to chit-chat online with everyone you know on company time." Candy, an anxious personalizer, just flips out. She thinks, "Oh, my gosh! I bet he saw me the day I left my door open when I was emailing Christina about her engagement party! Nobody else in here looks even the least bit guilty. There goes *another* job. I am *such* a loser!"

1. *Choose a type of thought to monitor and stop.* A mildly anxiety-provoking thought (with a SUDs level of 3 or less) is a good choice of an initial target. Examples might be hoping that you won't be late or wondering if a friend is going to call. A line from a song or ditty that is hard to stop once you begin replaying it in your mind can also be used for practice drills.

2. *Teach yourself to say "Stop!"* Do this sharply and convincingly in your mind. You may want to practice at first by saying it *out loud* when the thought or song you've selected enters your mind. Ultimately, your goal is to say "Stop!" mentally, without any vocal activity. Some instructions advise you to snap a rubber band on your wrist each time you say "Stop!"

3. *Each time you give the command, shift your attention to present-moment sensations.* This shift may consist of immediate implementation of a self-control relaxation technique like calming breaths, tightening and then relaxing your hands or feet, counting your toes, or else doing something more basic, like looking up at the sky or around the room and noticing the colors of everybody's shirts, taking a whiff from a vial of cologne, or glancing at photos you carry for this purpose.

4. *If at first you don't succeed . . .* If your target thought recurs within a few minutes, give the "Stop!" command and shift your attention to present-moment sensations once again. *If the thought still persists after two tries, it is probably not controllable through this simple technique.* But fear not—before this chapter ends, you will have more sharp anti-worry arrows in your quiver!

5. *If it works, keep using it.* Continue to use thought stopping for each thought that you successfully stop. After multiple successes, these thoughts will probably desist once and for all.

WORRY POSTPONEMENT

Worry postponement is another simple behavioral technique. Simply monitor your anxious thinking for specific types of target thoughts, and when they occur, make the decision to *postpone worrying about them* for a certain period of time. The length of the postponement can be as short as a few seconds or as long as part of a day, but after lengthy postponements, worries

Table 11.3

CORRECTING ANXIOUS THINKING

Type of Anxious Thinking	Example	Realistic Thought
Filtering	This week has been horrible.	There were a few bad incidents, but some positive things occurred as well.
Black and White Thinking	If I can't deliver my speech perfectly, then it's a total loss.	I think I made several good points in a nervous monotone. I'll ask people I trust for their reactions.
Overgeneralization	He frowned when he looked at me. He must disapprove of my outfit.	Maybe he has gas. Maybe he just had an upsetting phone call. My conclusion is not justified by the facts.
Personalization	My boss is lecturing everybody about the computers, but it's *me* he's really rebuking.	I feel guilty, but I will wait and see if any bad consequences occur. That way I'll have a clearer idea whether I really was "found out."
Shoulding	I shouldn't be so jumpy.	It's my first time. I'm nervous because I'm in awe of the other people on my team. I will get calmer after I have practiced more.

should be scheduled for specific times. For instance, say you are worrying about a call about your travel plans or a job, or about the size of an expense. Rather than saying you will worry about it "later," "after work sometime," or "today or tomorrow," plan more specifically—after dinner, for example, or at eight P.M., or tomorrow morning while applying makeup or shaving.

When the period of postponement has elapsed, either think about your target thought right then or decide to postpone it until a specific time once again. Try not to mentally avoid the thought by passively letting it slip away, because it *won't* stay out of mind! Remember the principle of thought suppression? The more anxiety-laden a thought is, the more likely it is to resurface and demand your attention at some point. Worry postponement may be utilized repeatedly until the "worry is worried" or fades away.

Significant fears are often tenacious. They may persist until they are dealt with through powerful techniques like self-control desensitization or worry exposure, described below. As we will discuss, worry postponement has important functions for utilizing worry periods and in worry exposure techniques.

WORRY PERIODS

Worry periods are blocks of time devoted to taking care of the day's worrying all at once. We will try to persuade you that worry periods are a valuable way to make major strides to overcome your anxiety. By intentionally devoting time and attention to your worries, your fears are exposed to the spotlight of consciousness. Since anxiety generally diminishes after a long enough contact with what is feared, worry periods are a fine venue for mental exposure to images of fears and worries. You will learn to use worry periods to study your anxiety—to consider how realistic, imminent, and likely it is, to work on becoming more comfortable, and to devise ways to master it.

Letting unhealthy worry continue is undesirable and contrary to your best interests, as evidenced by the dismay and anxiety contagion that result. Unlike other unpleasant processes like spring cleaning, paying taxes, and changing diapers, unhealthy worry is unmanageable and spills out all over the place. Worries have a tendency to get tangled, chained together, and shaped into anxious moods and glum mental habits.

Establishing worry periods helps to corral unhealthy worries and anxiety. Even better: Worry periods are just the kind of uninterrupted time periods that are needed to practice worry and imaginal exposure therapies, the most potent treatments of tenacious, GAD-type fears.

Setting Up Worry Periods

1. *Monitor and postpone tenacious worries.* Certain worries keep occurring and are difficult to relieve. Monitor your worries, examine

your Worry Records, and you will spot them. When you notice them coming up again during the course of daily living, postpone them to the worry period.

2. *Schedule daily worry periods.* Set up a definite time each day as a worry period. A half hour or longer is ideal, but plan on at least twenty minutes. When the time arrives, stop what you are doing, gather your notes about the particular worry or worries, and go to a setting where you can worry without interruption.

3. *Keep focused on substantial worries.* Worry about immediate, substantial concerns that you need to think about, or else recurrent, anxiety-provoking worries. Focus actively and consistently on one worry at a time. You may prefer to place the worries in a hierarchy, beginning with those that produce the least anxious discomfort, and work your way up to your most disturbing concerns.

4. *Think about it actively for a few minutes.* Try to exclude physical and mental distractions from worry periods. Choose a quiet place and arrange for responsibilities to be taken care of or put them on hold until after you practice.

5. *Use cognitive-behavior therapy.* During worry periods, do the structured, therapeutic techniques for rethinking your worry described above: uncoupling the train of thoughts and examining the evidence, ABC analysis of anxious thinking; and correcting thinking errors. Worry periods are also ideally suited for the exposure therapy techniques described later in this chapter: self-control desensitization, and reestimation and decatastrophization of tenacious worries.

6. *When one worry loses its oomph, go on to the next.* If you have several different unhealthy worries, such as a health concern, a problem at college or with your job, and concerns about a couple of personal relationships, untangle them, make them as specific as possible, and worry about each until your anxiety diminishes, ideally to a SUDs level of 1 or 2. Then proceed to the next worry on your agenda.

META-WORRY MODIFICATION

Psychologist Adrian Wells believes people with generalized anxiety would be likely to reply in the negative to the question, "If you were to stop worrying about X (a particular topic), would that solve your problem?" People who worry themselves sick are often afflicted with "meta-worrying," in which they interpret *the abundance of worry itself as a central problem.* Table 11.4 gives examples of meta-worries and the specious evidence that overworriers may use to validate them.

Since the presence of uncontrolled panic or anxiety attacks provides a foundation for many an unhealthy worrier's meta-worries about uncontrollable negative thoughts or loss of sanity, it's often very desirable to work on relieving these types of meta-worry by learning to control panic. Worry periods also provide a versatile arena for modifying meta-worries, using two types of meta-worry control techniques. *Worry postponement* is utilized to place worries on the worry period agenda, and in the *worry periods* themselves, worries are engaged in actively and then terminated at the end. Worry postponement helps modify beliefs in the uncontrollabililty

Table 11.4

SAMPLE META-WORRIES AND APPARENT VALIDATIONS

Meta-Worries	Evidence That Seems to Confirm Their Validity
My worries are uncontrollable.	Racing mind and inability to relax; worries recurring after attempts to suppress them
Worrying is harmful.	Constant fatigue, inability to sleep, elevated heart rate and blood pressure, impaired digestion
I could go crazy with worrying.	Anxiety attacks, catastrophic thinking
I could enter a state of worry and never get out.	Inability to remember the last time one went for a prolonged period without worry
My worries will take over and control me.	Panic attacks

Adapted from Wells, 1997

of worry, since postponement is a type of control. Worrying for a while and then stopping appears to refute fears that a person could enter a "ceaseless" state of worry. To derive the greatest effect from these techniques, the level of anxiety produced should be rated before and after worry periods.

The strength of meta-worries can also be weakened by several rethinking techniques. For instance, if worriers' fear of going crazy is based on the belief that high stress could devolve into psychosis, they should consider the evidence. Do they believe that soldiers who undergo the extreme stress of combat are especially likely to become psychotic? Shouldn't they consider whether they've heard of people getting psychiatrically hospitalized as a result of taking the bar exam or other difficult examinations at school? In keeping with this line of inquiry, if their fear is that intrusive thoughts of trouble will lead to acute psychosis, shouldn't they be wondering about the fact that 90 percent of the general population has intrusive thoughts, yet is not psychotic?

Putting Relaxation and Imagery to Work

In order to help you modulate your anxiety during the intensive experience of the worry period, we will recap Self-Control Relaxation Training (SCT) and provide you with advanced instruction for cue-controlled relaxation. In chronic and generalized anxiety conditions, physical tension and anxious thinking act in tandem: Each one can increase the other, and relief of either eases the other. Techniques for relieving tension can thus be as valuable as those for contending with anxious thinking, and strategies for utilizing *both* relaxation and cognitive therapy are especially powerful. The purpose of learning to relax on cue is to abbreviate SCT so that it is adaptable and portable enough to match the portability of GAD.

To develop an ability to relax on cue, the key steps are: practice, practice, and practice.

SCT Relaxation Training
1. Five calming breaths

2. Present-moment awareness of:
   - Sounds
   - Pressure sensations

3. Progressive muscle relaxation of:
   - Hands and arms
   - Facial muscles

4. Calming breaths, focusing on breathing

We encourage you to practice SCT for fifteen or twenty minutes twice a day. Keep this routine up for a couple of weeks. On days when you aren't able to practice twice, practice once. Every practice helps.

Cultivate the capacity to relax and focus, and it will serve as a valuable skill that will help you overcome unhealthy worry and generalized anxiety. There are three reasons for this. The mind of a person with excessive anxiety and worry gets littered with "anxietoids" (pronounced "anx-*eye*-eh-toids")—worry fragments and bits of recent tense experiences that keep him uneasy. Anxietoids also assert their presence by creating disturbance and distraction during SCT, but as you continue to practice, you will grow increasingly adept at contending with them. Practices can also become soothing breathers that help you moderate the high level of tension that can develop amid demanding days and stressful projects while protecting you from the ill effects of stress. And lastly, after a period of consistent practicing, you will become able to utilize your relaxation periods for deep relaxation, calm review of important personal issues, and real refreshment and renewal.

For instance, for days before untangling her intertwined worries about her daughter Tia's sleepovers, every time Tasha would attempt to practice SCT, anxietoids concerning her daughter would enter her mind. As soon as she set them aside and just breathed, others would creep in to take their place. As she continued to practice SCT, Tasha found herself growing increasingly capable of contending with anxietoids by setting them aside gently and relaxing deeply. Like Tasha, you will become adept through practicing.

After about fifteen or twenty practices, many people notice that inducing relaxation becomes pretty straightforward. You may want to abbreviate your practices. After you have become skillful at relaxing, start shortening the sessions with each technique while aiming for the same calming effect. For instance, an initial trial of "abbreviated relaxation practice" might consist of two or three calming breaths, then focusing on actively relaxing only your arms, hands, and face. After a number of practices in which you devote your attention to the process of controlling and releasing your tension, you will probably be able to achieve results similar to those that result from extended practices.

Once you succeed in shortening your practices, start relaxing on cue by saying, "Relax," "Breathe through," or "Be calm." Or else use the universal symbol that things are okay: make a circle by touching the tip of your index finger to the tip of your thumb. After you cue yourself, do an abbreviated relaxation session. Practice this technique numerous times a day. Once you have repeatedly relaxed on cue, you will find that you can relieve stress this way with little effort. Moreover, cue-controlled relaxation will have an important role in the more intensive worry exposure techniques that follow.

EMOTIONAL PROCESSING AND MENTAL IMAGERY

The fears that power GAD begin as everyday concerns. They grow increasingly complex as the anxious person becomes preoccupied with troubling possible outcomes. These tenacious worries continue to swell and get exaggerated as the worrier ruminates, procrastinates, and dreads facing them.

Once the worry process has gained momentum, the worrier unconsciously starts to avoid really thinking about what he dreads. Instead of managing the worries—like scheduling time to work on decisions and problems—he is barely conscious of them and brushes them aside. The anxietoids accumulate, and during anxious moods they preoccupy him by chasing each other around his brain, sustaining tension and adding to the sense of uncontrollability. The resulting anxious self-talk seldom morphs into anything really awful, like massive panic or frightening obsessions. Instead, the worrier feels oppressed or stays continually jittery while thinking things like:

- "Late again!" and tries to hurry up

- "That woman's voice drives me bananas!" and wanders away from his desk

- "I wish these steps weren't so steep," and feels noticeably more tired for a while or

- "Why does my manager stare at me every time he passes?" and feels growing apprehension

Can Relaxation Induce Anxiety?

Sometimes people become more nervous when they try to relax. Throughout the annals of anxiety treatment and our clinical experience, certain individuals begin to fear letting go of too much control during relaxation training and start to feel unsafe. This phenomenon is known as relaxation-induced anxiety (RIA). People with this problem might prefer relaxing with eyes open and may favor progressive muscle relaxation over more inward-directed, meditation-like techniques. We have developed a special relaxation procedure for people whose efforts to relax are stymied by RIA. Look in appendix C to learn Relaxation by Holding On and Letting Go, a way of relaxing that will help circumvent your concerns about the effects of reduced control.

Like the monster, whose presence or absence in the cave is obscured by the darkness at the entrance, the true nature of these tenacious fears lies concealed beneath these innocent phrases.

Aren't the fears represented in the right-hand column of table 11.5 much more vivid and disturbing than the worrisome phrases on the left? When worried thoughts like those on the left provoke strong anxiety, and when they aren't relieved by decision making, thought stopping, unchaining, or rethinking, often this indicates that they are just window dressing for tenacious, underlying fearful beliefs like those on the right.

Psychologists have discovered that an imbalance between verbal and imaginal thinking power is a fundamental characteristic of GAD. This predominance of mental self-talk over mental imagery is the result of impairment of the *emotional processing mechanism*—the basic fear-busting machinery in anxiety disorders—which causes frightening underlying fear to be entombed beneath a sea of words (see chapter 2 for a broader discussion). The cure? *Exposure therapy* to modify the "fear structure"—our entire package of catastrophic images and anxious feelings and thoughts—into realistic thinking about the nature of our fears and our capacity to cope with them. An effective means of modifying our fear structures would be to slip beneath all the worrisome phrases to the underlying catastrophic images and thoughts and "take a bite out of the fear." We can do this by vividly reactivating our fearful images or catastrophic thoughts.

Table 11.5

EXAMPLES OF WORRIES AND UNDERLYING FEARS

Worried Thought	Tenacious Fear
Late again!	I feel like a jerk. If I can't quit my delaying tactics and show up on time, my friends will abandon me and I'll be alone.
That woman's voice drives me bananas!	I can't concentrate hard enough to read a label on a carton of milk. What's wrong with me lately? Am I losing my mind?
I wish these steps weren't so steep.	I huff and puff like a tired old steam engine. I'm afraid I'm falling apart physically.
Why does my manager stare at me every time he passes?	I bet he's scheming up some creepy way to harass me. Something always happens to spoil every job I ever like.

Experiment with the examples in table 11.5 above and see how it feels to imagine each person's underlying fears. Spend a moment or two imagining as vividly as you can the person struggling up the stairs, fearing he or she is falling apart, or the scrutiny of the scheming manager described above. Then picture your own personal nemesis, the worry or the person who makes your nerves shriek the loudest. For a few moments, imagine it, him, or her vividly. Beneath the words, what feelings do you encounter? Do you feel envy, pain, uncertainty, or fear? When we tremble with fear or are consumed with worry, we generally are deeply engaged with a troubling situation and are sincerely trying to cope.

The imaginal desensitization and worry decatastrophizing techniques we will describe shortly are exposure and reverse engineering strategies. They will help a person with tenacious anxiety vividly re-create and actively work with anxious feelings and thoughts.

Imagery Training with Neutral Scenes

We suggest that you begin training for worry exposure by adding an exercise to your daily SCT sessions. After completing the relaxation, learn to induce neutral imagery. Follow the instructions below and see if the images "work" for you; if not, replace them with a vivid description of a different neutral scene of your choosing, one rich in sensory data but not emotionally charged. Read the description in your own voice or have another person with a pleasant voice read it onto a loop tape (an endless tape loop obtainable at audio suppliers or office supply outlets), or else record them two or three consecutive times onto a regular tape and replay it repeatedly to make up a twenty- to thirty-minute session.

Shut your eyes during imagery sessions to increase your focus and eliminate any outside competition with what you are imagining. While you imagine, activate all your senses as much as possible.

Imagine yourself strolling along a walkway, the stones hard and gray beneath your feet. You enter a spacious patio, sit down on a cushioned chair by a small white café table, and lean back. Bright flowers and lush shrubbery surround you. The patio looks out onto a large, still body of water. The day is warm and clear, and a light, cool breeze is blowing. The air feels cool on your skin, and the sun is warm.

On the table is an icy, clear glass pitcher brimming with cold liquid, and next to it is a tall drinking glass. You reach for the pitcher and pour yourself a drink. The ice cubes clink as the liquid flows into your glass. You lift the glass, feeling the cold against your palm, and take a long, refreshing sip.

Now write out a pleasant imagery scene of your own, something you enjoy picturing and remembering. The scene can come from your own experience, a photograph, or film, or it can be inspired by a painting or a story. It can be a special place where you feel calm and secure, or a deliciously exciting imaginary scene. The key elements are you—the central character of the scene—and a lot of detailed sensory impressions, so that you can imagine vividly.

Practice actively evoking these two images one or more times a day for a week, and you will strengthen your "imagery muscles" and become increasingly adept at imagining. Next we will discuss how to utilize imagery techniques to *reverse engineer anxiety by activating it and then getting it to subside.*

SELF-CONTROL DESENSITIZATION (SCD)

A vital part of treatment is *active control or relief* of the tension and emotional discomfort that occurs while facing your fears. Without the elements of activation and control of anxiety, learning and therapy would not occur. In addition, you may be relieved to know that the best treatments limit your exposure to a measure of anxiety that you can tolerate.

Once you have practiced enough to be adept at consistently producing vivid neutral or pleasant imagery, you are ready to learn self-control desensitization (SCD), an anxiety control technique developed by psychologist and worry expert Thomas Borkovec. The "self-control" involves both placing the controls for regulating the intensity of anxious exposure in your hands and including self-control relaxation techniques in treatment. The "desensitization" is the process of decreasing disturbance in response to the stimulation of anxiety.

As we discussed above, the most potent way to relieve tenacious symptoms of unhealthy worry and generalized anxiety begins with activation of the whole package of catastrophic images and anxious feelings and thoughts. In SCD, imagery of the underlying worry or fear should be evoked vividly enough to cause a physical and mental anxiety reaction. A moderate level of fear should be evoked for the best results. Excessively anxiety-provoking imagery would be hard to keep in focus and hamper your ability to learn to cope effectively with fear. To ensure that the fears you focus on are manageable, do the following:

- List them on a hierarchy or stepladder, sequenced from least to most anxiety-provoking.

- Start with a low-SUDs-level tenacious worry and imagine vividly what you fear. What is the worst-case scenario? If things start getting bad, what then? If the outcome you fear occurs, what would it mean or say about you or the person you worry about? After considering these heavy questions for a couple of minutes, take a break!

- Perform SCD (see below). Learn the procedure and follow the steps to reduce the intensity of your fearful imagery using brief self-control relaxation techniques.

- Continue to practice until the fear subsides.

Steps for Self-Control Desensitization (SCD)

1. Warm up your sensory imagination with calming breaths and neutral imagery.

2. Vividly imagine a scene depicting the worst-case scenario of your worry and keep focused on the imagery for at least a minute or two.

3. Next, focus on an image of *actively coping with your fear until your SUDs level starts to decrease.* If you worry about being fired, for example, imagine telling your boss how you feel and then asking for a severance package and a reference. If you fear a loved one having an accident, imagine coping compassionately and wisely with the aftermath until the situation is stabilized.

4. Spend about twenty seconds focusing on neutral or pleasant imagery.

5. Do the self-control relaxation exercise of your choice for twenty seconds.

Continue to work on SCD for at least fifteen or twenty minutes a day or more. Specify the worries that you plan to focus on before each session. Imagine graphically the challenges to your catastrophic thoughts and thinking errors and use them to grapple with your fears and shift your perspective. If you worry about fire, for instance, imagine the flames, feeling the heat and the fear, and then extinguishing it. If you dread feeling oppressed by a confrontation, perhaps you can imagine feeling strong enough to act assertively, even to grin down your adversary. Use SCD as an opportunity to rehearse challenging your tenacious worries with flexible coping responses.

REESTIMATION AND DECATASTROPHIZATION

Catastrophization is an integral part of the process that ensnares the unhealthy worrier. An innovative, effective cognitive-behavioral program for mastering worry by contending with catastrophic thinking has been developed by Michelle Craske and her associates at the Center for Anxiety and Stress Disorders, SUNY–Albany. According to their model of worry, catastrophic thoughts prey on the mind of the person with generalized anxiety by predicting disaster with daunting certainty, while evidence of probable safety is excluded from consciousness. Thus, alarming catastrophic thoughts may virtually compel the anxious person to react vigorously with every ounce of energy and resource at his command, to put forth the utmost effort to overcome these appalling threats that seemingly are imminent.

To illustrate: Deshana worried herself sick whenever family members whom she'd invited to her home were delayed. Even the fact that they called before leaving to apologize and reassure her gave her no relief. Until they actually walked through her door, images of them being victimized by predators and incapacitated in a horrible car wreck would cascade through her imagination. Again and again her sister's and brother-in-law's efforts to reassure her fell on deaf ears: never mind that they were both terrific drivers, that the drive was in broad daylight on good roads, and that they often ran late. Deshana had catastrophic thoughts to counter every reassurance. Eventually, her significant others became cynical and made light of her fears.

At first blush it would appear that an unhealthy worrier could seldom emerge from anxiety-provoking situations unscathed. Demoralization and dread are thus among the immediate consequences of this raw deal. How many times have you or another worrier you know said, "I just *know* something bad will happen!"? In these cases, your "knowing" is *not* actually based on objective thinking or scientific evidence, but on *feeling consumed by dread.*

What is the worst thing that *may actually* occur? Using the approach of Craske and her associates, you would arrive at the most realistic outcome by using *reestimation* and *decatastrophization*—two techniques introduced in the chapters on panic and phobia treatment—to rethink your worst-case scenarios. Their application for worry treatment is described in detail below, but first a short summary.

Reestimation

When consumed with worry, the anxious person may find himself saying *with near certainty and almost 100 percent conviction,* "I can't face my doctor! He'll tell me I have TB!" or, as Deshana thought, "I just *know* that Dwight and Cynthia have been in a horrible car wreck!" To reestimate, one confronts these exaggerated estimates of the likelihood of a bad outcome, ponders the facts and anxious misinterpretations, and arrives at a *more realistic* estimate of the risk of a catastrophe. For instance, Deshana's sister and brother-in-law could just be running very late—after all, didn't they already call to apologize for the lateness of their departure? They could have been sidetracked on their way out the door by a long-distance call from Grandmother or Aunt Stephanie. They might have decided to stop and pick up flowers or a special dessert. They may be caught in a traffic jam. Even if they *were* in a motor vehicle accident, isn't it "black and white thinking" to assume anything beyond a fender bender?

Decatastrophization

At highly anxious times, we predict dire outcomes that seem unbearable, almost overwhelming. The Four Horsemen of our personal Apocalypse—humiliation, loss of dear ones' lives, financial catastrophe, or severe incapacitation—are events that seldom occur through most of individuals' lifespans but are commonly predicted during episodes of unhealthy worry. To decatastrophize, rethink your worst fears during worry periods repeatedly and at length until the apprehension starts to fade. Psychologist Richard Zinbarg and his associates explain: "It is safe to let go of excessive worry because by doing so, the individual is not in reality placing himself at greatest risk of negative things happening."

Worry Exposure Therapy: The Rethinking Technique

1. Spell out the worst outcome you fear from a tenaciously anxiety-provoking situation, and rate the likelihood that it could occur on a scale between 0 (where it definitely won't happen) to 100 percent (an absolute certainty that it will). Also, rate the level of discomfort (SUDs) you experience while thinking about the worst-case scenario.

2. Use a worry period to consider the evidence for your rating. What could turn the worst-case scenario into a sure thing? What might prevent it from coming out so badly? Relax on cue from time to time to keep your anxiety manageable. Once you have thought about the matter thoroughly, rate anew the likelihood of the dreaded outcome.

3. If your probability estimate has dropped to around 50 percent or lower, rerate your SUDs level. See if it is low enough to permit you to contemplate the matter comfortably and make decisions or brainstorm about how to resolve it. If so, then handle it by brainstorming or planning solutions.

4. If the estimate of bad outcome or your discomfort level stays high, think for a few minutes about ways you would cope with the worst-case scenario if it occurred. If the worst happened, what then? (Or: So what?)

5. If your SUDs level drops substantially (to 3 or below), rethink the situation again and again until the anxiety either stops rising above 2 or 3 or drops at least this low *right away.*

6. If your SUDs level remains high throughout your rethinking of a particular worry topic, relieve discomfort through use of relaxation on cue, but *stay with the topic* for an exposure of at least fifteen to twenty minutes. Return to it during subsequent worry periods until your anxiety starts to decrease and ultimately drops below a SUDs level of 2 or 3.

7. Once a worry has lost the power to make you anxious, go on to the next, more anxiety-provoking item on your hierarchy of tenacious worries. Now that you have mastered the lesser anxiety, you will confront this new challenge with more confidence.

Learning to Quit Acting So Nervous!

By learning to relieve your anxious thinking, you have made tremendous strides toward liberation from unhealthy worry and generalized anxiety. Much of our unhealthy anxiety is based on thoughts, attitudes, and beliefs. You will discover that you are really ahead of the game when you take the next step of tackling your anxious behaviors and learning to act differently.

Every anxiety disorder is sustained by certain behaviors. Anxious behaviors associated with generalized and chronic anxiety may include nervous habits, actions based on superstitious beliefs, and playing it safe—erring on the side of safety and caution due to unhealthy worries.

NERVOUS HABITS

Nervous habits develop as a way to relieve anxiety temporarily and may be maintained until the anxiety diminishes. Many nervous habits can be altered or eliminated by *focused appropriate efforts,* although certain ones, like smoking, involve hard-to-change physiological processes in addition to the anxiety and qualify as addictions.

You already have the tools to change many nervous habits. First, revisit and update your list of nervous habits on page 221–222 ("My Anxious Habits"). Designate a particular habit as your first target—biting your nails or tapping your foot, for instance—and monitor it. Start catching yourself doing it as early as possible. Next, *without trying to prevent it yet,* simply label it as a nervous habit. You have begun taking control by "calling a spade a spade," because identifying it is a temporary anxiety reliever.

Now bring in additional resources to relieve the anxiety that drives this habit. As soon as you have begun *consistently* detecting and relabeling it, try *relaxing on cue.* An additional technique is to follow the relaxation by *postponing performance of your nervous habit* for thirty seconds. If you succeed *consistently* with thirty-second postponements, up the ante: Try systematically expanding postponements until they last a few minutes. Once you are successfully contending with "urges to indulge" in this way, you may discover that the impulses that drive them have largely subsided or weakened by the time several minutes have elapsed. If you meet with success, resolve to persist in utilizing this approach, because it will help you master your nervous habits. If your success is limited by difficulty controlling the targeted habit twenty-four hours a day, seven days a week, then try the techniques on weekends only, or for a couple of hours each day, and you can still master habit control.

SUPERSTITIONS, RITUALS, COMPULSIONS, SAFETY SIGNALS, AND COVERTLY AVOIDANT BEHAVIORS

These terms give you but a taste of the plethora of descriptors of anxious behaviors based on errors on the side of safety and caution. But aren't safety and caution among the best of reasons to commit errors? Whether or not you should work on modifying a behavior based on this kind of anxious thinking depends on your frank answers to several questions:

- Is your anxious behavior more likely the product of your anxiety disorder than your concern for the welfare of yourself and others?

- Does your caution in this matter serve primarily to reinforce your own fears?

- Is your behavior inappropriately restrictive?

- By continuing this behavior, are you inadvertently acting as an example to other people and modeling attitudes and beliefs that increase their fearfulness unnecessarily?

If you conclude from your consideration of these issues that you wish to overcome these kinds of anxious behaviors, proceed by spelling out the specific behaviors that you would like to target.

My Overcautious Behaviors

1. _____

2. _____

3. _____

4. _____

Many everyday behaviors are governed by superstition. When we avoid walking under ladders, or we shudder upon breaking a mirror or when a black cat crosses our paths, we know we are engaging in common superstitions. Superstition-based behaviors that may impair functioning include avoiding situations that involve the number 13 (like never leaving the house on Friday the 13th) and governing major life decisions by palmistry or astrological readings.

Superstitions sometimes include prescribed rituals—observable sequences or patterns of behavior like throwing salt over one's shoulder to prevent bad luck and avoiding cracks in the sidewalk lest stepping on one breaks Mother's back. Commonplace rituals and compulsions include checking locks, burners, and switches repeatedly and adhering rigidly to self-devised routines and procedures, like checking mirrors in a set order while driving or touching certain things in sequence before leaving a room.

Then there are behaviors labeled "safety signals" by Craske and her associates. This category includes actions performed "just in case," such as:

Peculiar Compulsions

Some people experience strong anxiety in connection with the rituals and compulsions they perform and may perceive them to be inappropriate or peculiar. Their anxiety may be mingled with feelings of guilt, shame, or disgust. If this is the case for you, we suggest that you read about OCD in the next chapter.

- Reading the obituary column religiously to see if someone you know has died

- Avoiding newscasts so as to avoid hearing things that would be too disturbing

- Calling a spouse or relative multiple times a day just to check in and make sure things are okay

The term "safety signals" also encompasses "safety behaviors" and "safety checks." Therapy for worry-based behaviors consists of *exposure to worrisome situations while refraining from engaging in anxious behaviors or "just in case" actions*. The anxious person might start listening to or watching newscasts instead of avoiding them. He or she would *pay careful attention* and deal actively with the anxiety that is generated. The italics indicate the importance of actively refraining from subtle avoidance of the anxiety-provoking aspects of the broadcast.

Zinbarg and his associates have postulated that the experience of anxiety is well expressed in terms of predictability, controllability, and safety, dimensions that resemble the ABC system of analysis we discussed on pages 228–229. The dimension of "controllability"—C—is the same, but instead of A for "activity," consider how *predictable* a worrisome situation seems to be. In place of B for the overall "badness," consider how *safe* or *unsafe* it seems.

Base your practices in modifying overcautious behaviors on analysis in these terms. For example, Kelly decided she should work on exposing herself to TV newscasts. She analyzed her selection this way:

1. *Controllability:* When I watch stories on violent crimes, I get anxious. My anxiety may reach a SUDs level of 3 or 4 and lasts at most a couple of minutes, so I feel pretty confident that I can control it.

2. *Predictability:* My prediction? Even if my anxiety is harder to bear than I expect, I know I can tolerate it.

3. *Safety:* TV stories on violent crimes represent no actual threat to my safety.

Thus, broadcast news avoidance sounded like a good choice of a target behavior Kelly could really hope to master, so she went ahead to practice modification of this behavior. She tempered her anxious behavior by watching gradually more news while successfully coping with increased anxiety through thought stopping and cue-controlled relaxation. During worry periods, she dealt with the occasional worry that was precipitated by her news watching. After a few weeks, her anxiety became wholly manageable.

Experimenting with Worry Prevention

A number of men and women who have succeeded in overcoming much of their generalized anxiety tried experiments in worry prevention such as modifying long-term safety behaviors that held their worries at bay at the cost of restricting their liberties. Consider Tasha, whom we met earlier in this chapter. Ever since her husband died, her anxiety had prevented her from allowing Tony, her eleven-year-old son, to spend weekend days away from home. After Tasha succeeded in easing her excessive anxiety about her teenage daughter, she decided to employ a strategy of worry prevention to tackle this tenacious safety behavior. First she let Tony stay all day one Saturday with trusted friends. Rather than worrying herself sick, she went for a "stress management" swim and diligently documented her intense anxiety about him in copious Worry Records. After the first practice day went smoothly, Tasha devised a series of graduated practices that enabled her to continue coping with her exaggerated concerns for Tony's safety. Ultimately, she was comfortable enough to permit him to participate in a day-long school outing to Disneyland during which she worried very little. Here are other examples of worry prevention:

- Ronnie used to worry about Judy whenever she came home late. He would worry that she'd been harmed, but he knew that his distress was excessive, so they decided to experiment. Ronnie found that he was much less anxious when Judy gave him advance notice that she would be late. On the basis of this discovery, Judy helped Ronnie practice by planning and informing him of the number of days of each week that she would be late without letting him know in advance which days those would be. Ronnie discovered within just a few weeks that he was strong enough to subdue this monster in the cave.

- Andre had always assuaged his worry about the possibility of being unprepared for unforeseen eventualities by avoiding going out of the

When to Seek Professional Mental Health Treatment for Generalized Anxiety

- When physical tension symptoms, such as stomach irritation, sleep disturbance, body tension, or headaches, become highly uncomfortable or interfere with daily functioning

- When important areas of living, like academics or work, relationships, parenting, or health concerns, become "infected" by anxiety to the point where they become top-heavy with worry or unmanageable

- If you often become very nervous or afraid

- If you find you are unable to progress using the techniques in this chapter, or if you become highly anxious while working on relieving your worry

- When marked insecurity develops while attempting to modify safety behaviors

- If you are considering medication treatment for your anxiety

house unless he had at least fifty dollars in his pocket. He challenged his fear of the unforeseen by decreasing his pocket cash by ten dollars a week and cognitively restructuring his worries, until one day he wound up comfortably taking a day-long excursion with just five dollars and a gasoline credit card.

- Rosie liked to clean but she felt trapped; she wasn't really sure whether she actually chose to clean or if cleaning chose her, since she could "never" leave home without cleaning the bedroom, bathroom, and kitchen and washing all the dishes. She decided to experiment with deliberate omission of one of her cleaning duties every time she went out. At first, she was apprehensive—it almost felt like insubordination. But the process she began with this step eventually resulted in her feeling so emancipated that she hired a cleaning service and started taking yoga and aerobics classes.

Worry and anxiety take up far too much room in many of our lives, but concerted efforts can shrink anxiety so we can feel better—calmer, more secure, yet more vital. This chapter began by focusing your attention on the earliest, smallest indicators of anxiety—seeming trifles like nervous smiles or jumpiness and fleeting thoughts of impatience or inadequacy—and enabled you to discern their links to your substantial anxious discomfort. Then, recruiting both your rational and your imaginative powers, you learned to implement a plethora of strategies for tackling unhealthy worries of almost every size and shape and easing the distress and tension that anxiety engenders.

As we have seen, success in treatment of anxious thinking and generalized anxiety helps improve our lives. Have you increased your ability to dissolve worry and to shrink apprehension and dread? Relieving worry and generalized anxiety activates and enhances our capacity for contending with vital concerns and problems and liberates us to enjoy life more brightly and heartily.

Chapter Twelve

The Doubting Disease: Obsessions, Compulsions, and OCD

Everyone has doubts. Things are never quite perfect. We may picture an absolutely idyllic afternoon, the ultimate cheeseburger, a perfect floral arrangement, or the totally balanced checkbook, and devote every effort to achieving it. Yet absolute certainty is very elusive, and so is total satisfaction—even with good things.

Doubt, like worry, is not bad in itself. But add a hefty dose of anxiety to doubting, and uneasiness, guilt, and shame are born. And when a sense of urgency or deep-seated uneasiness intensifies urges to adjust, align, repeat, or redo until things seem "just right," we might feel our self-control beginning to slip. Although everyone has these obsessive and compulsive moments, nobody likes them much.

Obsessive-compulsive disorder, or OCD, affects 2.5 percent of the population at some point in their lives—over 6.5 million people. Approximately equal proportions of men and women have the disorder. The peak ages for females to develop OCD are between twenty and twenty-four, while for males onset is typically between thirteen and fifteen, although many people also develop the disorder as younger children. Often people recall that the first signs of the disorder emerged in their teens. One woman confided that she started to have obsessive thoughts of punching pregnant women in the stomach around the time of her seventeenth birthday party, when she learned that her aunt gave birth to a child. A male client of ours remembered that he first started engaging in the compulsive ritual of counting everything he laid eyes upon when he was thirteen years old.

Like the name and the examples imply, the crux of OCD is recurrent obsessions or compulsions. When compulsions are markedly disturbing or when the time devoted to obsessions and compulsions exceeds an hour a day, formal diagnostic criteria for the disorder are met.

Worry vs. Obsession

The boundary between obsessions and the sorts of worries we encountered in the last chapter is fuzzy, but we can make it more distinct. Much more than simply realistic but excessive worries about everyday problems, obsessions are likely to contain very disturbing, unrealistic, or inappropriate images or ideas. They often center on "unacceptable" thoughts—images of or memories about such topics as contamination, sex, aggression, or religion. An example of an obsession from the *DSM-IV* is "the intrusive, distressing idea that 'God' is 'dog' spelled backward." Other examples are the unfounded belief that one has contracted an undetected HIV infection by merely being in a room with an apparently healthy homosexual person, or a case of anthrax by simply opening one's mail, or a motorist's notion, without an actual basis, that he may have run over an animal and failed to notice or stop. By contrast, the content of worries is just "*somewhat* unrealistic."

Obsessions are seldom the direct result of stress. While worries are typically exaggerated reactions

> ### The Essential Features of OCD
>
> The essential features of OCD are recurrent obsessions or compulsions that are severe enough to take more than one hour a day, or cause marked distress or significant impairment. Obsessions are persistent ideas, thoughts, impulses, or images that are experienced as intrusive and inappropriate and that cause marked anxiety or distress. Compulsions are repetitive behaviors or mental acts the goal of which is to prevent or reduce anxiety or distress, not to provide pleasure or gratification. In most cases, the person feels driven to perform the compulsion to reduce the distress that accompanies an obsession, or to prevent some dreaded event or situation. At some point during the course of the disorder, the person has recognized that the obsessions or compulsions are excessive or unreasonable.

to everyday stresses, they are generally briefer and usually take the form of mental verbalizations or reasonable "self-talk," whereas obsessions more commonly occur as intense ruminations, images, and impulses. Despite the significant differences between worrying and obsessing, they are similar enough to enable the use of select worry control techniques to relieve obsession, as you will discover in chapter 13, where the treatment of OCD is discussed.

According to psychologist Paul Salkovski, the obsessive-compulsive (OC) person will interpret obsessive thoughts as very significant, perhaps as important revelations about "crazy" or repulsive aspects of his true personality. Such misinterpretations of obsessive thoughts as indicators that one is crazy, evil, or egregiously malfunctioning provoke the intense anxiety so characteristic of OCD-type thinking. The second main process that fuels OCD is the person's relentless effort to try vigorously to erase, neutralize, or otherwise detoxify these disturbing thoughts. Thus, although both worries and obsessions are experienced as uncontrollable, a person with OCD will typically make more vigorous, but not particularly more successful, attempts to *suppress* his obsessive thoughts than a person with GAD does his worries.

Table 12.1
MAIN DIFFERENCES BETWEEN WORRIES AND OBSESSIONS

Unhealthy Worries	Obsessions
Realistic but excessive	Very disturbing, unrealistic, unacceptable, often "bizarre and alien" in content
Topics are related to work or school, family or friends, finances, daily chores, health	Topics include contamination, sex, aggression, or religion
Usually mental verbalizations	Usually images or impulses
Less vigorous attempts at control	More vigorous attempts to resist and control, known as *neutralization strategies* and *undoing*

OCD-TYPE COMPULSIONS OR RITUALS *DECREASE* ANXIETY (BUT AT GREAT COST)

For people with OCD, obsessions are linked with compulsions, behaviors aimed at reducing anxious distress that is either generated by obsessions or apprehensive thinking about a dreaded event or situation. For instance, a woman with OCD might feel anxious distress at both her inability to control thoughts of her child being abducted by a stranger and her fears that she will never see her child again. As a result, she could feel compelled to recite a prayer one hundred times, without interruption, in a futile effort to neutralize her intrusive thoughts and insure her child's safety.

Compulsions are temporary, *ineffective* means of coping with anxiety triggers. To be precise, compulsions are anxiety-relieving in the short run (especially hand washing), but don't help in the long run. The person with OCD may find her own compulsions peculiar or even disturbing but nevertheless feels driven to continue performing them. Even though they are ineffective, as long as the disorder persists, compulsions can become consistently associated with the issues, thoughts, or images that trigger them.

Common OCD-type rituals include repeatedly checking locks, electrical and electronic controls, and ranges and ovens; performing tasks in set ways by counting the number of steps, taps, touches, or glances; arranging and rearranging things in an effort to make them look "just right"; saying a prayer or ditty every time a particular obsession comes into mind; and washing or grooming repeatedly and unnecessarily.

Compulsions are difficult to resist and are experienced as intense inhibitions of one's liberty. Thus, both the intensely disturbing quality of obsessive thinking and the sense of being driven to *ritualize against one's will* contribute to the disheartening sense of *uncontrollability* that permeates the lives of people with OCD.

It's useful to think of OCD in terms of the common subtypes of the disorder, categories of obsessions and compulsions within which a number of symptoms often appear together.

Common Subtypes of OCD

- Harming/religious/sexual obsessions and checking rituals

- Contamination obsessions and washing/cleaning rituals

- Symmetry/ordering/certainty concerns and counting/repeating/checking compulsions

While this list imparts more structure to this complex disorder, it is not hard and fast, since many people with OCD suffer from multiple symptoms that overlap more than one subtype. However, according to the research that produced this list, a compulsion to hoard possessions typically appears independently of the subtypes.

Regardless of the precise nature or type of OCD symptoms, the time and energy devoted to obsessing and performing rituals numerous times a day can be substantial. Performance of rituals frequently delays ritualizers and may make them chronically late. In addition, many families become dysfunctional as a consequence of a family member's OCD symptoms and the family's overinvolvement in those symptoms.

Obsessions, Compulsions, or OCD?

Various kinds of thoughts seem virtually to insert themselves into people's minds and hence qualify as obsessions, and many people, acting on their urges, perform repetitive physical or mental actions. In this section, we take a look at these types of obsessive thoughts and compulsive behaviors and discuss distinguishing characteristics that qualify some of them, and not others, as OCD.

INTRUSIVE THOUGHTS AND IMAGES

Many people who do not meet the formal criteria for OCD, but seek therapy nevertheless, report intrusive thoughts, images, and impulses, and compulsive activities. In fact, 80 percent of the general population have had intrusive thoughts within the past year, and as many as 90 percent have had them at some time in their lives. In one of the studies measuring the prevalence of these intrusions, typical reports by *non-OCD participants* included impulses to attack and harm people, thoughts about sexual assault or unacceptable sexual acts, or ruminations about their families getting harmed. Zany or deeply disturbing, intensifying at times of stress, intrusive thoughts seem to rise "out of the blue," and most of us really don't know what to make of them.

However, people with OCD think differently about their intrusive thoughts and images. They misinterpret them negatively. They generally judge their intrusive thoughts as significant and feel responsible for them. An obsessive person is likely to misjudge and misinterpret his own motives in three fundamental ways: badness (immorality), madness (insanity), and danger (aggression). For example, Nick grew consumed with the fear that he was bad because he dreamed of enjoying his inheritance while his terminally ill mother was still alive. Ashley was convinced that she'd completely lost her sanity when her mind started to run rampant with numerological associations to every birth date she would read or hear. Matt was disgusted with his secretary's ineptitude but grew horribly obsessed after he imagined slipping poison into her Diet Coke. Nick, Ashley, and Matt believe that the occurrence of their intrusive thoughts proves they are bad or crazy or dangerous people and are likely to act on these thoughts.

Suppose this image occurs to a nonobsessive person: He tongue-lashes a coworker, an offensive, critical person, and reduces him to a gibbering pulp. This image might remain in the person's mind for mere seconds before fading and cause minimal discomfort. An obsessive person, on the other hand, could become very disturbed by such an image, perhaps because it seems to be proof of his aggression and unwholesomeness. As a result, he could have unsettling self-recriminations that continue on and off for hours or days.

Do you find that you're uncomfortable with certain intrusive thoughts and images that enter your mind? Do some of your intrusive thoughts get charged up with anxiety and build disturbing momentum in your mind? Some examples and a worksheet will help heighten your awareness of the unique spin you impart to some of your intrusive thoughts and help you determine whether you misappraise them and turn them into OCD-type obsessions. Read the examples below and fill in the right-hand column with examples of your own thoughts and images.

Many of our clients wonder whether their intrusive thoughts and compulsive activities qualify as OCD. We reassure them that many intrusive thoughts and seemingly compulsive activities have little or nothing to do with OCD. Besides being ineffectual as coping behaviors, OCD-type compulsions are neither pleasurable nor gratifying, *not even for a moment*. Thus we will exclude several common types of compulsive problems from our discussion here. As much misery as they cause—and despite the fact that they are indeed "repetitive behaviors or mental acts"—compulsive gambling, overeating, overshopping, shoplifting, drinking, drugging, and excessive or indiscriminate sexual activity are all interlaced with periods of pleasure and gratification.

Shouldn't I Feel Guilty About My Urge to Slap My Silly Friend Silly?

Many people, both with and without OCD, feel morally bound to be guilty for *thinking about* slapping a silly or hysterical friend or kicking a dog. After all, if the fantasizer is truly a respectable, upright citizen, shouldn't pangs of misgivings accompany such mean-spirited mental images?

At such times, people with OCD experience substantial anxious distress. But OCD or no OCD, such common intrusive thoughts don't actually prove a thing. Objectively, they are very unlikely to produce bad consequences. Just because people *think of* bad actions doesn't mean they will *really do* them.

Two exceptions to this rule are thinkers of these thoughts who have trouble controlling aggressive impulses and people who have bad values, like sociopaths and abusers of children, spouses, elderly or dependent people, or animals. If you don't belong in either of these categories, maybe try to let yourself off the hook. Many intrusive thoughts are normal.

IDEALIZATION

It is almost a cultural cliché to accuse a person who fervently idolizes entertainment, bodybuilding, or sports figures of having an obsession. Where is the line between obsession and idolatry? A teenager proudly remarked to her parents, "A girl's got to have an obsession, and mine is [teen music star] Justin Timberlake!" She showed them her Justin Timberlake light switch plate, fan club membership certificate, computer screen wallpaper, T-shirt, and mouse pad as proof of the dominant role her idol had assumed in her life.

Idealization refers to an intense identification with a fantasized ideal of another person—or an altered body, as when weight lifters sweat and strain to condition themselves to resemble images in magazines or in their minds. These "idealizing obsessions" differ from OCD-type obsession thinking. Rather than centering on *our own negative ideas, mental images, or memories* (the actions we've taken, errors we've committed, accidents we fear we've caused, or diseases or infections we'd hate to contract), idealizing obsessions draw our focus toward *the positive qualities of another person or group* (the person's looks, talent, or the way he or she moves).

Worksheet 12.1

INTRUSIVE THOUGHTS THAT BECOME OCD-TYPE OBSESSIONS

Type of Misappraisal or Obsessive Spin	Example of Disturbing Thought or Image	Examples of My Own Disturbing Thoughts or Images
Exaggeration of the importance of intrusive thoughts or images	If I think about harming my children or my parents, I must be an abuser.	
Overestimation of danger	Fear of contracting anthrax from touching anything that has been handled by unknown other people; or, belief that any food that's been sitting out of the refrigerator for more than three minutes before cooking must be discarded, because it's likely to be spoiled.	
Mistaken estimation of dire consequences	If I don't keep my home neat as a pin, my family will die.	
Need for certainty	A student was unable to hand in *any* paper unless he felt it comprehensively and impeccably covered the assigned topic and was written in perfect style. He had to drop out of college, because he couldn't hand anything in.	

Type of Misappraisal or Obsessive Spin	Example of Disturbing Thought or Image	Examples of My Own Disturbing Thoughts or Images
Need for perfect control over thinking	If I have bizarre or nonsensical thoughts, I can't be sure that I'm not a bad, dangerous, or crazy person, rather than a decent human being.	
Degree of personal responsibility	If I imagine my relative/friend dead, I must wish he/she would die.	

Adapted from McLean & Woody, 2001; Freeston, Rheaume & Ladouceur, 1996

And rather than disturbing us by provoking anxiety, idealizations stimulate pleasant excitement.

Adoring fans of media stars, figure skaters, and sports figures fantasize pursuit of and encounters with their heroes. Around 1970, for example, a dedicated cadre of individuals fanned out across the British Isles, determined to find evidence that their adored Beatle, Paul McCarney, had *not* died, as rumor had it. Energizing, frequently exciting, and seldom anxiety-provoking, idealizing obsessions are often synonymous with what young men and women wish to be when they grow up and, arguably, with what the media would like them to strive for. Idealizations are often a normal, uplifting part of development that we frequently, and sometimes reluctantly, outgrow.

DELUSIONS AND PSYCHOSES

Sometimes problems with obsessions and compulsions are linked with delusions and other symptoms of psychosis, and a different type and level of mental health care is needed which we believe must be administered by mental health professionals. To qualify as clearly *nonpsychotic*, OCD symptoms must be recognized as excessive and unreasonable, and obsessions must cause marked anxiety or distress.

The following are examples of psychoses—defective, distorted perceptions of reality. Suppose a man is so profoundly concerned with germs that he is utterly incapable of functioning on a job or as part of his family, but does not recognize that his germ obsession is excessive. Indeed, he is consumed with the certainty that the entire world *truly is* hopelessly disease-ridden. Some stalkers are utterly convinced of a "divine" link between them and their "prey"; and psychotic sexual predators may be motivated by certainty that their victim is evil incarnate. Or consider a person who believes she has a flashing orange light on the top of her head, but does not feel distressed about it at all. The treatments described for OCD in the next chapter would *not* be appropriate means of relieving these unfortunate individuals' mental conditions.

Peter McLean and Sheila Woody give a related example from their clinical practice. A twenty-seven-year-old woman in an OCD therapy group had cleaning and checking rituals, but was not responding to treatment. The therapist took her aside and interviewed her individually in order to discuss her feeling that she was "evil" for making minor mistakes or checking insufficiently. She disclosed her belief that she was being watched by "the shadow," an entity that mocked and threatened her whenever she erred. Her belief in this entity's terrible power over her constituted a delusion disorder, another example of a psychosis that resembled OCD but would not be likely to respond to the treatments we describe in this book.

MORBID PREOCCUPATIONS AND FIXATIONS

Have you ever become annoyed with yourself for staring with rapt fascination at a person with a deformity or disfigurement? Warts, birthmarks, and scars are frequent targets of such unnerving attention and intrusive thinking. People with Down syndrome, dwarfs, and people with markedly misshapen physical features are often objects of such commonplace obsessions, labeled *morbid (unhealthy) preoccupations*. But strikingly beautiful or handsome people, women's feet, large bosoms, and tiny waists are also focal points for many people. These preoccupations are called *fixations* because they involve attraction, rather than focus on deformity or disfigurement. A fixation is an abnormal attachment to a person or object.

Morbid preoccupations and fixations further illustrate differences between OCD-type and other obsessions, because people commonly experience them as the brief, fleeting products of an encounter or other reminder of the overfocused object. Only a minority of individuals (most of whom suffer from a type of OCD) finds them to be consuming, dominating their thoughts, stimulating efforts to resist thinking about them and mental tugs-of-war that sometimes last for hours. These persons may experience their preoccupations or fixations as significant losses of mental control. For instance, Lucy considered herself entirely heterosexual, but she complained that she got anxious whenever other females were near her because she obsessed about their bodies. Alicia, a forty-year-old dental technician, reported that whenever she was around mentally retarded people she grew afraid she would become one.

Body Dysmorphic Disorder

A kindred type of disturbance is body dysmorphic disorder (BDD), which we introduced you to in the Introduction. BDD is a so-called "OCD-spectrum disorder"—with a number of symptoms that overlap with those of OCD—whose sufferers are "preoccupied with an imagined defect in appearance. If a slight physical anomaly is present, the person's concern is markedly excessive" (DSM-IV).

Many people share in smaller measure the concerns that distress and significantly impair the functioning of the person with BDD, and this is quite normal. Ralph, handsome though he is, occasionally gets disturbed at the traces of teenage acne still visible on his cheeks and forehead when he examines his face in the mirror. And like most women her age, Linda seldom goes a day without spending a few minutes pondering the imperfections in her figure or facial features, a practice she recalls doing even when she was ten years old. If we get down on ourselves for such physical or aesthetic defects, we may get nervous or even feel a little depressed when preparing for situations where we feel we must perform, like a date or job interview, or our mood may turn gloomy when a friend's offhanded critique of our appearance adversely affects our self-esteem.

But BDD is much, much more. Sufferers' thinking is actively disrupted by recurrent images of physical defects, real or imagined, that intrude into their thoughts and cause them marked anxiety or distress. They go to great lengths to cover up or neutralize exaggerated or imagined defects.

Shawn and Evan both suffer from BDD. Shawn checks the size of his mouth in the mirror for thirty to sixty minutes every time he prepares to leave his apartment. Evan has spent a fortune on hair transplants and drugs he reads about or learns of from infomercials to rejuvenate his slightly thinning hair, but he still feels tormented by embarrassment. He has broken off a number of relationships because of his suspicions that his girlfriends secretly had aversion to his hair.

Interpersonally, an individual with BDD is likely to be highly sensitive about any conceivable reference to his or her "flaw" and may seek excessive reassurance yet gain little respite from the obsession. BDD is considered full-fledged OCD "only when the obsessions or compulsions are not restricted to concerns about appearance."

The Physiology of OCD

Like those with other anxiety disorders, OCD sufferers have too much anxiety that interferes with their daily functioning. Biology—not psychology—is considered the most important factor in the development of OCD. Genetic studies confirm the primacy of biology, since approximately 40 percent of those with the disorder have a relative with OCD.

Neurologically, the obsession-compulsion response is distinctive. It involves a significant malfunction of the caudate nucleus, a portion of the basal ganglia located in the emotional brain that primarily initiates and controls body movement. Brain scans also indicate increased activity in portions of the frontal lobes where information is filtered, prioritized, and organized. This area of the thinking brain also serves to suppress or delay responses to extraneous or unimportant stimuli, engage in rational decision-making, set aside doubts and misgivings, and regulate and "fine-tune" movements and complex behaviors activated by the basal ganglia. "These functions are critical to spontaneity and the expression of emotion," according to psychologists Gail Steketee and Teresa Pigott.

According to psychiatrist Jeffrey Schwartz, when "the smooth, efficient filtering and the shifting of thoughts and behavior are disrupted by a glitch in the caudate nucleus," the result is like a car that is stuck in gear. "The person with OCD has a sticky manual transmission; he or she must [learn] to shift gears through behavior therapy."

When we feel confident and safe, or even when we are coping with a manageable degree of stress, our minds function as though they are in drive gear. The frontal lobes strongly signal the basal ganglia to facilitate proactive thinking and active, adaptive behavior. At times when stress is high, however, it may be more prudent to act warily or to worry before acting in error. When highly stressed or overwhelmed with dread, the basal ganglia in effect "disengage the mental gears," thereby facilitating coping by preventing a misstep that might put us in a "dangerous" situation.

The thoughts of any person whose mind is "stuck in gear" circle around and around the pivot point of the dreaded matter, the body virtually paralyzed with fear, and behavior is confined to stereotyped, minimal, often overcontrolled actions. *To a limited extent,* this development is productive, since it buys time for careful analysis of an imminently threatening situation and enables planning to precede action. When the *non*-OCD person determines how to handle the situation, his frontal lobes transmit a "green light" (the basal ganglia activate and enable his mental gears to shift into drive), and these neurological changes in turn release him to deal effectively with the stressors.

What happens to a person with OCD? His emotional brain sends overpowered signals to the thinking brain, causing acutely anxious thinking. Instead of providing relief, the signals the thinking brain sends to the emotional brain at times of stress cause too quick and too complete disengagement of the mental gears, and obsessions and compulsions are the results. Once triggered, *the anxiety of persons with OCD stays higher for a longer time* than for people without the disorder, so anxiety must be reduced much more drastically before they can regain the ability to think and act normally.

Let's consider the case of Ray, an "orderer" whose rituals required that he arrange objects in a certain order to relieve uneasiness. Just before Ray got home from work, his son had finished unpacking his new computerized scanner as a surprise.

Ray was dismayed. His anxiety spiked the instant he entered the room and saw the brand-new addition. However, he became very uneasy when he tried to leave, and kept rearranging his equipment on the desk, repetitively moving a stapler, pens, a desk calendar, and computer components a couple of inches one way and then back. He found that he could easily spend twenty or thirty minutes lost in thought about the possibilities and pitfalls of various action plans. He struggled in vain to keep from getting caught up, until he was very frustrated. Despite Ray's efforts to evaluate the situation and retain self-control, neither his attempts at reassuring self-talk, like "You can get back to it later" and "It's just your OCD, nothing's really wrong," nor his wife's soothing remarks made a dent in his fear.

If we peeked inside Ray's skull, what would we see? Certainly negative activation of his emotional brain, since he became very anxious as soon as he laid eyes on the new scanner on his desk. Because of the change in the room layout, Ray felt like his world was knocked out of orbit. Right after the anxiety centers of his brain signaled his basal ganglia and frontal lobes, his mind went into "OCD mode," in which he couldn't organize his thoughts or arrive at a reasonable plan of action, and his basal ganglia would not "let him off the hook" by modulating or suppressing his excessive nervous behaviors and thoughts. Ray was immobilized, his mental wheels spinning. The results were his compulsive attempts to rearrange the objects on his desk until they "felt right" and the obsessive doubts and misgivings that bothered his mind. Try as he might, though, Ray couldn't restore his equilibrium. Finally, his wife persuaded him to tear himself away after more than an hour, but he was still upset.

The Psychology of OCD

Psychologists Gail Steketee and David Barlow underscore the extremely disturbing quality of obsessive thinking and the catastrophic reactions precipitated in people with OCD. Obsessive thoughts can evoke a phobic or panic reaction, along with the conviction that the bizarre and alien thoughts must be avoided or resisted at all cost.

Psychologist Adrian Wells proposes that *negative beliefs* and *worries about intrusive thoughts* are central factors for OCD-type obsessions. These disturbing patterns of thinking are linked to compulsive behaviors impelled by urges to avoid or neutralize the anxiety that actually wind up adding to it. As we learned in our discussion of phobias, as long as you practice *avoidance* by staying

---

Brain Scan Evidence of Effectiveness of Medication and Therapy

Controlled brain scan research indicates that OCD is associated with hyperactivity in the orbital-frontal region of the brain and to a lesser extent with the caudate nucleus in the basal ganglia. Findings from several studies show that *successful treatment (either behavior therapy or SRI/SSRI medication) results in normalization of activity in these regions, with changes in OCD symptoms correlated with changes in the brain."* (Italics ours.)

These studies provide strong evidence that behavior therapy triggers changes in brain biochemistry *identical* to those resulting from medication treatment.

Steketee & Barlow, 2002; Baxter et al., 1992; Steketee & Piggott, 1999, p. 62

away from what you fear, you continue to miss the opportunity to learn that you can be safe in its presence. A woman who fears contamination may avoid hospitals, while a man who fears harming someone else may avoid sharp objects.

Neutralization, a mechanism commonly mentioned in discussion of OCD, is an attempt to "put an obsession right" by canceling the effects of a thought or action or doing something to prevent a feared outcome. Washing, checking, and hoarding are examples of *overt* neutralization, and mental ritualizing through such activities as compulsive praying, reciting ditties, or counting are examples of *covert* neutralization. Like avoidance, neutralization fails to diminish fears overall.

How People with OCD Worry Themselves Sick About Intrusive Thoughts

1. As we discussed earlier, attempts to use thought suppression to silence disturbing, unwanted thoughts can actually *increase* their frequency and intensity.

2. Obsessive "mechanisms" promote increased overawareness of disconcerting intrusive thoughts and images. Rumination, efforts to "tear one's thoughts away" by creating distractions, and attempts to erase bad thoughts by neutralizing (counting, compulsive praying, or reciting ritualized phrases) actually draw mental focus to the intrusion and so increase distress. These mechanisms "sensitize" the anxious person to intrusions, because disturbing feelings so regularly accompany intrusions that they become increasingly prominent and consistent and thus grow more likely to occur.

3. Thought suppression and mental neutralizing are counterproductive efforts to cope with the disturbing thoughts and images of OCD, resulting instead in increasing symptoms and loss of control. Instead of relieving anxiety, activities such as checking, rituals, ordering, repeating, and washing or cleaning become associated with a widening array of stimuli and actions.

Fortunately, we know more about effective treatment programs for OCD than about its precise causes. Our discussion in the next chapter will be limited to the nature and treatment of its milder forms, and we refer the reader to appendix G for a list of supplemental readings and sources of referral for psychotherapy treatment and help for more severe cases.

Chapter Thirteen

Treating Obsessions and Compulsions

Remember that great line from the *Zorro* TV series (or was it the *Lone Ranger*)? After he rescues the meek and the innocent, our hero rides away, and the announcer intones, "He disappears as mysteriously as he came." We wish the same could be said of OCD. Its onset is so insidious that it seems like one day it ought to just glide away. However, if you suffer from OCD, you have probably stopped waiting for obsessions and rituals simply to vanish.

People who develop OCD wait an average of ten years before seeking treatment, due to lack of public awareness, hopes for spontaneous recovery, and the intensity of their embarrassment about having it. OCD has a quite chronic course, although it sometimes remits spontaneously and is very responsive to the kinds of treatment now available. It is often misdiagnosed or unrecognized by mental health personnel, and sufferers often have managed to conceal their fears and compulsions for many years. An average of six years pass after diagnosis before a person with OCD receives appropriate treatment.

As table 13.1 shows, the rate of improvement of several different types of treatment for OCD is quite high. The recovery rate via medication treatment that we discuss near the end of this chapter is nearly as high as those from exposure and ritual prevention treatment (ERP), a rigorous form of cognitive-behavioral therapy (CBT), and a combination of ERP and med-

Table 13.1

TYPES AND OUTCOMES OF TREATMENT FOR OCD

Type of Treatment	Improvement Rate	Long-Term Improvement	Comments
No treatment	25–71% spontaneous recovery rate	14–61% stay the same or improve gradually	15% get progressively worse
Exposure and ritual prevention (ERP)	80–90%	75% maintain their improvement	About 20% relapse; about 25% aren't able to utilize ERP
Medication: SRI or SSRI	60–80% improve 20–40% in their OC symptoms	70–90% relapse rate within a few weeks after medication is discontinued	Medication generally controls OCD only as long as it is taken and does not cure it.
ERP plus Medication	Same as ERP	Same as ERP but relapse rate for medication is drastically lower for people who have also completed ERP	Since the effective medications are antidepressant, the efficacy of combined treatment is enhanced for OCD sufferers with concurrent major depression

Adapted from Steketee and Piggott, 1999, pp. 2–3

ication. However, 70 to 90 percent of the individuals who treat their OCD with *medication only* relapse after it is discontinued, as opposed to only 20 percent of those who complete ERP or who receive a combination of medication and ERP.

We will help you develop a repertoire of CBT techniques adapted from the evidenced-based self-help literature to help you begin to take control of your OCD. The techniques and strategies that we introduce will be equally applicable to "non-OCD but OCD-type" obsessions and compulsions—thoughts and behaviors that are anxiety-driven and disturbing but not of the magnitude of full-fledged OCD.

The input of a therapist, trusted friend, or concerned family member may be needed in order to gain a realistic viewpoint on this disturbing disorder. By researching the facts and available treatments and informing the OCD sufferer of their findings, significant others can help relieve worry and confusion and assist in steering the best course.

In order to progress toward recovery, it's necessary to face one's fears throughout the work on OCD and keep challenging fears and avoidance. Fear can be more unsettling when we are alone, and the threat presented by *this* monster in the cave affects many people profoundly and for years. Work on relief of obsessions and compulsions can be disconcerting because rethinking them and changing behaviors essentially requires you to practice a lot of "obsession exposure." We encourage you to rely on the support and consultation of significant others whenever necessary, and especially whenever you become uncomfortably anxious.

Edna Foa and Reid Wilson are recognized experts on self-help and therapy for OCD. They recommend cognitive-behavioral therapy treatment with a mental health professional for individuals who spend two or more hours a day contending with OCD, and also for any OCD sufferers who really cannot accept the idea that their thoughts and behavior may be irrational. For people with these types and this extent of discomfort, medication is also worthwhile to consider, or even treatment in an intensive, specialized setting.

In the following sections we will touch upon the important elements of empirically validated treatments and also introduce a number of procedures that our clinical experience indicates are helpful. In order to cover the widest range of effective self-help, psychopharmacological, and therapist-assisted treatment, however, we recommend two books with effective self-help sections for exposure and ritual prevention written by leading scientists and researchers into the nature and treatment of OCD: *Stop Obsessing* by Edna Foa and Reid Wilson and *When Once Is Not Enough* by Gail Steketee and Kerrin White. For people who respond best to books on tape, *Stop Obsessing* is also available as an audiotape set.

When to Seek Professional Therapy

- When a person with OCD spends two or more hours a day contending with his disorder

- If an OCD sufferer or significant others believe he may have delusions or another psychosis as part of his condition

- If an OCD sufferer has a concurrent problem with major depressive disorder

- When a person who has significant OCD cannot accept the idea that his thoughts and behavior may be irrational

- When an OCD condition does not respond to self-help efforts, the treatment techniques in this chapter, or medication treatment, and especially if it gets worse

- For intense exposure/ritual prevention therapy (see pp. 296–299)

Beginning OCD Treatment by Taking On the Four Challenges

In order to tackle OCD in an effective, minimally anxiety-provoking way, begin with skills you can develop in order to impart *a greater sense of self-control*. In *Stop Obsessing,* Foa and Wilson present "the Four Challenges," a cogent framework for beginning skill building. The first three address obsessions and will be discussed in the course of the next few pages. The fourth challenge deals with rituals, which we will explore later in this chapter.

The Four Challenges

1. Become determined to conquer your problem.

2. Accept your obsessions instead of resisting them.

3. Gain the perspective that your obsessions are irrational.

4. Consider that ritualizing is not the only way to reduce your distress.

Challenge #1: Become determined to conquer your problem. This challenge reflects the necessity of making a conscious decision to devote the necessary energy, persistence, and self-discipline to your efforts to overcome OCD. Overcoming even mild OCD will take quite a bit of work.

Is this a good time to work on overcoming your OCD? Yes? Are you quite sure? Well, then, clear the decks (and your schedule). Plan to devote significant time and effort—often at least five hours a week—to your treatment program over the next month or two. It's probably unwise to start working on OCD at the same time that you are implementing other major self-improvement efforts like weight management, smoking cessation, or stopping alcohol or drug use. If you have a problem with major depression, get treated for it first. Arrange for the cooperation or assistance of friends or family in your endeavor as needed.

Next, turn your attention to *Challenge #2: Accept your obsessions instead of resisting them.* Though many individuals with OCD are aware when they are going through symptoms, as a prerequisite for recovery it is extremely useful to *actively* recognize and accept when episodes of obsessing and ritualizing are occurring. Challenge #2 involves two main steps:

1. *Actively and consistently* identify *your obsessive thoughts and compulsions whenever they occur.* To help you become most objective, bring your old friend the "personal anxiety technologist" (your ally from the panic treatment chapter) onto the scene and utilize the Rituals and Obsessions Record on page 274 to organize your data, as described below. We recommend that you begin *now* to label your obsessions and compulsions/rituals and continue to do so consistently.

    On the surface, this may sound easy enough. When you're counting, cleaning, ordering, or hoarding, just say to yourself or out loud: "I'm ritualizing," "I'm acting compulsively," or "It's my OCD." When you notice you are repeatedly going over the disturbing possible consequences of making a mistake or not checking thoroughly, or when you ruminate over anxiety-provoking impulses or images, just remark to yourself, "I'm obsessing."

    When you *do* try labeling, however, you'll discover why it's called a challenge. You see, it's very difficult to do anything therapeutic, however small, while obsessing or ritualizing, because your emotional brain is trying to force you to continue your "anxiety program."

What Not *to Do with Obsessions*

When you notice that you are obsessing, *do* try to identify obsessions by labeling them explicitly; but *don't* succumb to the temptations to try to make your obsessions disappear on the spot or try to snatch your mind away from them! Start teaching yourself not to waste energy by trying to silence obsessions, because *they are not obedient to your will.* Don't order them to stop, and try to persuade other people in your life to cease urging you to "exert force" on your obsessions as well. Attempt to refrain from distracting your mind, too, at least not until after you have labeled your obsessions. These mental maneuvers amount to a futile game of hide-and-seek that you won't ultimately win: Research has demonstrated that such "neutralization" or "thought suppression" ploys have a paradoxical effect, in that they actually *energize* obsessive thinking.

Just to squeeze in a small labeling comment during an episode is a real accomplishment. Try it—and then try again and again! Remember: Be determined!

If you have problems identifying your obsession thoughts and compulsions, Gail Steketee and Kerrin White suggest a simple method: Notice the events, ideas, or situations that increase your anxiety and lead to your compulsions to ritualize. Most likely, you try to *avoid* these anxiety triggers, so recognition of what you avoid is another indicator that you have spotted an obsessive thought or image.

Whenever you perform a ritual, *trace it back* to the thoughts and images that preceded or triggered it. Record your rituals, the situations in which you perform them, and the obsessive thoughts and images that are linked to them, in worksheet 13.1. Allow just moments to do your recording—try not to obsess! Also, jot down anything that you think you are probably avoiding by performing rituals or obsessing.

2. *Journal or detail your obsessions, either in writing or on a tape.* Be as specific and accurate as possible. For instance, Kristen ruminated about members of her study group being badly hurt if she didn't clean off every speck of dirt in her kitchen. She felt that she would

Worksheet 13.1
RITUALS AND OBSESSIONS RECORD

Rituals I Perform	Situation: Who? What? Where?	Avoiding Anything? (If yes, what?)	Obsessive Thought or Image
Arranging and rearranging the mail on my desk	Paying bills in my office	Yes—thinking about paying to send our daughter to college	I'm afraid I'm failing my children.
Humming Jim Morrison music	Cruising the nightclubs	Trying not to touch or brush against anyone	There's so much dirt and so many germs in public places.

be responsible for the harm that befell them, although she couldn't say how that would work. So she wrote in her OCD diary: "I fear that members of my study group will be badly hurt because of me if I don't clean my kitchen thoroughly."

Recording your obsessions signifies your acceptance that they are occurring. Also, a load will lift from your mind and off your shoulders once you put them on paper or tape, because no longer are they simply swirling relentlessly in your head. Then, when you are *not* having an episode of OCD, you can review what you've written more objectively.

Challenge #3: Gain the perspective that your obsessions are irrational. You might meet this challenge easily if you already recognize that your obsessions are anxious misinterpretations of a triggering event or situation. During OC moments you exaggerate the likelihood of what you fear and the "badness" of its consequences. If you know that your obsessions are irrational, start adding this information, too, to your labeling of obsessions. When they occur, you could start by saying, "I'm thinking obsessively and irrationally," or more simply, just "Obsession. Irrational." Do this as consistently as possible.

Do you doubt whether your obsessions are irrational? We recommend that you revisit worksheet 12.1 on pages 260–261. Following the examples, copy the entries describing your own disturbing thoughts and images into column 2 of worksheet 13.2 on the following page. In column 1, write the subject or situation that triggered each of your obsessions. And very important: In column 3, write down what a person *without* OCD would make of the same subject or situation that concerns you. If you aren't sure, we suggest you consult with other people about how they would view this kind of subject or situation.

Rethinking Obsessions

In order to implement Challenge #3, you may choose to do more than recognize the irrationality of obsessions: You can also rethink them. You already began to rethink your obsessions when you filled out worksheet 13.2 and wrote down what a person without OCD would think.

A person with OCD is likely to irrationally blame himself for a bad situation or feel guilty about a problem for which he would *not* blame others in comparable positions. This type of misinterpretation is known as a *double standard,* a "very OCD" thinking error that results from taking on too much personal responsibility.

For instance, Ms. Wilner blames herself for her daughter developing

Worksheet 13.2
ARE OBSESSIONS REALLY IRRATIONAL?

1. Subject or situation that is obsessed about	2. The disturbing thoughts or images	3. How would a person *without* OCD be likely to think of or picture the situation?
Use of the toilet at Luke's home.	Microorganisms are left on the toilet seat after every use. Luke fears his children will be contaminated and infected with terrible diseases as a result of contact with the toilet seat.	The amount of microbes is minuscule and unlikely to cause health problems. The chances of anybody catching anything are very small as long as the seat is cleaned every few days and any obvious mess is cleaned up.
Ms. Wilner blames herself for her daughter developing breast cancer and believes that everyone will condemn her.	"If I had never given birth to a daughter, I would not have transmitted the gene that predisposed her to cancer."	If the daughter of a dear friend developed breast cancer, she would not think that she had caused her daughter's illness and neither would Ms. Wilner. Ms. Wilner utilizes a double standard here.

breast cancer and believes that everyone will condemn her. Her therapist asks her to consider a hypothetical situation: Would she blame a dear friend whose child contracted cancer? By answering her question in the negative, Ms. Wilner realizes that she was applying a harsh standard to herself while holding her friend blameless. Her therapist enabled her to recognize her double standard, thus exonerating her guilt and relieving her anxiety.

In rethinking your obsessions, think of them as being made up of two components:

- *The tangible source* of the fear

- *The dreaded consequence* of failing to ritualize or otherwise neutralize the threat

Intrusive thoughts are considered the tangible sources of the fear. For instance, wouldn't it be frightening to have the intrusive thought, "I could drop this infant down that escalator?" *Intrusive thoughts trigger obsessions by giving rise to automatic anxious thoughts* like "I must want to kill babies." These thoughts simply link intrusions and dreaded consequences, but the linkages they create are fraught with anxiety because the person who is obsessing imputes bad, mad, or dangerous motives to herself.

To rethink obsessions, identify the intrusive thoughts that raise your anxiety. Reason with yourself about them, and evaluate the likelihood and actual severity of the consequences you dread.

Rethink automatic anxious thoughts by identifying them and changing them into realistic, reasoned-out "nondistressing thoughts." To that end, we reintroduce you to the rethinking strategies of ABC analysis, examination of the evidence, and reestimation so you may apply any of them or a combination of techniques to your work with OCD.

ABC ANALYSIS

Review "ABC analysis"—analyzing anxiety in terms of its *a*ctivity, *b*adness, and *c*ontrollability—on pages 228–229. Then compare your responses in column 2 of worksheet 13.2 with those of a person without OCD in column 3 in terms of the activity, badness, and controllability of the anxiety-provoking aspects of the situation. In the example above, for instance, do Luke's thoughts and images seem like a more accurate assessment of the activity, badness, and controllability of actual microbes than that of the person without OCD, or are they less realistic? Does momentary contact of a person's body with a toilet seat usually produce hoards of aggressive, highly toxic microbes, or is the actual scenario probably far lower key? How do *your* responses in column 2 compare with your entries in column 3? If you find your thoughts to be even slightly less accurate than a non-OCD person's would be, try to exercise your valor and determination by labeling your obsessions as irrational despite any lingering doubts you might have.

EXAMINATION OF THE EVIDENCE FOR YOUR OBSESSIONS

Also in chapter 11, we discussed "examining the evidence" for your anxious thoughts in order to relieve their dreadful power. *Although obsessions are very frightening, at their root they are no more than anxious thoughts and catastrophe theories.* Their capacity to stimulate anxiety may diminish as you think carefully and reasonably about them.

Follow these steps in order to examine the evidence behind your obsessions:

1. First, write out your intrusive thoughts and feared consequences as clearly as possible in column 1 of worksheet 13.3 on page 281. Utilize the blank worksheet on page 281 following the example of the completed worksheet that precedes it on page 280.

2. Next, review the following list of thinking errors associated with *intrusive thoughts* that people with OCD commonly make. Identify any thinking errors that you might be making and enter them into column 2 of worksheet 13.3.
   - Exaggeration of the importance of the thoughts or images
   - Overestimation of danger
   - Misestimation of dire consequences
   - Need for perfect certainty
   - Need for perfect control over thinking
   - Excessively strong sense of personal responsibility

3. Once you have identified your anxious thinking errors, answer the following three questions to help reevaluate the accuracy or inaccuracy of your obsessions:
   - *Past Experience*—Has what I'm worrying about happened in the past? For example, in the past how often has someone died because I haven't bathed thoroughly?

- *General Rules*—Does what I am worrying about usually happen?
- *Alternate Explanation*—What other explanations are there?

Put all relevant answers to these questions in column 3, and *reason with yourself* about the anxious thinking errors and evidence you've amassed for your obsessive thoughts.

4. In column 4, write out all the modified, compromise, or alternative thoughts that you come up with.

REESTIMATION: CALCULATING CUMULATIVE RISK

Although catastrophic images materialize automatically and full-blown in the obsessive person's mind, in real life the bad events that people obsess about seldom just come out of the blue. *Bad events are often the "cumulative consequence" of a series of mishaps.* For example, a match dropping from someone's hand does not turn instantly into a three-alarm blaze. A number of events, each depending on the one before it, actually intervene between most initial or triggering events and "total catastrophes." Each "mini-event" is only so likely to occur, despite the anxious person's sense of imminent danger.

Calculating the *cumulative risk* of a catastrophe occurring is a reestimation technique tailor-made for the extensive catastrophic ruminations of OCD. Here is a method of calculating the cumulative risk of an event occurring:

1. Estimate the "anxious probability" of the feared event—your rating of the likelihood of its occurrence when you feel the most anxious.

2. Analyze the sequence of events that would lead to the feared catastrophe.

3. Estimate the chance of *each of the events* in the sequence occurring separately.

4. Compute the cumulative risk by multiplying the chance of each of the events occurring by the chance of the previous event in the sequence occurring.

5. Compare the cumulative risk of the full sequence of events occurring—the overall product of the multiplication steps—with your original estimate of the likelihood of catastrophe.

Worksheet 13.3
Examining the Evidence for Your Obsessions and Transforming Anxiety Propositions

1. Obsessions and Anxiety Propositions: Intrusive Thoughts and Feared Consequences	2. What Are My Anxious Misinterpretations?	3. Replies to Questions for Examining the Evidence	4. Modified, Compromise, or Alternative Thoughts and Realistic Propositions
Ms. Wilner blames herself for her daughter developing breast cancer and believes that everyone will condemn her.	Excessively strong sense of personal responsibility	I couldn't have caused my daughter's cancer, and rarely do people blame the parents for their children's cancer.	My sense of responsibility is excessive, because it's very unlikely to be my fault, and other people don't blame me.
Luke fears his children will be contaminated and infected with terrible diseases as a result of contact with the toilet seat at his home.	Overestimation of danger Misestimation of dire consequences	No one has ever gotten infected from our toilet seat. I've hardly ever heard of that happening. Microorganisms probably don't get a foothold by that means.	Probably they could pick up no more than a few microbes, and they won't pay bad health consequences.
Kayla thinks she's going crazy because thoughts of gaudily clad chickens cross her mind when studying for finals. She avoids taking tests because she's afraid that her craziness will prevent her from scoring 100%, and that would be awful.	Exaggeration of the importance of intrusive images Need for perfect control over thinking Need for extreme certainty	Alternatively, the chicken images could be just plain intrusive thoughts, not signs of craziness. She generally has at least *some* distracting thoughts when studying. She knows many people who don't get 100% without it turning catastrophic.	The distracting images are reducing her efficiency at studying, and there are a number of reasonable explanations for them. Her inconsistent studying probably won't earn her a perfect grade, but that's not the end of the world.

Worksheet 13.3

EXAMINING THE EVIDENCE FOR YOUR OBSESSIONS AND TRANSFORMING ANXIETY PROPOSITIONS

1. Obsessions and Anxiety Propositions: Intrusive Thoughts and Feared Consequences	2. What Are My Anxious Misinterpretations?	3. Replies to Questions for Examining the Evidence	4. Modified, Compromise, or Alternative Thoughts and Realistic Propositions

We will illustrate use of the technique with an example of a woman who told her therapist that it would be her fault if a park burned down because she failed to check properly and make sure her cigarette was out. She felt compelled to check again and again to make sure it was extinguished. She estimated a probability of 60 percent (or odds of 3 in 5) that this would occur. However, when her therapist helped her calculate the cumulative risk of her burning down the park, the odds were much different. He first asked her to evaluate the odds of her not putting out her cigarette properly, and she estimated that there was a 1 in 10 chance that she would do this. Table 13.2 illustrates the rest of the steps in the calculation.

As you can see, although her anxious estimate of the odds that she would be responsible for setting the park on fire because she didn't put out her cigarette was 3 in 5, her *realistic reestimate* of the odds was 1 in 10,000,000.

Now you try it. Choose a situation or two where you obsess about the possibility of causing terrible consequences that you'd feel responsible for—perhaps where you feel a compulsion to check or an impulse to return and undo—and use worksheet 13.4 below to help you calculate the cumulative risk.

If you have been reestimating the cumulative risk and rethinking obsessions as we have been describing, then you have been creating *mental representations of the obsessional process* and trying out various strategies for working with your fears. You've been remembering situations where you had intrusive thoughts and images that provoked your anxiety, and you worked on thinking differently about them. Rethinking misinterpretations of obsessions actually amounts to an *imaginal exposure technique*.

Table 13.2

EXAMPLE OF CUMULATIVE RISK CALCULATION

Step	Chance	Cumulative Risk
1. I didn't put my cigarette out.	1/10	1/10
2. A little spark falls on some dry leaves.	1/10	1/100 (= 1/10 × 1/10)
3. The leaves catch fire.	1/10	1/1,000 (= 1/10 × 1/100)
4. The underbrush starts burning, and I don't notice the fire right away.	1/100	1/100,000 (= 1/100 × 1/1,000)
5. I notice the fire when it is burning out of hand, and I can't do anything about it.	1/100	1/10,000,000 (= 1/100,000 × 1/100)

Worksheet 13.4
CUMULATIVE RISK CALCULATOR

Step	Chance	Cumulative Risk
1.		
2.		
3.		
4.		
5.		

Cumulative Risk = (step 1 chance) × (step 2 chance) × (step 3 chance) × (step 4 chance) × (step 5 chance) = _____

Have you "taken bites out of your anxiety" as you rethought your obsessions? Have these techniques helped relieve your anxiety and started to weaken OCD's hold on you? If change has been too difficult or uncomfortable, if excessive anxiety has been provoked, or if your progress seems very halting or nonexistent, we suggest that you consider seeking professional mental health help. On the other hand, if you have been progressing and beginning to improve, we congratulate you.

Using Exposure Techniques

The techniques described in the following sections emphasize work with obsessions and compulsions that deliberately and gradually stimulates a measure of anxiety. The difference between these techniques and the ones described above—rethinking obsessions and reestimating cumulative risk—is primarily one of emphasis. Exposure—direct confrontation with obsessive fears—is apt to relieve anxiety most effectively when you specifically try to *provoke some anxiety during practices and use the techniques to reduce the level of discomfort while controlling or preventing rituals.* When you cannot accomplish these steps during a practice, try again, move back or on to a different technique, or get assistance from family, friends, or a professional.

ANXIOUS THINKING ERRORS, OBSESSIONS, AND META-WORRIES

In chapter 11, we studied special rethinking techniques for contending with "meta-worries," psychologist Adrian Wells's term for fearful concerns about worrying too much or too often (such as "If I am worrying this much, then I must be out of control" or ". . . then I'm losing my mind"). Anxious thinking errors of intrusive thoughts resemble meta-worries. They are virtually "obsessions about obsessions," the emotional brain's automatic reactions to the disturbing quality of intrusive thoughts and images.

In earlier chapters, we developed the skills to reverse engineer the anxious misinterpretations that occur during panic and phobias and make them more realistic. As with phobias, anxiety proposition is a useful description of the thinking processes in OCD. Recall that an anxiety proposition links specific anxiety-provoking thoughts and images with specific feared consequences. Here is the form that OCD anxiety propositions take:

> In obsessive anxiety propositions: Intrusive thoughts and images are subject to anxious thinking errors that result in dread of feared consequences.

Now that we've introduced this useful way of thinking about obsessions, how can you practice transforming the anxiety propositions that you obsess about into reality propositions?

OBSESSING PERIODS

Set aside regular obsessing periods to *actively rethink* your feared thoughts— your obsessive anxiety propositions. During these obsession exposure periods (based on the concept of "worry periods" explained in detail in chapter 11), implement the cognitive strategies of your choice to help modify your anxiety propositions into more realistic propositions. Also, we suggest that you implement "cue-controlled relaxation" (see pp. 80–81), a simple but generally effective means of modulating your anxious discomfort to help make your obsessing periods manageable and productive.

Before each obsessing period, choose the obsessions you would like to think about and use your time to think hard and steadily about them. Since this is *exposure* rather than *rethinking* practice, deliberately try to *provoke anxiety about your obsessions before you start to work on modifying your thinking.* Think actively about everything that provokes your anxiety while obsessing—intrusions, feared consequences, and anxiety propositions—*before* relieving your anxiety. Then, don't ruminate, but instead devote your energy to correcting thinking errors. Apply all the skills you know: relieve your anxiety through use of cognitive restructuring techniques for working with obsessions, anxious thinking errors, and anxiety propositions, and modulate your anxious discomfort with cue-controlled relaxation.

Once you start to progress, as evidenced by your decreasing anxious discomfort, keep working with a particular obsession until you have reduced your level of discomfort by about 50 percent. We suggest you schedule obsessing periods that last at least twenty to thirty minutes a day. Set an alarm to signal when to stop and do something different afterward—preferably an enjoyable, change-of-pace activity. Finish up each obsessing period by noting the techniques that helped the most and writing down your modified thoughts.

Besides demonstrating the value of examining the evidence for your obsessions, worksheet 13.3 illustrates the transformation of anxious, obsessive propositions into realistic propositions. Utilize the blank worksheet form found on page 281 by filling in column four only after you have devoted concerted effort to rethinking your obsessions and anxiety propositions.

Acceptance of Uncertainty in Exposure to Obsessions

Note what the realistic propositions in Column 3 *do not say.* Ms. Wilner is *not* perfectly absolved of responsibility; there is *no guarantee* that Luke's children will be microbe-free or that Kayla's mind is so clear and strong that she can be sure to ace the test. After Ms. Wilner, Luke, and Kayla work successfully to relieve the anxiety of obsessions by correcting their thinking errors and exposure during obsessing periods, a measure of safety, sanity, and fairness is likely to be as good as it gets for them.

Acceptance theory rests on the recognition that few things in our lives are certain, and you can train yourself to accept the fact that you possess neither perfect control over outside events nor your emotional reactions to them. From this point of view, your anxiety is relieved by gaining acceptance of the reality that you cannot be totally safe, clean, and morally impeccable. At the same time, it *is* possible to be safe most of the time, clean enough to avoid contagion or infection most of the time, and moral enough to lead a generally virtuous life. The benefits of acceptance might be augmented by listening extensively to a loop tape on which you repeat the realistic proposition that you arrive at in your obsessing periods—such as "Even though I repeatedly touch unclean surfaces, I am uncertain whether I am actually contaminating my family."

DIRECT TESTS OF ANXIETY PROPOSITIONS

Beside rethinking obsessions and challenging anxiety propositions by reasoning with yourself, direct testing of anxiety propositions can be an effective way to weaken obsessive fears. With this technique, experiments are devised to see if the frightening or catastrophic event predicted by an anxiety proposition is borne out in reality. For example, Ray was obsessing about the proper placement of the new scanner in his computer nook. He decided to test his fear that family members would fall ill if the scanner wasn't "correctly" placed by letting his teenager carelessly plop the scanner down every day in a different site of her choosing and finding out whether relatives got sick. By testing whether or not his frightening prediction came true, Ray could gather evidence that enabled him to form more realistic, alternative propositions about his obsession, such as the following: "It makes little difference where the scanner is placed" and "When I let my daughter arrange the computer nook, I feel much less anxious," and "There doesn't seem to be a connection between placement of the scanner and family members' health."

Let's consider an assortment of behavioral experiments with the common anxiety proposition that *thinking repeatedly about an event can make it more likely to happen or actually make it happen.* This proposition would apply for positive as well as negative outcomes.

Mark Freeston and his colleagues gave examples of a couple of their clients' successes in being treated behaviorally to help modify this anxiety proposition. One client bought a Quebec provincial lottery ticket and then devoted an obsessing period every day for a week to imagining winning the

Worksheet 13.6
TESTING A FEAR THAT THOUGHTS CAN KILL OR HARM

Behavioral Experimental Hypothesis	Feared Outcome	Anxious Probability of Feared Outcome	Anxiety Level	Actual Outcome
Thinking about the toaster breaking down 100 times this week will cause it to break down.	The toaster breaks down.	40%	Low	Toaster doesn't break down.
Willing my neighbor's noisy dog to die will kill her.	The dog dies.	30%	Medium	The doggy lives to bark on.

jackpot, but he didn't win. Another client agreed to select a functioning appliance to target with repetitive thoughts about a negative outcome. She chose the breakdown of her toaster, thinking about it a hundred times a day for a week, but it continued to work. The actual outcomes of these experiments were then compared to their clients' subjective predictions. On the basis of these comparisons, they helped their clients generate the realistic proposition about their obsessive thoughts that repeated thinking about unlikely events, whether positive or negative, has no actual effect nor dreadful consequence.

Peter McLean and Sheila Woody give the example of a client who believes that her thoughts can kill. Her anxious thinking error involves *an excessively strong sense of personal responsibility* for images of destruction that intrude into her everyday thoughts. She is first asked to kill a houseplant with her thoughts, then the goldfish, the neighbor's noisy dog, and finally someone she knows—all by thinking. Throughout these practices, she agrees not to ritualize, and so she refrains from touching the religious pendant that she wears on a chain around her neck. When none of the experimental subjects died because of her thoughts, the client was able to think more realistically about her anxiety proposition and gain more conviction that her destructive mental images do not actually produce fatalities.

INTENSIVE EXPOSURE WITH IMAGINAL EXPOSURE TAPES

Intensive exposure to obsessions with imaginal exposure tapes involves listening carefully, repeatedly, and at length to vivid narrative descriptions of the situations, activities, or events that trigger your obsessions while refraining from ritualizing during practices, and eventually in between practices, as well. The purpose of this technique is to stimulate graduated amounts of OCD-type anxiety so that the OCD sufferer can build strong mental habits of coping effectively with his fears.

Through preparation and use of precautions, intensive imaginal exposure practices can generally be manageable and productive. Since this procedure is *literally* anxiety provoking, people often enlist their family's or friends' support or enter professional mental health treatment before initiating this phase of treatment.

The biggest obstacle to intensive exposure is fear that tackling obsessions directly could "do you in"—drive you crazy or cause the types of harm or the catastrophe you have felt driven to prevent through your OCD. Although intensive exposure is challenging, you can do this.

- Review how far you've come in overcoming your obsessions and compulsions.

- Recognize the extent to which you have proven that the thinking that drives your obsessions is irrational and fear-based and that you can relieve your anxiety by means other than ritualizing.

Hesitation to embark upon a course of intensive imaginal exposure is just another behavioral freeze due to anxiety. Like so many times before, your mind may initially reel with catastrophic possibilities; but haven't you surmounted enough obstacles and worked with yourself long and well enough to relieve your fears and control your urges to act out of anxiety?

If you feel ready to try out intensive imaginal exposure, here is what to do:

1. *Carefully inventory the situations, intrusive thoughts, and feared consequences that currently result in your episodes of OCD. List them and describe each anxiety proposition as clearly as you can, including plenty of sharp detail.* For instance, "Every time I drive near the woods of Cypress Park, I mistake bumps in the road for animals I've accidentally driven over. I fear that I've killed innocent critters and kindly people's household pets." Or, "Whenever I touch door-knobs or anything in a public restroom, I fear that I will pick up disgusting contaminants on my hands, like anthrax, Ebola, and salmonella, and transfer them to my mouth. Then I will be infected with a virulent wasting disease."

2. *Give each item a SUDs rating.* Scale your ratings from 1 (no anxiety) to 10 (the absolute maximum imaginable). (See p. 85 to brush up on this rating system.) Sequence your list so that items that produce the least significant discomfort are at the top and those that produce the most are at the bottom.

3. *Start your exposure practice with one of the least anxiety-provoking items on your hierarchy. Write out a thorough vivid description of the scene that would trigger your obsessions.* How would it smell? How would the air feel? Fresh or stale? Breezy or rank? Is it night or day? Inside or outdoors? Imagine yourself vulnerable, in an anxiety-prone state where you believe the triggering situation or events would provoke a powerful onslaught of anxious feelings. Would you be lying on the floor, alone and afraid and exhausted? Pull out all the stops in your description.

In the first of the examples above, for instance, the person preparing for exposure would write out a vivid description of finding the animals gruesomely mauled and maimed by his careless driving; being confronted and accused by agonized elderly persons, angry parents, and baleful children for his misdeeds; and arraigned and publicly humiliated. In the second example, she might describe touching foul substances from the filthy floor of a public restroom, seeing and feeling the dirt and scum on her fingers, touching her lips and face, the foul taste, and getting sick. A checker afraid of neglectfully causing a fire might describe the searing flames shooting through his building, the terrified shrieks of innocent victims, walls charring and melting; and the person with OCD being held responsible and condemned.

4. A critical element of imaginal exposure practice is active, prolonged experiencing of the anxiety with which the obsession is imbued. *Record two or three anxiety-provoking scenes that evoke the same fears onto a tape or endless loop tape* (available from audio suppliers in lengths up to six minutes). *Play the tape repeatedly or run the loop tape for the duration of the practice period you've decided on.* We suggest that you try to arrange uninterrupted time for exposure, and—like during obsessing periods—use the time exclusively for intensive work on OCD. Practices should last at least twenty minutes and as long as two hours, preferably daily, but probably not close to bedtime. Make sure you end your practices at predetermined times by setting a timer or arranging for someone to let you know when the time has elapsed.

5. If the scene you are working on produces a significant but manageable amount of anxiety, you're in the right neighborhood. *You may use any of the cognitive techniques we've discussed to work on your anxiety during practices, but keep your main focus on the anxious discomfort.* Modulate your tension with brief, cue-controlled relaxation, but promptly resume working with the anxiety. Continue practice with a particular obsession until your discomfort drops to 50 percent or less of what it was originally. Then move on to the next scene on your hierarchy or to any obsession that you'd like to target that provokes at least somewhat greater discomfort.

6. *Do not ritualize during exposure practices.* If rituals are a part of your OCD, *response (or ritual) prevention* (see pp. 296–298) will play a very important part in your recovery. At least control and limit your compulsions between practices or eliminate them entirely if you can. Use prompting and shaping to help you. People often utilize the support and assistance of others in setting up the environment and reminding them to limit ritualizing or not to ritualize, and they often wait until they are engaged in psychotherapy with a mental health professional before instituting this practice. We suggest you utilize the guidelines for support people described on pages 143–145.

Altering Rituals

Exposure techniques for confronting obsessions go hand in hand with techniques for altering compulsions or rituals. Again, rituals are activities or behaviors geared to reduce the anxious distress produced by obsessing. In order to enrich your strategic repertoire for relieving OCD, we begin this section by introducing you to the fourth challenge from Foa and Wilson's *Stop Obsessing.*

Challenge #4 is to consider that ritualizing is not the only way to reduce your distress. We will assist you in tackling this challenge by helping you learn to gradually and systematically alter rituals in order to render them more controllable. Then we will discuss useful, double-barreled approaches that couple techniques for altering rituals with exposure to manageable amounts of obsessive anxiety.

RESIST YOUR COMPULSIONS

You *can* resist your compulsions to ritualize, and it would therapeutically be in your interest to do so. We suggest that you start by targeting one or several of your compulsions—checking, counting, cleaning, or ordering—for *ritual postponement treatment.* Recall "worry postponement" from chapter 11? We introduced you to this behavioral technique as a means of controlling tenacious worries by intentionally putting them off until scheduled worry periods, which are very similar to the obsessing periods.

You can utilize postponement to enhance your control of compulsive behaviors. Here's how. Choose certain specific rituals to target. When you have an impulse to clean, check, order, count, or repeat, make the decision to postpone carrying it out for a certain period of time. Start by postponing for just a few seconds. Time each interval, and when it's over decide either to ritualize *right then* or to postpone again. Try to postpone the ritual(s) you are targeting that day *consistently*—each and every time you feel the urge to do them. After you have consistently postponed particular rituals for a few seconds for one day, the next day increase the length of your postponements to between thirty seconds and three minutes, and the following day, to between five and thirty minutes.

You are likely to find that you begin forgetting to perform certain rituals after you have postponed them often and long enough. Should this development occur, it does not portend memory impairment. Rather, it represents your successful use of ritual postponement for anxiety reduction, since postponements diminish the sense of urgency that helps sustain ritualizing.

Accomplish as much as you comfortably can. Through successful use of postponement, you are implementing Challenge #4, since *you've begun reducing anxious distress while decreasing reliance on rituals.*

PLAY WITH RITUALS

Since compulsions are attempts to relieve great anxiety, they are carried out intensely. Like safety signals for generalized anxiety, the anxious person vests in them the power to neutralize or undo obsessions and often has high hopes for relief. Compulsions generally make minimal sense and are quite limited in their capacity to relieve anxiety. While it's safety wise to check one's mirrors while driving, checking five times before putting the car in gear is no longer sensible and garners no extra benefit. We should wash our hands after handling dirty diapers or cleaning up a mess, but should not use up half an hour to do it properly nor harm ourselves by rubbing or bleaching our skin raw, as "cleaners" with OCD may do.

A person may be able to progress in overcoming OCD by *altering compulsions so that they are performed with less intensity*. These ways to "play with rituals" can help OCD sufferers meet Challenge #4 by accomplishing this alteration while increasing their sense of control.

Foa and Wilson introduce two self-help practices for relieving compulsions, by playing with rituals:

- *Slo-mo ritualizing:* Perform and think about rituals in slow motion.

- *Altering the details:* Change some of the specifics of your ritual. For instance, modify the sequence of specific kinds of actions, number of repetitions, setting or location, or your physical position.

We would add a third technique:

- *Speeded-up ritualizing:* You might wish to speed your rituals up. Perform them quickly, perhaps even using a timer to pace yourself.

Playing with rituals using any of these techniques enhances your sense of control because your thoughts and actions are less in the grip of your OCD. Betsy, a woman with checking rituals, was afraid of accidentally setting her apartment building on fire. She'd devoted literally thousands of hours over the past ten years to "safety checking" in her efforts to prevent her fears from turning into catastrophic reality. Because she doubted her ability to remember vital safety information, Betsy would check and recheck the controls of her stereo, TV, stove, and microwave oven, as well as all the light switches and door locks in her place, before leaving for work each weekday morning.

Betsy decided to work on relieving the intensity of her doubts by playing with rituals. After years of allowing half an hour every morning for her rituals, she started to carry out daily "slo-mo practices." Several times per morning she practiced *really looking* at the front of her stereo with all its controls and operating lights for a minute or two, and then she would s-l-o-w-l-y reach for the power switch while maintaining keen awareness of every movement and all her perceptions and sensations. She turned the control gently to the left for "off," pausing midstream to say in her mind, "Left is 'off.'" Then she turned the set on again, paused, turned it off, and repeated, "Left is *'off.'*"

EXPOSURE AND LIMITED RITUAL PREVENTION: THE CASE OF LUCINDA

Lucinda took a long time to wash her hands and face and then applied and impeccably reapplied her makeup several times a day. In her stressful workplace environment, she often had mean thoughts about her coworkers and, because of her OCD, she was immensely uncomfortable. Her mischievous thinking felt so dangerously uncontrolled that she believed that unless she washed thoroughly and made up perfectly, she would mentally cause her coworkers illnesses and accidents.

She devised an experiment in exposure therapy. She planned to restrict her washing and making up to ten minutes before work and ten minutes every three hours thereafter. In addition, for fifteen minutes every morning, during the coffee break, she would deliberately, vividly imagine two annoying coworkers getting injured or sick. By doing so, she could test out the proposition that her sarcastic thoughts about the coworkers would harm them. She also decided to "try" to injure one coworker with her thoughts by actively, mentally repeating several of her own mean, sarcastic remarks about him that made her so anxious.

Since Lucinda exercised regularly at the same gym with her coworker, she could check this "victim's" health out for herself. She recruited her boyfriend as a confederate to observe her other "victim," with whom he regularly practiced and played baseball, and he dispassionately gave Lucinda clean bills of health for the guy four times a week. Within weeks, Lucinda's obsessing and urges to ritualize decreased dramatically.

Lucinda utilized two behavioral techniques, *prompting* and *shaping,* in order to control her grooming rituals. She "prompted" herself to maintain the ten-minute limit she'd set on washing and making up by activating a timer, and she placed little reminder notes on her lip gloss and mascara to prompt her when she'd start fixing her makeup at work. She "shaped" her grooming ritual—a behavioral technique defined by psychologist Lee Baer in *Getting Control* as slowly decreasing the amount of time spent on a target behavior so that it increasingly approximates the norm—by reducing the time limit by a minute every three days. After two weeks, Lucinda was washing and touching up her makeup at work in only five minutes, which she considered normal.

In order to derive the greatest benefit from behavioral experiments like Lucinda's, the predictions and outcomes should be carefully charted, as Lucinda did, on worksheet 13.7. By this means, the person with OCD has the opportunity to discover the truth about his or her anxious misinterpretations of these particular intrusive thoughts.

Compulsive Hoarding

We have treated hoarders whose problems have fed family and marital conflicts and even led to separation and divorce. Hoarding impedes sufferers' major life endeavors, like the case of a man who couldn't move to the city where his wife found work because he couldn't discard enough of his mountainous hoard to enable a realtor to show their home. *Many hoarders doubt they have a problem* until their families become really disturbed and pressure the hoarder to discard or rearrange his collections or even to quit collecting.

When the pressure is applied, what makes hoarders anxious? Psychologists S. Rachman and Roz Shafan believe that indecisiveness and a dread of making mistakes are the prime suspects. Hoarders' indecision causes them tremendous difficulty in determining what to treasure or to trash. They dread the consequences of failing to measure up because of erroneously discarding or donating a necessary item. According to Foa and Wilson, hoarders fear the day when they would be unable to find a needed item or lack an object that is truly necessary for their well-being or peace of mind.

The case of Donna, described by Foa and Wilson, illustrates successful therapy for hoarding. Donna's therapist visited her home and disorganized her vast, carefully arranged collections in order to provide her with the opportunity for real-life exposure to disarray. After several days of exposure came several weeks of daily practice, consisting of systematically discarding items, starting with those that had no conceivable value. By the time three weeks had passed, Donna's "collectibles" were drastically reduced, and she no longer felt much distress about throwing things out.

Foa and Wilson observe that treatment for hoarding is likeliest to succeed if continuance of the compulsion threatens to force an end to an important interpersonal relationship. Psychologist Lee Baer suggests that before embarking on therapy—exposure and gradual or rapid response (or ritual) prevention—the person should spend time imagining how he would feel in the future looking back on his now satisfactorily resolved problem with hoarding as if it were a weird episode of ancient history. Psychologists Melinda Stanley and Patricia Averill stress the importance of flexibility in planning exposure to a hoarder's fears: For instance, it might be best to start eliminating stuff by practicing quickly tossing out trash from his home into a support person's Dumpster or wastebasket.

Combining Exposure and Ritual Prevention Therapy

"Exposure/Response (or Ritual) Prevention," often abbreviated as "ERP," was developed in 1966 by Victor Meyer, a British psychiatrist. The first effective treatment for OCD, ERP was initially utilized at the psychiatric hospital where a number of his patients were hospitalized. Meyer instructed the staff to prevent OCD patients' ritualizing while exposing them to the anxiety-provoking stimuli that would lead to their compulsive behavior. In his original treatment, Meyer actually had the staff turn off the water supply to the hospital ward in order to prevent a washer from washing. Patients improved significantly through his innovative approach to treatment, and the improvement in their conditions generally lasted long-term. Subsequently, numerous other mental health professionals have validated and refined his treatment. One of the changes in modern versions is that forced ritual prevention is no longer considered acceptable clinical practice.

In modern-day ERP treatment, the average optimum number of exposure sessions is twenty, occurring between daily and once a week, each session usually lasting between one and two hours. People derive the greatest benefit from very direct, realistic exposure. In quite a number of research studies, as many as three-quarters of those who complete ERP treatment are moderately to much improved.

You might wonder, if ERP is so effective, why doesn't everybody with OCD undergo it? Individuals must be very motivated for ERP treatment to be successful. They should be capable of structuring themselves consistently and tolerating several weeks of anxious discomfort. Accordingly, intensive ERP is usually carried out as part of intensive therapy, often in collaboration with a case manager. An intensive three-week ERP program is detailed in the second part of Edna Foa and Reid Wilson's book, *Stop Obsessing*.

Also, therapist-assisted exposure is more effective than self-directed exposure. The therapist can first model the exposure practice for the client to show that it can be done. Then the therapist can help persuade the client to engage in exposure to what is feared while therapy is in session. Clients collaborate with a therapist to devise a plan to undergo sessions of extended exposure to gradually intensifying aspects of their fears. Remember, a key theory of therapeutics for OCD is that [anxiety] "arousal is necessary for fear reduction" (Foa and Kozak, 1986).

Worksheet 13.7

TESTING A FEAR THAT THOUGHTS CAN HARM, COMBINED WITH PROMPTING AND SHAPING

Behavioral Experimental Hypothesis	Feared Outcome	Anxious Probability of Feared Outcome	Anxiety Level	Actual Outcome
Without ritualizing, Lucinda thinks repeatedly that her coworker will get into a car crash.	Her coworker will get hurt in an auto accident.	60%	High	Nary a hair on her head is ruffled.
The catastrophe theory or anxiety proposition that you are testing:				

In its most intensive form, the therapist and the client plan for the client (and her family or significant others, if available) to carry out complete ritual prevention—abstaining from the ritual or rituals that were temporarily relieving the fear during the active phase of the OCD. Steketee and Barlow observe that "preventing rituals that have come to be equated with everything that is safe and comfortable [requires] that the patient confront his or her worst fears." But unlike time-limited, graduated exposure to phobic anxiety, "exposure is really in effect 24 hours a day for weeks at a time . . . since patients are unable to use rituals to escape their overwhelming fears of disaster or thoughts of impending catastrophe."

Because some people with OCD cannot adhere to complete ritual prevention, therapists may conduct intensive exposure along with partial ritual prevention. For example, the number of repetitions or time spent ritualizing is reduced *slowly* or else a hierarchy of ritual prevention is established—that is, one type of ritual at a time is banned. Such "lax" ritual prevention decreases exposure to intense anxiety, mental processing of the fear, and fear reduction. It probably does not activate the curative mechanisms that intensive ERP does, so it has not proven to be very effective. When strict ritual prevention can't be tolerated, a more gradual approach may be instituted, like cognitive therapy and changing, prompting, and shaping rituals.

In ERP with a therapist, the clinician shoulders an important part of the responsibility for the OCD sufferer's progress. He or she helps the client look beneath the surface of anxiety to discover his or her core fears. The therapist models exposure practice and guides the client in implementing the program. Professional therapy can provide what may be the keys to treatment success—reassurance, dialogue, motivation, and clarity of purpose.

The Role of Medications

A lot of research has implicated parts of the midbrain and the frontal lobes of the cerebral cortex as components of the brain mechanism responsible for OCD, but the precise nature of this mechanism has not been determined. The metabolism of the neurotransmitter serotonin also has a central role in the disorder, and the arousal-producing neurotransmitter dopamine also takes part, but the exact neurochemical "script" is not yet known.

Fortunately, a number of antidepressant medications have potent serotonin-enhancing effects that enable them to serve as very effective OCD treatments. Anafranil (Clomipramine), a TCA (tricyclic antidepressant), reduces OCD symptoms the most, but has a number of uncomfortable side effects and safety problems. Among the new-generation antidepressants, the SSRI medications fluvoxamine (Luvox), fluoxetine (Prozac), sertraline (Zoloft), and paroxetine (Paxil) are all effective, popular treatments with relatively tolerable or even negligible side effects.

The U.S. Food and Drug Administration currently has approved all of these medications for OCD treatment, and relatively few other medications are effective. Prozac, Zoloft, and Paxil are also very widely used for treating depression and other anxiety disorders, but the dosages needed for treating OCD are higher, and onset of their therapeutic effects on the disorder takes considerably longer. Also, the fact that individuals with OCD do not respond to one SRI or SSRI medication does not predict whether they will respond to another.

Since OCD is difficult to control, we believe it is important to receive medication treatment from a knowledgeable psychiatrist. When a case of OCD is complicated by a major depression, medication is strongly indicated. The consensus of many clinicians is that medication treatment should generally be continued for at least a year once it proves helpful in improving a person's condition.

Remember: A few compulsions and obsessions are part of normal life. Nearly everybody checks things that extra time "just to make sure" about safety or personal concerns. Part of recovery from anxious obsessions and compulsions is restraining a desire to pursue the impossible dream of perfect control. Perhaps rituals impart a necessary sense of order and manageability to the complexities of life and our uncertain world, yet they restrict the liberty of OCD sufferers and keep them in orbit around feelings of anxiety. Once the anxiety has dissipated, the mental energy trapped in obsessions and compulsions can be released and transformed into more productive, creative ways of thinking.

Chapter Fourteen

Now You've Done It!

By exercising courage and persistence, you have illuminated the darkness in the cave and seen the monster for what it really is. Your strength and mental clarity enabled you to spring the trap that your anxiety ensnared you in.

Now that you have confronted and conquered some of your fears, in this chapter you will learn about what may lie ahead. In most cases, cognitive-behavioral treatment for anxiety problems is a one-way street: Once treatment for panic, phobias, generalized anxiety, or OCD is complete, full relapse seldom occurs. When attacks or episodes have been relieved through therapeutic efforts, only infrequently do they recur, often months or even years apart, and seldom produce more than mild discomfort. If panic or OCD was a significant problem, mild attacks or episodes may develop from time to time. If you continue exposure therapy until your important phobic situations and life activities no longer provoke anxiety, then you can probably ensure that with only minimal "maintenance treatment" they will no longer loom large in your life.

A good source of "insurance coverage" against recurrence of each disorder consists of devoting special attention to actively contending with stimuli that are similar to the original events that triggered it. Linda originally got obsessive about contamination after a dear friend was hospitalized for an infectious disease, so she fortified her recovery by doing volunteer work at a hospital and spending time on medical units. Men and women with histories of phobic avoidance might actively seek out formerly phobic situations and reenter them from time to time, if for no other reason than to fortify their realistic perspectives and deter "anxiety creep." Similarly, if you suffered from social or general situational phobia and wind up "out of commission" due to a prolonged illness or injury, we suggest you celebrate your recovery by deliberately venturing out to phobic situations and engaging in the activities that used to be hampered by anxiety.

It's wise to practice self-control training long after anxiety symptoms fade, so that relaxation training or present-moment focusing becomes almost second nature. Many people like to foster the integration of SCT into their day-to-day functioning. If that's the case for you, you may find the study of meditation helpful and pleasant.

In the event that anxious distress recurs, resume keeping a worry diary or a record of panic, phobic, or obsessive anxiety. Review what you wrote before when you worked with your anxious thoughts and feelings and monitor any recurrence of the "tricks of your thinking" that were characteristic of the anxiety problem that you relieved or overcame. For relapse prevention, Adrian Wells underscores the importance of recognizing these uniquely problematic types of anxious thoughts that lead to anxious discomfort.

Try to identify any tendencies toward apprehension, rumination, and catastrophic thinking. For instance, the trick of thinking with GAD is a tendency to believe that negative events—generally involving daily activities, health, work or school, family, friends, or finances—are laden with disturbing meaning and beyond one's coping ability. According to Wells, the trick of panicky thinking involves selective attention to—and often obsession with—the physical sensations of anxiety. In obsessive-compulsive thinking, watch for selective attention to particular disconcerting thoughts. In general situational phobias, tricky thinking consists of feeling irrationally trapped or cut off in nonthreatening situations; while in social phobia the individual hyperfocuses on his or her publicly conspicuous actions and emotions.

After undergoing disturbingly stressful events, apprehension and rumination may return with a vengeance and catalyze a recurrence of one's anxiety disorder. For instance, after a person who has overcome social fears suffers great embarrassment at a family gathering, he could temporarily be at somewhat greater risk of "relearning" his social anxiety condition. As a preventive measure, it would be helpful for him to start recording and mentally processing incidents of increased social anxiety for a while, at least until his sensitivity subsides.

Craske and her associates both researched this "return of fear" and the best ways for individuals who have undergone cognitive-behavioral therapy to "maximize long-term retention and generalization of new learning" and recover fully from anxiety disorders. In general, fearful reactions after the completion of treatment are not at all portentous of relapse, but the way you practice boosting your cognitive-behavioral skills is likely to make the difference in your stability. Spacing booster sessions—so called because they boost your therapeutic benefits—days or weeks apart is preferable to "cramming" intensive refresher courses. Also, diversification will enable you to generalize your learning better. Practice in coping with a variety of former phobic fears is preferable to focusing on only one situation or activity.

Following this principle, then, your prognosis for long-term recovery from general situational phobia will probably not improve by spending a long weekend doing *all* of the following:

- Riding an elevator to the top of the Empire State Building
- Jogging two hundred yards through rush hour crowds at Grand Central Station
- Going to a Yankees game
- Having a shopping spree in Times Square
- Hopping a shuttle flight from JFK to Washington National Airport and back

Performing all these activities over the course of a couple of months, on the other hand, could be excellent exercise of your anxiolytic skills and help ensure your continued recovery.

Another good "preventive medicine prescription" involves periodic self-taught refresher courses in fighting fear in the venues where it was triggered in the first place. For instance, a kindergarten teacher with social anxiety who became phobic during a semester of covering eighth grade classes could arrange to pinch-hit for eighth grade teacher colleagues from time to time, making sure to mentally process anxieties that arise.

Imagery can also play an important part in maintaining long-term recovery from anxiety disorders. Individuals can often cope effectively with unexpected fears or highly anxiety-provoking situations if they recall the coping imagery they developed and utilized to recover from their anxiety conditions. Some recovered phobics or panickers report imagining how they and their therapists would discuss such challenging situations. Other individuals refer to their Worry, Panic, Phobia, or Rituals and Obsessions Records and jog their memories by reviewing the alternative perspectives they arrived at as they were recovering. Those who utilized self-control desensitization (SCD) can use the coping imagery they employed as a ready-made resource for imaginal fear prevention.

When life's major stresses strike, actively deal with the emotional reaction. Get involved in psychotherapy or a grieving group after loss of a loved one, and find a support group or supportive therapy after divorce or separation.

Exercise and health practices also help manage stress and augment preventative behavioral medicine. Rod devoted several months to self-help treatment for GAD and succeeded in mastering his unhealthy worry and tension. When his employer assigned him the lion's share of responsibility for fulfillment of a major new contract, he responded by a) carrying an organizer, prioritizing the activities on his to-do list, and actively letting go of things he could not complete; b) joining a gym and setting up a schedule for regular aerobic exercise; and c) planning regular restaurant outings and weekend trips with his family.

Stress management techniques are invaluable for the ex-anxiety-disordered person. They relieve tension, impart pleasure and enjoyment of life, restore and maintain the sense of control, renew the sense of being a healthy animal, and help normalize sleep, appetite, and cardiovascular health.

Anxiety sensitivity remains a part of life for people who have suffered from anxiety disorders but ceases predisposing them to recurrences after successful completion of therapy. Perhaps the old-fashioned term, *emotionality*, would fit better, with its emphasis on abundant strong feelings, intense emotional reactions, and the individual's sensitivity to her and others' emotions. These characteristics can be germane to a variety of fulfilling creative and interpersonal pursuits, from work in crafts to writing, art, or music, practicing psychotherapy, or acting as an advocate of the indigent.

In fact, a growing literature validates the special strengths of people who identify themselves as "highly sensitive," and it can be argued that people who master anxiety disorders have strengthened their minds and actually made themselves smarter. *Emotional intelligence* is the term popularized by psychologist Daniel Goleman in his popular book of the same name for the versatility and coping potential derived from mastering the facility for working with one's emotions.

After anxiety recovery, painful feelings are still sometimes a fact of life. Emotional distress may be dealt with effectively as a symptom of an imbalance in the individual's way of living, and devoting care to establishing a healthy, balanced lifestyle can be the remedy. If emotional distress persists, psychotherapy can be a wise choice.

Appendix A

Worksheets

Worksheet 5.3
PANIC RECORD

Situation: Who, What, When, Where?	Length of Time of Attack	SUDs (Rate 0–10)	Physical Symptoms	Automatic Thoughts (Put realistic thoughts that are included in parentheses.)	How Would I *Rather* Think?

Worksheet 7.2

TRANSFORMING YOUR ANXIETY PROPOSITIONS INTO REALITY PROPOSITIONS

Anxiety Propositions	Physical Anxiety Symptoms	Facts about the Symptoms and SCT Techniques	Anxious Thoughts	Reasoned Challenges to Anxious Thoughts	Realistic Propositions: How Would I *Rather* Think?

Worksheet 9.7
EXPOSURE WORKOUT WORKSHEET

Situation	Highest Anxiety Level (0–10 SUDs)	Physical Anxiety Symptoms	Anxious Thoughts	What Would I *Rather* Think?

Worksheet 11.1
WORRY RECORD

Situation: Who, What, When, Where?	Worry Topic and Specific Worrisome Thought	Anxious Behaviors	SUDs (0–10)	Actual Outcome

Worksheet 13.3
EXAMINING THE EVIDENCE FOR YOUR OBSESSIONS AND TRANSFORMING ANXIETY PROPOSITIONS

1. Obsessions and Anxiety Propositions: Intrusive Thoughts and Feared Consequences	2. What Are My Anxious Misinterpretations?	3. Replies to Questions for Examining the Evidence	4. Modified, Compromise, or Alternative Thoughts and Realistic Propositions

Relaxation Induction

Please make yourself comfortable. Close your eyes if you want, or keep them open. It doesn't matter. The important thing is that you begin to let yourself relax. Take a few slow, deep breaths, and notice that as you exhale, you can feel yourself becoming more relaxed. Notice that when you breathe in, your shoulders rise, and that when you exhale . . . fully and completely . . . your shoulders fall. Maybe you hardly notice the easy, gentle, natural way your shoulders move up and down . . . with your breaths . . . and you know, you don't even have to think about it a lot . . . but as you continue to relax in this easy natural way . . . with each breath . . . each time you exhale, let it happen . . . let your shoulders and your entire upper body relax even more. That's it . . . more and more . . . more and more relaxed . . . more and more relaxed. Perhaps you notice that as you exhale, you can enjoy a sense of becoming more and more relaxed . . . more and more relaxed . . . as you experience yourself resting more and more easy . . . more and more easy . . . calm . . . relaxed . . . peaceful . . . easy . . . serene.

And as you go deeper into a state of comfortable relaxation, you probably are beginning to have a sense of what the experience of a more complete sense of relaxation is like. As you continue to relax even more, you may feel a slight tingly feeling in your fingers . . . or in your toes . . . and if you do, you will know that it is a sign that your body is relaxing. Let your body relax. Just let the tension drain from your body, and just relax . . . more and more . . . feeling more and more at peace . . . calm . . . more deeply relaxed, as you enter into a pleasant, comfortable state of relaxation, all the while remaining alert, wide awake, and mentally keen.

To help you relax even more, focus your attention on your toes . . . your right toes . . . and your left toes. Feel any tension that may be there, and just let it drain from your right toes . . . and from your left toes . . . letting all the tension drain out and letting your toes relax . . . more and more . . . more and more relaxed. And let the relaxation spread from your toes into your feet, and let your feet relax. Let all the tension drain from your feet, and let them become more and more relaxed. And now pay attention to your ankles and to your calves. I wonder if there is any tension in your ankles or your calves, in your right leg or in your left leg. And if there is, you can let it go right now. Just let your legs relax . . . more and more relaxed . . . more and more completely relaxed.

And the relaxation can spread into your thighs . . . your thighs can relax more and more . . . just letting go. And you can let your pelvis relax. Just let it go loose and limp . . . loose and limp . . . relaxing more and more. Relax your stomach. Let your stomach become completely relaxed. Notice how it feels, and if you feel any tension at all, just let it drain from you . . . loose and limp . . . completely relaxed. And let the relaxation spread upward into your chest. Let all the nerves and muscles in your chest relax . . . completely relaxed . . . loose and limp . . . all the tension draining away. And now your back can relax, and your shoulders. Let yourself feel the relaxation in your back and your shoulders . . . more and more relaxed . . . loose and limp . . . completely relaxed.

Let the relaxation spread through your arms, down into your hands and your fingers. Focus on the feelings in your arms and hands. Notice any tension that may still be there, and let it drain out through your fingers. Focus on your right upper arm . . . right lower arm . . . your right hand . . . and fingers . . . relaxing completely . . . more and more relaxed . . . completely relaxed. And now your left arm . . . relaxing completely, the tension draining out . . . completely relaxed . . . completely relaxed.

Now relax the muscles of your neck . . . just let go and relax . . . loose and limp . . . completely relaxed. And relax your jaw muscles. Just let them go limp. All the nerves and muscles in your jaw relaxing completely. And relax all the rest of the muscles in your face . . . your mouth . . . nose . . . eyes . . . eyebrows . . . eyelids . . . forehead . . . all the muscles going loose and limp . . . loose and limp . . . completely relaxed . . . at peace . . . calm and relaxed . . . completely at ease. And now take a minute or two to just thoroughly enjoy your experience of relaxation.

If you wish you can enter an even deeper state of comfort and relaxation by using a simple counting procedure. Just say to yourself with each count, "Deeper and deeper." And begin to count to yourself as you remain alert and awake, yet so relaxed, comfortable, and at ease. Count to yourself from one to ten, and with each count, feel yourself becoming increasingly comfortable and relaxed. With each count, take a nice, slow, deep, easy breath.

One . . . more relaxed . . . even deeper . . . more and more relaxed . . . two . . . more and more comfortable . . . three . . . four . . . wouldn't it feel good to let yourself relax even more? Would you like to experience relaxation even more completely? Feel even more calm and at ease? Five . . . halfway there . . . six . . . can you feel even more safe . . . secure? . . . seven . . . calming yourself down . . . even more relaxed than before . . . yet alert and fully awake . . . eight . . . nine . . . ten . . . relaxed, alert, wide awake, yet calm, and at ease. If you chose to close your eyes, open them now or when you are ready. You will be alert, relaxed, yet wide awake and able to think clearly, with a body that is relaxed and at ease.

And you can take this technique with you. Practice the complete relaxation procedure at least once a day, perhaps in the morning or before sleep. It will become increasingly easy for you to relax at will. This relaxation procedure begins from the toes up. However, some readers may prefer to relax from the head down to the toes. At different times during the day, practice counting your breaths from one to ten and feel your body relaxing progressively as you have learned in this exercise. If you need to count another ten breaths, feel free to do so. You might also attach a phrase to this practice, such as saying, "Relax" or "Calm" with each exhalation, or whatever you discover facilitates your experience of relaxation.

Another practice that some people find quite helpful is to touch their thumb and index finger together to "anchor" their sense of relaxation. It is possible to feel tension draining from your body while feelings of relaxation are flowing and spreading the comfortable sense of inner calm. Practice the breathing and anchoring in a variety of different everyday life situations. Discover for yourself the pleasures of feeling relaxed, calm, and at ease.

Appendix C

Relaxation by Holding On and Letting Go

Some people have fears that if they relax completely they will be vulnerable, and they actually experience an *increase* in anxiety following relaxation procedures. The following induction, while relaxation-based, can be used to decrease the likelihood that such a "paradoxical anxiety reaction" will occur during relaxation. Note that some people may prefer to relax from the head down to the toes, rather than from the toes up.

During your relaxation practice today, I would like you to hold on to only as much tension as you need in order to feel comfortable and relaxed, safe and secure. You know that you need a certain amount of tension in your body to sustain your everyday functions. You need a certain amount of tension in the muscles of your mouth to talk, but you don't have to talk during relaxation practice . . . unless you want to. You need a certain amount of tension in your legs to walk, but you don't have to walk during your relaxation practice, unless you want to. And you need a certain amount of tension in your eyes to open them and keep them open, if you want to. But you don't have to open your eyes during relaxation today, unless you want to. In fact, you might wish to close your eyes right now, if you like. Whether your eyes are open or closed doesn't really matter. What matters is that you release all of the tension in your eyelids and eyes that you do not need . . . relax your eyes and, if you would like, let them close . . . let them close, knowing you could summon up just as much tension as you would need at any time to open them. Now create just enough tension to open your eyes a little and then release the tension in your eyes and let them relax even more completely . . . more completely, and let your body begin to release some of the tension that it does not need. And as you begin to do this, you notice that your body relaxes. Actually, you need to have very little tension in your body for you to breathe, walk, talk, and see, because much of these basic processes occur automatically, with little conscious awareness and relatively little tension required to sustain these activities. So, if you want, your body can become relaxed, very relaxed, while you remain fully alert and awake. Today, you can discover just how much tension you need while your body releases and relaxes as much as it possibly can.

And as your body begins to relax, I would like to draw your attention to your breathing. As you notice your breathing, perhaps you notice a certain amount of tension when you breathe in, and then a relaxation of tension when you breathe out, although your breathing may be very effortless, and you may not even notice the steady rhythm of your breathing in and out . . . in and out. But for now, take a very deep breath and hold it for as long as you can. And then you will notice some tension, I am sure. And when you can hold that breath no longer, let it out. Release the breath completely. Let the tension out and experience how deeply relaxed you feel when you release the breath completely . . . release the breath completely and hold on to only as much tension as you need to feel relaxed and comfortable, comfortable and at ease. And now take another breath . . . hold it for as long as you can and then release it, just as you did before . . . tensing and releasing . . . releasing and relaxing . . . holding on and letting go. And now feel your breathing becoming easier and easier . . . easier and easier . . . with each breath you release tension you do not need and you become more and more relaxed, peaceful and relaxed.

Actually, you have had a lot of experience in holding on and letting go. When you were a child and learned to walk, you held on to the walls when you needed support. The stronger you became, the more agile and confident you became . . . and as you sensed you could release you did . . . and you were able to let go of the walls. You had to hold on less and less as you became more confident in your abilities. You learned to train your muscles to support the activities your mind wanted you to engage in. And today, you can walk on your own. You can talk on your own. You can stand on your own two feet and make decisions for yourself. And today, you can become more confident in your abilities to practice relaxation as you experience yourself holding on and letting go . . . releasing and relaxing.

Now you can practice releasing and relaxing various muscle groups in your body to help you relax. Remember if you need to hold on to tension, hold on to it, but only as much as you need to in order to sustain the vital workings of your body. When you let go, you allow yourself the privilege of feeling as relaxed and at ease as you would like to be . . . as you can be.

As you release the muscles in the bottom part of your body, from your waist down through your legs, feel the tension flowing out of your toes and your body relaxing just the right amount. As you move through the muscles in your upper body, you will feel the tension flowing out through your fingertips.

Focus your attention on your toes . . . your right toes . . . and your left toes. Feel any extra tension that may be there, and just let it drain from your right toes . . . and from your left toes . . . letting any extra tension drain out and letting your toes relax . . . more and more . . . more and more relaxed. And let the relaxation spread from your toes into your feet, and let your feet relax. Let all the unnecessary tension drain from your feet, and let them become more and more relaxed. And now pay attention to your ankles and to your calves. I wonder if there is any tension in your ankles or your calves, in your right leg or in your left leg. And if there is any that you don't need, you can let it go right now. Just let your legs relax . . . more and more relaxed . . . more and more completely relaxed.

And the relaxation can spread into your thighs . . . your thighs can relax more and more . . . just letting go. And you can let your pelvis relax. If you need to tense it first to see how much you really need, do so, and then, just let it go loose and limp . . . loose and limp . . . relaxing more and more. Relax your stomach. Let your stomach become comfortably relaxed. Notice how it feels, and if you feel any tension at all that you don't need, just let it drain from you . . . loose and limp . . . more and more relaxed. And let the relaxation spread upward into your chest. Let all the nerves and muscles in your chest relax as completely as you would like . . . loose and limp . . . so good to let yourself relax. And now your back can relax, and your shoulders. Let yourself feel the relaxation in your back and your shoulders . . . more and more relaxed . . . loose and limp . . . relaxed.

Let the relaxation spread through your arms, down into your hands and your fingers. Focus on the feelings in your arms and hands. Notice any

tension that may still be there, and let go of any that you would like to release more completely, so that you can relax even more, let the tension
drain out through your fingers. Focus on your right upper arm . . . right
lower arm . . . your right hand . . . and fingers . . . relaxing . . . more and
more relaxed . . . so relaxed. And now your left arm . . . relaxing completely, excess tension draining out . . . relaxed . . . so relaxed.

Now relax the muscles of your neck . . . let it go a bit more if you
like . . . and relax . . . loose and limp . . . even more relaxed. And relax
your jaw muscles. Just let them go limp, if you are willing to do so . . . so
relaxed. All the nerves and muscles in your jaw relaxing so comfortably.
And relax all the rest of the muscles in your face . . . your mouth . . .
nose . . . eyes . . . eyebrows . . . eyelids . . . forehead . . . all the muscles
going as loose and limp as you like . . . loose and limp . . . so relaxed . . .
at peace . . . calm and relaxed . . . completely at ease. And now take a
minute or two to just thoroughly enjoy your experience of relaxation.

If you have even a bit of residual tension in your body that you would
like to release so that you can relax even more completely, make a fist now.
That's it. Make a fist. A strong fist. Scan your body now, from your head
to your toes. Be aware of any tension that remains that you would like to
let go of . . . release it because you don't need it. And now you can do
something you will find interesting. See whether you can gather all of that
tension into your hand and make your fist even stronger with this tension.
Take your tension and convert it into a feeling of strength. A strong and
powerful fist. A fist of strength. This strength that you can feel will remind
you that strength is within . . . strength is within. And as you release the
fist, you notice something interesting . . . you can release any and all tension that is within your body that you do not need. And that you can be
strong without being tense at all. Say to yourself, "Strength is within," as
you relax more and more. Feel your entire body becoming more and more
comfortable as you become more in tune with the strength that is within
your body, strength you can access any time you wish . . . and as you are
even more aware of this strength, you can relax completely . . . relax completely . . . relax completely.

And now I would like to suggest that you can have this feeling of
strength combined with relaxation any time you wish. You can establish a
cue or what I call an "anchor" to remind you in any situation that you can
remain strong and mentally keen, even while you relax. All you have to do
instead of making a fist is to simply bring your thumb and forefinger together in a way that nobody will notice.

Practice the complete relaxation procedure at least once a day, perhaps in the morning or before sleep. And be sure to use your anchor in a variety of different situations. As you continue to practice, you will learn more about just how much tension you need to hold on to in different situations. You will learn that it is possible to replace excess tension with feelings of relaxation, comfort, and ease in an increasing number of everyday life situations.

Appendix D

Body and Breath:
A Simple Meditation

Traditionally we learn to meditate while sitting. Meditators are often seen cross-legged in a lotus or half-lotus position, often using a cushion beneath their backsides. However, a cross-legged position isn't necessary. You can also sit in a straight-backed, comfortable chair. Here are some basic instructions:

- Straighten your body and sit erect. Don't lean to either side, and try not to bend forward or backward. Let your shoulders drop naturally.

- Try to keep your nose in line with your navel and keep your head placed so that your ears are over your shoulders. Keep your head on straight.

- Let your tongue rest lightly on the roof of your mouth, with lips and teeth gently closed.

- Place your hands in your lap or on your knees.

- Keep your eyes closed or half closed.

- Allow yourself to experience some spaciousness, ease and clarity, letting the mind settle naturally into its own natural state.

- Begin by breathing in through the nostrils, then out through the nostrils. Concentrate on the physical sensation of air going in and out of the nostrils. Simply observe your breathing at that very sensation point, and focus on nothing else. Connect to your present experience by maintaining contact between your mind's concentrated attention and that sensation of breathing.

- Whatever occurs while you are meditating—noises, an itchy foot, a memory, be it pleasant or unpleasant—let it go and return your focus to the breathing.

- Keep your body still and breathing free and easy.

- Stay loose, open, and accepting.

- Enjoy the moment.

From *Awakening the Buddha Within*
by Lama Surya Das, copyright © 1997 by Lama Surya Das.
Used by permission of Broadway Books, a division of Random House, Inc.

||||||

Appendix E

How Safe Are Elevators?

levator phobia is a type of claustrophia, a fear of confining spaces. Whether large or small, swift or poky, an elevator is a people-moving box whose big mechanical doors temporarily cut riders off from the outside world, so that men and women with elevator phobia are flooded with frightening sensations and disturbing images.

According to statistics cited by Ray Lapierre, executive director of the Elevator Escalator Safety Foundation, out of an estimated 120 billion U.S. rides per year, only one injury occurs per *12 million* elevator rides a year.

Like other claustrophias, elevator phobia often includes the fear of having insufficient air to breathe. A warm, crowded, stuffy car will stimulate anxiety more than an elevator with cool, freely flowing air. Fortunately, it is essentially impossible to run out of air in an elevator, since it shares the air supply with the entire building that houses it. Our information review indicates that there has never been a single mishap caused by lack of air.

In the scenario that many elevator riders fear the most, the cable snaps and the car plummets out of control and smashes into the bottom of the shaft. Older, slower, noisier elevators more easily stir this image than nearly silent, high-tech lifts that glide smoothly up and down. But perhaps this fear will dissipate when you realize that while only one cable is necessary to support the car, between four and eight cables, each strong enough to manage the entire weight of a fully loaded elevator, are attached to it. Besides multiple cabling, multiple safety systems are installed—gripping devices and brakes designed to slow and stop a fully loaded elevator that has begun to descend too fast.

Still unsure whether elevators can be trusted? In order to soothe your anxieties, let's consider other common fears and the aspects of elevator design that help keep them from becoming realities:

- Why do elevators refuse to move? What is supposed to prevent them from getting stuck?

- What mechanisms ensure that the elevator doors won't open on a brick wall or a gaping hole?

- If elevators are inspected regularly, what is likely to go wrong anyway? What are the best ways to contend with the rare mishap?

An Open-and-Shut Case

Most modern-day elevators have devices that control their every move, that check and double-check to make certain that all the doors are closed before the car starts to move. When the car stops, the devices ensure that it is properly lined up with the building floor before the doors will open again.

BEFORE MOVING

Up to three mechanisms perform the following checks before transmitting the "go" signal:

1. The doors to *both* the building floor and the elevator car are closed.

2. The elevator doors are solidly in contact with each other.

3. An "overseer" circuit is satisfied that steps 1 and 2 have been completed before sending a pulse that closes an electronic switch that sets the car in motion.

When a elevator has left a floor landing, federal regulations require that the opening be covered by a door or gate to prevent accidental falls.

After Stopping

After a run, but before the elevator doors open fully to permit passengers to exit, electronic confirmation is received that the car has arrived and come to a stop within a half an inch of the floor landing. Modern elevators restrict the door opening to four inches when the elevator is more than three inches from the building floor. This ensures both that an elevator won't stall as soon as the "leveler" gets even slightly out of adjustment and that the elevator doors do not one day open on a brick wall or a gaping hole.

Safety and Security

What should you do in the rare event that the elevator stops too long with the door shut? First, push the Door Open button when the elevator stops too long with the doors shut. If the doors remain closed, use the alarm bell, telephone, or intercom with which the elevator is equipped to call for help, and then wait for assistance. These devices, and all of the elevator's safety equipment, should be inspected regularly to make sure they are in good operating condition. The federal Safety Code for Elevators calls for a minimum of semiannual inspections by state-certified inspectors, and a certificate of inspection should be displayed in each elevator or viewable in the building superintendent's office.

In the extremely rare event that the elevator stops between floors, we suggest that you do the following. Use the alarm bell, telephone, or intercom with which the elevator is equipped to call for help, and then wait for assistance. Do not attempt to force open the doors. Do not attempt to leave the elevator. The elevator hatch is designed for professional personnel who will provide assistance from outside of the elevator cab. Try to maintain or restore composure and be patient. Sit down on the floor and perform mini-practices. There is plenty of air, and the interior of the elevator is designed for passenger safety. Be reassured that help will come.

Always keep the statistic in mind that the likelihood of an elevator accident is infinitesimally small, and it is very improbable that you will be involved in a mishap with an elevator. Happy trails!

Appendix F

Frequently Asked Questions (FAQs)

Q: *I read somewhere that antidepressant medications accomplish their changes in neurotransmitter brain chemistry almost immediately after you start taking them. Why does it take three to six weeks for them to become clinically effective in relieving anxiety and depression?*
A: The immediate effects of antidepressants are changes in the way the brain processes negatively arousing emotions like acute anxiety. After the feelings have changed, it seems to take most people at least a month or two of trying before they figure out how to think and act differently.

Q: *The Internet has such a wealth of ideas about new medicines and treatment for anxiety and panic, people's experiences, and which professionals to use and avoid. What are the pros and cons of using this information to overcome anxiety disorders?*
A: The Internet is a vast, wonderful avenue for free information that is most useful for people who have the means of evaluating its *accuracy,* when necessary. With so many types of Internet information, this is not essential—for instance, opinions of Pink's or Garth Brooks's latest CD; and with others, there is no certified standard of accuracy—like the quality of food on Carnival cruises or how safe visitors to New Orleans are from pickpockets.

Anxiety disorders treatment is part of a new generation of mental health services that are being carefully researched for their safety and effectiveness. Great amounts of enthusiasm, time, intellect, and funds have been and are being devoted to strengthening scientific understanding of anxiety and bringing the results to as many people as possible. In order to get the greatest benefit from this movement, it's important to question whether information reported on the Internet is accurate. When in doubt, ask the informant to document his or her sources of information, and ponder whether you'd trust it in trying to overcome *your* fears.

Q: *I hear so much about people with anxiety disorders having too little serotonin and GABA available in their brains. Since there are all sorts of dietary supplements and natural sources of these chemicals available through health and nutrition firms, would it hurt to add the best of these to my diet or take them as pills?*
A: Might hurt, probably won't help. The brain does not directly accept things that we eat, no matter how badly they're needed. Our brains manufacture the brain chemicals we need. When we have anxiety disorders and they are in short supply, anxiolytic medications are the best ways known to science to remedy the problem. They usually get the brain to make or retain more of the chemicals and eliminate the shortage.

Q: *Relaxation training is mentioned a lot in connection with stress management training and in instructions for coping with panic and anxiety. But I prefer to relax my way. I like to come home from work or school and veg out in front of the TV. During a weekend or holiday, I surf the channels endlessly or else I enjoy watching a ball game. Is there any problem with TV viewing as a relaxation technique?*
A: Of course TV viewing has its value. It certainly can be very enjoyable and can serve as a tremendous contrast from a busy, demanding day or a hard work week. Television viewing is similar to self-control relaxation practice in that, in both activities, the person is sitting and not working physically—but there the resemblance ends. TV viewing is very passive, in the sense that the viewer is not getting his mind to do anything but focus on the program and let it more or less captivate him. During self-control relaxation, even though the individual is sitting quietly, he is actively guid-

ing his mind to engage in certain activities or focus on certain things while putting others into the background.

Besides differing in activity and focus, TV viewers and self-control relaxation practitioners also differ in their emotional processing. By practicing self-control relaxation, the person learns to put anxiety, certain kinds of fear, and possibly anger into the background of his thinking. The TV viewer, by contrast, is consumed by anger, fear, excitement, envy, or disgust, depending on what's on the screen. That's entertainment!—but not anxiety therapy.

Appendix G

Anxiety Treatment Resources

Professional Organizations

American Psychiatric Association
Dept. NASD, 1400 K Street, NW
Washington, DC 20005
Phone: 202-682-6000
Names of psychiatrists

American Psychological Association
750 First Street, NE
Washington, DC 20002-4242
Phone: 202-336-5700
        800-964-2000 (referral line)
Website: www.apa.org
Names of psychologists

Anxiety Disorders Association of America (ADAA)
11900 Parklawn Drive, Suite 100
Rockville, MD 20852
Phone: 301-231-9350
Website: www.adaa.org

Newsletter for mental health consumers and clinicians
Names of anxiety treatment professionals
Support group information

Association for the Advancement of Behavior (AABT)
305 Seventh Avenue, 16th Floor
New York, NY 10001-6008
Phone: 212-647-1890
        800-685-AABT
Website: www.aabt.org
Names of professionals who treat anxiety disorders
Brochures and articles on anxiety disorders

Mental Health Consumer Organizations

Anxiety Disorders Association of America (see above)

Obsessive-Compulsive Foundation, Inc. (OCF)
337 Notch Hill Road
North Branford, CT 06471
Phone: 203-315-2190
Website: www.ocfoundation.org

Trichotillomania Learning Center, Inc. (TLC)
303 Potrero #51
Santa Cruz, CA 95060
Phone: 831-457-1004
Website: www.trich.org

Internet Resources

Anxieties.com: www.anxieties.com
Includes information on fear of flying, OCD, panic, and agoraphobia

Anxiety Disorders and Their Treatment: A Critical Review of the Evidence-Based Literature, by M. M. Antony and R. P. Swinson (Health Canada, 1996):
www.hc-sc.gc.ca/hppb/mentalhealth/pdfs/anxiety_review.pdf

Anxiety Disorders Association of America: www.adaa.org

Expert Consensus Treatment Guidelines: www.psychguides.com
Includes the experts' consensus on treatment of epilepsy, depression, ADHD, and OCD

National Institute of Mental Health Anxiety Disorders Education Program: www.nimh.nih.gov/anx

Obsessive-Compulsive Foundation: www.ocfoundation.org

PanicBuster: www.panicbuster.com
David Mellinger's website includes information about GAD, panic, and phobias, including social phobia and agoraphobia

Trichotillomania Learning Center: www.trich.org

Notes

Introduction

Total number of Americans with anxiety disorders: Narrow et al., July 1, 1998.
Total of anxiety-disordered people seeking mental health help: ibid.
Incidence of panic: NIMH ECA 1991: Eaton et al., 1991.
Prevalence of anxiety disorders in a given year: NCS 1994: Kessler et al., 1994.
DSM-IV: 1994.
Insufficient awareness of anxiety: De Becker, 1997.
"A disparity": Dalai Lama & Cutler, 1998, p. 158.
The symptoms of panic: APA, 1994.
The case of Wendy: ibid., p. 397.
Prevalence of shyness among college students: Zimbardo et al., 1974.
Prevalence of dissatisfaction with appearance and BDD.
Stages of positive change: Prochaska et al., 1995.

1. A Brief History of Anxiety Disorders and Their Treatment

Physical proximity in colonial America: Dalai Lama & Cutler, 1998, pp. 81–82.
Hikikomori: *Newsweek,* August 28, 2000, p. 37.
Specter of potential BZD addictiveness: Susann, 1966.
Panic disorder and Xanax: Sheehan, 1983.
Little Hans: Freud, 1909/1955.
Albert: Watson & Rayner, 1920.
Behavior therapy for phobias: Wolpe, 1958 and 1969.
Two-factor theory: Mowrer, 1960.
Acquisition of fear: Rachman, 1977.

Awfulizing and perfectionism: Ellis & Harper, 1975; Ellis, 2002.
Automatic negative thoughts in cognitive therapy: Beck & Emery, 1985.

2. Fundamental Concepts
Fight or flight: Cannon, 1915.
Stress: Selye, 1950.
Anxiety as loose structure of feelings: Barlow, 1988.
Anxiety sensitivity: Reiss & McNally, 1985.
Physical sensations become threatening: Clark & Watson, 1994.
Anxiety Sensitivity Inventory: Peterson & Reiss, 1987.
Inheriting behavioral inhibition: Kagan, 1994.
Outgrowing anxiety proneness: Wilson, 2000.
Triggers of anxiety: Fridja, 1994.
The impact of perfectionism on anxious thinking: Flett & Hewitt, 2002. Flett, G. L. & Hewitt, P. L. (2002). Perfectionism and maladjustment: An overview of theoretical, definitional, and treatment issues. In G. L. Flett & P. L. Hewitt (Eds.), *Perfectionism: Theory, research, and treatment.* (pp. 5–31). Washington, D.C.: American Psychological Association.
Brain structures that underlie narratives: Gazzaniga, 1998.
Distortions caused by automatic thoughts: Eckman, 1992; Epstein & Brodsky, 1993.
False alarm: Barlow, 2002, p. 220.
Thinking about a pounding heart: Foa, 1988.
New perspective on agoraphobia: Goldstein & Chambless, 1978; Chambless & Goldstein, 1982.
Agoraphobia is a self-confirming expectancy disorder: Kirsch & Lynn, 1999.
The effects of expectancies on panic, social anxiety, and agoraphobia: Turk, et. al., 2001.
Emotional processing of phobic fears: Foa & McNally, 1996.

3. The Brain on Anxiety
The emotional brain: LeDoux, 1996.
The HPA axis (illustration): *Alcohol Health & Research World,* 1998.
Distressing childhood memories and the hippocampus: Lenderhendler, 1995.
The thinking brain: LeDoux, 1996.
Anxiety disorders and the emotional brain: ADAA *Reporter,* Spring 2000, p. 14.
Emotional brain activity (table): ibid.
Adverse side effects of beta-blockers: *Merck Manual: Home Edition* (Internet edition), section 3, chapter 27.
Unlikelihood of BZD abuse: Fogelson, Feb. 1987.
BZD addiction potential: Gordon, 1981; Hofsiss, 1982.
Slowly tapering off BZDs: Crocker, 1996.
Preferred dosing with BZDs: Shiovitz, 2001.
CBT vs. medication vs. placebo: Barlow & Lehman, 1996.
Expectation of improvement on medicine: Craske, 1999.
Stopping Anxiety Medications: Otto et al., 1996.
Loss of tolerance of emotional discomfort: Krystal, 1993.

4. How Does Panic Happen?

Panic attacks in the general populace: E.g., Brown & Deagle, 1992; Wilson et al., 1991.

Prevalence of panic disorder: Kessler et al., 1994; NIMH, accessed April 2002.

Frequency of panic attacks in anxiety disorders: Antony & Swinson, 2000; Kessler et al.; McNally, 1994.

Panic peaks in ten minutes: Antony & Swinson, 2000.

Panic symptoms in the *DSM-IV*: APA, 1994.

Types of panic fears (table): Taylor & Cox, 1998.

When medical conditions lead to anxiety disorders: APA, 1994.

False alarms: Barlow, 1988.

Learning to release fight-or-flight hormones: Hellhammer, 1992.

Learned alarms evolving outside of conscious awareness: Barlow, 1988.

Suffocation false alarms: Klein, 1993 and 1994.

An easy, effective technique for regulating your breathing: McNally, 1999.

To think scientifically about anxiety: Feyman, 1998.

Emergency response symptoms: Otto et al., 1996.

"There are three things": McNally, 2002, March.

Globus hystericus: Davidson, 2001.

Interoceptive exposure: Antony & Swinson, 2000.

"Taking a bite out of the fear": Borkovec, 1999.

Worriers' negative predictions: Borkovec, 1999, March.

Worst-case scenario method of decatastrophizing: Craske & Barlow, 1994.

The "So what?" technique: Rapee, 1998.

6. The Many Faces of Phobias

Incidence of specific phobias: Eaton, 1991; Kessler et al., 1994.

Gender differences in specific phobias: Bourdon, 1988.

The subtypes of specific phobias: APA, 1994.

The course of common childhood fears (table): Ages when the fears emerge: Curtis et al., 1998. Lifetime prevalence: Antony et al., 1997; Öst, 1987; Marks & Gelder, 1966; Himle, et al., 1989; Craske et al., 1989.

Phobias interfere with functioning: APA, 1994.

Prevalence of agoraphobia: Eaton et al., 1991.

Medications and specific phobias: Antony & Swinson, 2000.

Occurrence of agoraphobia in panic disorder: Barlow, 2002.

Features of BPD and DPD: APA, 1994.

Commonalities of agoraphobia and claustrophobia: McNally, 2003.

Biological preparedness to neutralize evolutionary threats: Seligman, 1971.

Physiological evidence for preparedness: Ohman et al., 1974.

Our evolultionarily derived behavioral fear systems: Ohman et al., 1985.

The role of disgust in phobias: McNally, 2002.

Disgust as a factor in avoidance: Woody & Tolin, 2002.

The psychodynamic symbolism of phobias: Cameron, 1963.

Suppressing or avoiding anxious thoughts: Wegner, 1989.

Avoiding thoughts of what is feared: Lynn & Kurzhals, 2000.

7. Phobia Therapy

Valor defined: *Webster's Dictionary*, 1997.
Combating catastrophic thoughts: Craske & Barlow, 1994.
Reasoning with yourself: Rapee, 1998.
Learning to predict panic makes it less likely: Rescorla & Wagner, 1972.
Effects of reestimating on likelihood of panic (table): McNally, 1994.
"So what?" if the worst occurs: Rapee & Sanderson, 1998.
Choosing starting points for phobia practice: ibid., p. 103.
Dimensions of exposure practice: ibid., pp. 99–103.
Importance of support persons: Wilson, 1996, p. 253.
Breathing as first aid for panic: Radomsky et al., 1998.
Coping cards: Beck, 1995.
Interoceptive exposure practice: Craske & Barlow, 1994, p. 4-4.

8. Social Anxiety and Phobia

Most adult anxiety is social anxiety: Rycroft, 1968.
Excerpt from diagnostic criteria for social anxiety disorder: APA, 1994.
NIMH estimates of prevalence of mental disorders: National Institute of Mental Health website, 2001.
Lifetime occurrence rate of social phobia: ADAA *Reporter,* Spring 2000, p. 14.
Popular misconceptions about social phobia: Hope & Heimberg, 1993.
Marital patterns among the anxiety disorders: Sanderson et al., 1990.
Celebrities who have admitted to stage fright: Infoxchange net, accessed February 2002; Currie, Performance Anxiety Coping Skills Seminar, Chapter 2, accessed on the Internet, February 2002.
Central features of social phobia: Wells, 1997.
Range of social phobics' fears: Rapee & Sanderson, 1998.
Prevalence of "generalized" social phobia: Mattick, 1990.
Cognitive biases, beliefs, physical changes, and thinking errors of social phobia: Foa, et al., 1996; Beck & Emery, 1985; Wells, 1997; Rapee & Heimberg, 1997.
Vicious circle that compounds the mortification of the socially anxious: Gray & McNaughton, 2000, p. 362.
Attention impairment during social anxiety: Wells, 1997; Rapee & Sanderson, 1998.
Minimizing the value of past social successes: Hope & Heimberg, 1993, p. 105.
The 3-component "anxiety program" begins when a social phobic enters a feared situation: Based on Clark & Wells, 1995.
Basis for shyness in nervousness among infants: Kagan, 1994.
Peer and adult relations among socially anxious children: Leary & Kowalski, 1995.
Families of socially anxious children: Rapee & Sanderson, 1998, p. 18.
Direct conditioning may lead to social anxiety: Barlow, 1988.
Learning social anxiety: Rachman, 1977.
Genetic factors in social phobia: Fyer, et al., 1995; Kendler, et al., 1992.
Biological aspect of social anxiety: Leary & Kowalski, 1995, p. 105.
Prevalence of shyness in the general population: Pilkonis & Zimbardo, 1979.
Differences between shy people and those treated for social phobia: ibid.
Distinction in perceptions of shy and socially phobic people: Stopa & Clark, 1993.

"Socially anxious" vs. "socially phobic": Gray & McNaughton, 2000, p. 321.
Social anxiety in GAD: Borkovec, 1999.

9. Treatment of Social Anxiety
Recovery rate with CBT treatment: E.g., Heimberg et al., 1990.
Relapse rates after CBT and medication: Hofman & Barlow, 2002.
Cyrano de Bergerac: Rostand, 1897.
Common thoughts and beliefs of social phobia: Rapee, 1998, pp. 51–52.
Questions to help specify what you are afraid of: Wells, 1997.
Generating alternative beliefs: Antony & Swinson, 2000, p. 252.
Thinking patterns of "the old, socially anxious you": Wells, 1997, pp. 170–171.
Attention bias in social phobia: ibid.
The three tasks of social evaluation situations: Rapee, 1998.
Rationale for attention training: ibid., p. 55.
Imaginal desensitization: Lazarus, 1977, p. 82.
Strategic planning of opportunistic exposure workouts: Leahy & Holland, 2000.
Common errors of socially anxious thinking: Wells, 1997, pp. 189–190.
Behavioral experiments to challenge rigid, unrealistic expectations: ibid., p. 196.
Discontinuing safety behaviors: Craske, 1999, p. 226.
Symptom exaggeration and remembering coping statements: Craske, 1999, p. 227.
Effective cognitive treatment of public speaking fears: Craske, 1999, p. 234.
Prevalence of bashful bladder syndrome: Soifer et al., 2001.
Triggers of BBS: ibid., p. 22.
The tyramine-restricted diet: "Tyramine-Free Diet," accessed 2003.
Efficacy of Luvox, Zoloft, and Prozac: Greist, 1999 (audiotape); Barlow, 2002.
Efficacy of Effexor: Altamura et al., 1999.
Efficacy of Celexa: Greist, 1999.
Relative effectiveness of Klonopin vs. CBT: Otto et al., 2000.
Relative effectiveness of Xanax vs. placebo: Gelernter et al., 1991.
Effectiveness of Neurontin: Greist, 1999.
Use of beta-blockers by professional musicians: Fishbein et al., 1988.
Use of beta-blockers by cardiologists: Greist, 1999.
Use of beta-blockers without a prescription: Fishbein et al., 1988.
Effect of medications on CBT practice: Rapee, 1999, videotape.

10. Dismantle GAD and Stop Worrying Yourself Sick
Relative prevalence of worry in GAD: Craske et al., 1989.
GAD nearly synonymous with anxiety: Gray & McNaughton, 2000, p. 328.
GAD as the core anxiety disorder: E.g., Barlow, 1988; Borkovec et al., 1991.
Main diagnostic criteria: APA, 1994.
Nationwide prevalence of GAD: Kessler et al., 1994.
Prevalence of coexisting disorders: Borkovec, 1999.
"Tricks of thinking" in GAD: Craske, 2000.
Anxiety and depression: Barlow, 1991.
What *is* worry?: Borkovec et al., 1983.
Worry as negative reinforcer: Borkovec, 1999.

"Worry contrasts with fear": Craske, 2000.

Exaggeration of worries in GAD: Butler & Mathews, 1983.

Three disturbing thought patterns: Borkovec, 1999.

"If only . . ." thinking: ibid.

Rumination and anxious moods: Blagden & Craske, 1996; Morrow & Nolen-Hoeksema, 1990.

Vigorous attempts to suppress obsessive thoughts: Becker et al., 1998, p. 30; Turner et al., 1992.

Impairment of immune system during high stress: Bloom, 1985.

Prevalence of GI complaints in anxiety disorders: Lydiard, 1996, pp. 1 and 22.

Histories of people with chronic anxiety: Zinbarg et al., 1993.

Improvement in worry rate and coexisting conditions: Borkovec, 1999.

11. Relieving Worry and Generalized Anxiety

Worry detection going through doorways: Borkovec, 1999.

Key processes that maintain anxiety: Zinbarg et al., 1993, p. 7-2.

Activity, valence, and controllability: E.g., Izard, 1985; Ellsworth, 1994.

Kinds of anxious thinking prevalent in GAD: Craske, 1999; Borkovec & Costello, 1993.

Sample Meta-Worries and Apparent Validations (table): Wells, 1997, pp. 202 and 207.

Relaxation-induced anxiety: Heide & Borkovec, 1983 and 1984.

Fears that underlie worries: E.g., Barlow, 1988; Foa & McNally, 1996; Borkovec, 1999.

Exposure therapy can modify the "fear structure": Foa & McNally, 1996.

"Taking a bite out of the fear": Borkovec, 1999.

Self-control desensitization (SCD): Borkovec, 1999.

Decatastrophization: Craske et al., 1992.

"It is safe to let go of excessive worry": Zinbarg et al., 1993, p. 3-3.

Safety signals: Craske et al., 1992.

Therapy for worry-based behaviors; dimensions of anxiety: Zinbarg et al., 1993.

Worry prevention: ibid.

12. The Doubting Disease: Obsessions, Compulsions, and OCD

Prevalence of OCD: Regier et al., 1988; Robins et al., 1984.

Equal proportions of males to females with OCD: Swinson et al., 1998.

Age of onset: Riggs & Foa, 1993.

The essential features of OCD: APA, 1994.

Example of an obsession: ibid., p. 421.

Comparisons between worries and obsessions: Turner et al., 1992.

Characteristics of obsessive thinking: Salkovski, 1985.

Attempts by people with OCD to suppress their thoughts: Becker et al., 1998, p. 30.

Common subtypes of OCD: Leckman et al., 1997.

Hoarding and the subtypes of OCD: Steketee & Barlow, 2002.

OCD and consequent family dysfunction: Steketee & Pruyn, 1998, p. 121.

Disturbing qualities of OCD thinking errors: Wells, 1997, p. 238.

Annual rate of intrusive thoughts in the general population: Craske, 2000.

Lifetime rate of intrusive thoughts in the general population: Turner et al., 1992.

Typical kinds of intrusive thoughts of people without OCD: Rachman & DeSilva, 1978.

Misjudgment and misinterpretations of motives in OCD: Turner et al., 1992.

Intrusive thoughts that become obsessions (worksheet): Adapted from McLean & Woody, 2001; Freeston et al., 1996.

Delusional disorder can resemble OCD: McLean & Woody, 2001.

Defining characteristics of body dysmorphic disorder: APA, 1994, p. 468.

Biology and psychology in development of OCD: Steketee & Pigott, 1999.

Percentage of OCD sufferers who have relatives with OCD: Billett et al., 1998.

Functions of the areas of the brain affected by OCD: Steketee & Pigott, 1999, pp. 60–61.

OCD likened to a sticky manual transmission: Schwartz & Bayette, 1996, pp. 209–210.

Brain scan evidence of effectiveness of OCD medication and treatment: Steketee & Barlow, 2002, p. 521; Baxter et al., 1992; Steketee & Piggott, 1999, p. 62.

Obsessive thoughts evoking a phobic reaction: Steketee & Barlow, 2002, p. 518.

Central factors of OCD-type obsessions: Wells, 1997.

Neutralization, a mechanism of OCD: Rachman & Shafran, 1998, pp. 52 and 56.

Compulsive activities become associated with a wide array of stimuli and actions: Wells, 1997, p. 243.

13. Treating Obsessions and Compulsions

Concealing OCD fears and rituals: McLean & Woody, 2001, p. 185.

Six years between diagnosis and onset of treatment: Hollander et al., 1996.

Types and outcomes of treatment for OCD (table): Steketee & Pigott, 1999, pp. 2–3.

Self-help and therapy for OCD: Foa & Wilson, 2001.

The four challenges: ibid.

Method for identifying obsessive thoughts: Steketee & White, 1990.

The "very OCD" double standard thinking error: Van Oppen & Arntz, 1994.

Two-component model for rethinking obsessions: ibid.

Calculating the cumulative risk of a catastrophe: Hoekstra, 1989.

Use of the technique of reestimation of cumulative risk: Van Oppen & Arntz, 1994.

Meta-worries and obsessions about obsessions: Wells, 1997.

Direct testing of anxiety propositions: McLean & Woody, 2001.

Acceptance of uncertainty in cognitive treatment of OCD: Grayson & Kirby, 2003.

Treatment successes resulting from directly testing anxiety propositions: Freeston et al., 1996.

The client who believes that her thoughts can kill: McLean & Woody, 2001.

Playing with rituals: Foa & Wilson, 2001.

Who is a hoarder?: ibid., p. 42.

What makes hoarders anxious?: Rachman & Shafran, 1998.

The case of Donna, a hoarder: Foa & Wilson, 2001.

A prognostic consideration for hoarding: ibid.

Imagining looking back on resolution of the compulsion: Baer, 2000.

Start small and plan to be flexible: Stanley & Averill, 1998.

Prompting and shaping: Baer, 2000.

Victor Meyer's exposure/response prevention therapy: Meyer, 1966.

Therapist-assisted vs. self-directed exposure therapy: Abramowitz, 1996.

"Arousal is necessary for fear reduction": Foa & Kozak, 1986, p. 23.

"Exposure is . . . in effect 24 hours a day": Steketee & Barlow, 2002, p. 542.

Drawbacks of "lax" ritual prevention: Stanley & Averill, 1998.
Effective medication treatment for OCD: Steketee & Pigott, 1999.
How long to stay on effective medication: Pigott & Seay, 1997.

14. Now You've Done It!
Relapse prevention through monitoring problematic anxious thoughts: Wells, 1997.
Tricky thinking of social phobia: ibid., p. 268.
"Relearning" an anxiety disorder: Craske, 1999, p. 103.
"Maximize long-term retention . . . of new learning": ibid., p. 145.
Emotional intelligence: Goleman, 1995.

References

Abramowitz, J. S. (1996). Variants of exposure and response prevention in the treatment of obsessive-compulsive disorder: A meta-analysis. *Behavior Therapy, 27,* 583–600.

Alcohol Health and Research World, 22, 1, 1998. Accessed online at www.niaaa.nih.gov/gallery/endocrine/hpa.htm.

Altamura, A. C., Pioli, R., Vitto, M., & Mannu, P. (1999). Venlafaxine in social phobia: A study in selective serotonin reuptake inhibitor non-responders. *International Clinical Psychopharmacology, 14,* 239–245.

American Psychiatric Association (APA) (1994). *Diagnostic and statistical manual of mental disorders* (4th ed.) [DSM-IV]. Washington, DC: American Psychiatric Association.

Antony, M. M., & Swinson, R. P. (2000). *Phobic disorders and panic in adults: A guide to assessment and treatment.* Washington, DC: American Psychological Association.

Antony, M. M., Brown, T. A., & Barlow, D. H. (1997). Heterogeneity among specific phobia types in DSM-IV. *Behaviour Research and Therapy, 35,* 1089–1100.

Anxiety Disorders Association of America. ADAA *Reporter* (Spring 2000), *12,* 2, p. 14.

Baer, L. (2000). *Getting control* (rev. ed.). New York: Plume.

Barlow, D. H. (1988). *Anxiety and its disorders: The nature and treatment of anxiety and panic.* New York: Guilford Press.

—— (1991). The nature of anxiety: Anxiety, depression, and emotional disorders. In R. M. Rapee & D. H. Barlow (eds.), *Chronic anxiety: Generalized anxiety disorder and mixed anxiety-depression.* New York: Guilford Press.

—— (2002). *Anxiety and its disorders: The nature and treatment of anxiety and panic* (2nd ed.). New York: Guilford Press.

Barlow, D. H., & Lehman, C. L. (1966). Advances in the psychosocial treatment of anxiety disorders: Implications for national health care. *Archives of General Psychiatry 53*, 727–735.

Baxter, L. R., Schwartz, J. M., Bergman, K. S., Szuba, M. P., Guze, B. H., Mazziota, J. C., Alazraki, A., Selin, C. E., Ferng, H. K., Munford, P., & Phelps, M. E. (1992). Caudate glucose metabolic rate changes with both drug and behavior therapy for obsessive-compulsive disorder. *Archives of General Psychiatry, 49*, 681–689.

Beck, A. T., & Emery, G. (1985). *Anxiety disorders and phobias: A cognitive perspective.* New York: Basic Books.

Beck, J. S. (1995). *Cognitive therapy: Basics and beyond.* New York: Guilford Press.

Becker. E. S., Rinck, M., Roth, W. T., & Margraf, J. (1998). Don't worry and beware of white bears: Thought suppression in anxiety patients. *Journal of Anxiety Disorders, 12*, 1, p. 30.

Billett, E., Richeter, M., & Kennedy, J. (1998). In R. P. Swinson et al., op. cit., pp. 181–206.

Blagden, J. C., & Craske, M. G. (1996). Effects of active and passive rumination and distraction: A pilot replication with anxious mood. *Journal of Anxiety Disorders, 10*, 243–252.

Bloom, F. (1985). Neuropeptides and other mediators in the central nervous system. *The Journal of Immunology,* 135:743s–745s.

Borkovec, T. D. (1999, March). New developments in the treatment of worry. Advanced practice symposium at the national conference of the Anxiety Disorders Association of America, San Diego, CA.

Borkovec, T. D., & Costello, E. (1993). Efficacy of applied relaxation and cognitive-behavioral therapy in the treatment of generalized anxiety disorder. *Journal of Consulting and Clinical Psychology, 61*, 611–619.

Borkovec, T. D., Robinson, E., Pruzinsky, T., & DePree, J. A. (1983). Preliminary exploration of worry: Some characteristics and processes. *Behaviour Research and Therapy, 21*, 9–16.

Borkovec, T. D., Shadick, R. N., & Hopkins, M. (1991). The nature of normal and pathological worry. In R. M. Rapee, & Barlow, D. H. (eds.), *Chronic anxiety: Generalized anxiety disorder and mixed anxiety-depression.* New York: Guilford Press.

Bourdon, K. H. (1988). Gender differences in phobias: Results of the ECA community survey. *Journal of Anxiety Disorders, 2*, 227–241.

Brown, T. A., & Deagle, E. A. (1992). Structured interview assessment of nonclinical panic. *Behavior Therapy, 23*, 75–85.

Butler, G., & Mathews, A. (1983). Cognitive processes in anxiety. *Advances in Behaviour Research and Therapy, 5*, 51–62.

Cameron, N. (1963). *Personality development and psychopathology: A dynamic approach.* Boston: Houghton Mifflin.

Cannon, W. B. (1915). *Bodily changes in pain, hunger, fear and rage: An account of recent researches into the functions of emotional excitement.* New York: Appleton.

Chambless, D. L. & Goldstein, A. J. (eds.). (1982) *Agoraphobia: Multiple perspectives on theory and treatment.* New York: Wiley.

Clark, D. M., & Wells, A. (1995). A cognitive model of social phobia. In R. Heimberg, M. Liebowitz, D. A. Hope & F. R. Schneier (eds.), *Social phobia: Diagnosis, assessment, and treatment.* New York: Guilford.

Clark, L. A., & Watson, D. (1994). Distinguishing functional from dysfunctional affective responses. In P. Ekman & R. J. Davidson (eds.), *The nature of emotion: Fundamental questions* (pp. 131–139). New York: Oxford University Press.

Craske, M. G. (1999). *Anxiety disorders: Psychological approaches to theory and treatment.* Boulder, CO: Westview Press.

———— (2000, November). *New developments in the treatment of anxiety disorders: Generalized anxiety disorder, social phobia, and obsessive-compulsive disorder.* Professional Psych Seminars, Los Angeles, CA.

Craske, M. G., & Barlow, D. H. (1994). *Agoraphobia supplement to the Mastery of Your Anxiety and Panic II program.* Albany, NY: Graywind.

Craske, M. G., Barlow, D. H., & O'Leary, T. (1992). *Mastery of your anxiety and worry.* Albany, NY: Graywind.

Craske, M. G., Burton, T. M. Rapee, R. M., Rygh, J., & Barlow, D. H. (1989). *Simple phobics presenting for treatment: What are their fears?* Unpublished manuscript.

Craske, M. G., Rapee, R. M., Jackel, L., & Barlow, D. H. (1989). Qualitative dimensions of worry in DSM-IIIR generalized anxiety disorder subjects and non-anxious controls. *Behaviour Research and Therapy, 27,* 397–402.

Crocker, B. (1996). Personal communication.

Currie, K. A. Performance Anxiety Coping Skills Seminar. On the Internet at http://scholar.lib.vt.edu/theses/available/etd-06132001-125529/unrestricted/02CHAPTER_1.pdf.

Curtis, G. C., Magee, W. J., Eaton, W. W., Wittchen, H.-U., & Kessler, R. C. (1998). Specific fears and phobias: Epidemiology and classification. *British Journal of Psychiatry, 173,* 212–217.

Dalai Lama, H. H. the, & Cutler, H. (1998). *The art of happiness.* New York: Riverhead Books.

Davidson, T. M. (2001). Globus hystericus. Article in Univ. of Calif., San Diego online ENT surgery manual. www-surgery.ucsd.edu/ent/davison (Terence M. M.D.)/Pathways).

De Becker, G. (1997). *The gift of fear.* New York: Dell.

Eaton, W. W., Dryman, A., & Weissman, M. M. (1991). Panic and phobia. In L. N. Robins & D. A. Regier (eds.), *Psychiatric disorders in America: The Epidemiological Catchment Area Study* (pp. 155–179). New York: The Free Press.

Eckman, P. (1992). An argument for the basic emotions. *Cognition and Emotion, 6,* 169–200.

Ellis, A. (2002). The role of irrational beliefs in perfectionism. In G. L. Flett & P. L. Hewitt (eds.), *Perfectionism: Theory, research, and treatment.* Washington, D.C.: American Psychological Association.

Ellis, A., & Harper, R. (1975). *A new guide to rational living.* Hollywood, CA: Wilshire Books.

Ellsworth, P. C. (1994). Some reasons to expect universal antecedents of emotion. In P. Ekman & R. J. Davidson (eds.), *The nature of emotion: Fundamental questions.* New York: Oxford University Press.

Epstein, S., & Brodsky, A. (1993). *You're smarter than you think.* New York: Simon & Schuster.

Feynman, R. P. (1998). *The meaning of it all.* Reading, MA: Addison-Wesley.

Fishbein, M., Middlestadt, S. E., & Ottati, V. (1988). Medical problems among International Conference of Symphony and Opera Musicians (ICSOM): Overview of a national survey. *Medical Problems of Performing Arts, 3,* 1.

Flett, G. L. & Hewitt, P. L. (2002). Perfectionism and maladjustment: An overview of theoretical, definitional, and treatment issues. In G. L. Flett & P. L. Hewitt (eds.), *Perfectionism: Theory, research, and treatment* (pp. 5–31). Washington, D.C.: American Psychological Association.

Foa, E. B. (1988). What cognitions differentiate panic disorder from other anxiety disorders? In I. Hand & H. Wittchen (eds.), *Panic and phobias: Treatment and variables affecting course and outcome* (pp. 159–166). Berlin: Springer-Verlag.

Foa, E. B., Franklin, M. E., Perry, K. J., & Herbert, J. D. (1996). Cognitive biases in generalized social phobia. *Journal of Abnormal Psychology, 100,* 156–162.

Foa, E. B., & Kozak, M. J. (1986). Emotional processing of fear: Exposure to corrective information. *Psychological Bulletin, 99,* 1, 20–35.

Foa, E. B., & McNally, R. J. (1996). Mechanisms of change in exposure therapy. In R. M. Rapee (ed.), *Current controversies in the anxiety disorders* (pp. 329–343). New York: Guilford Press.

Foa, E. B., & Wilson, R. R. (2001). *Stop obsessing: How to overcome your obsessions and compulsions* (rev. ed.). New York: Bantam Books.

Fogelson, D. (1987, February). Panic disorder: seminar on natural history, biology, and treatment. Paper presented at the meeting of the Western States Psychiatric Institute, Los Angeles, CA.

Freeston, M. H., Rheaume, J. L., & Ladouceur, R. (1996). Correcting faulty appraisals of obsessional thoughts. *Behaviour Research and Therapy, 34,* 433–446.

Freud, S. (1909/1955). Analysis of a phobia in a five-year-old boy. In S. Freud, *The Standard Edition (Vol. 10).* Translated by James Strachey. London: Hogarth.

Fridja, N. H. (1994). Emotions require cognitions, even if simple ones. In P. Ekman & R. J. Davidson (eds.), *The nature of emotion: Fundamental questions* (pp. 196–207). New York: Oxford University Press.

Fyer, A. J., Mannuzza, S., Chapman, T. F., Martin, L. Y., & Klein, D. F. (1995). Specificity in familial aggregation of phobic disorders. *Archives of General Psychiatry, 52,* 564–573.

Gazzaniga, M. (1998). *The mind's past.* Berkeley and Los Angeles, CA: University of California Press.

Gelernter, C. S., Uhde, T. W., Cimbolic, P., Arnkoff, D. B., Vittone, B. J., Tancer, M. E., & Bartko, J. J. (1991). Cognitive-behavioral and pharmacological treatment for social phobia: A controlled study. *Archives of General Psychiatry, 48,* 938–945.

Goldstein, A. J., & Chambless, D. L. (1978). A reanalysis of agoraphobia. *Behavior Therapy, 9*(1), 47–59.

Goleman, D. (1995). *Emotional intelligence.* New York: Bantam Books.

Gordon, B. (1981). *I'm dancing as fast as I can.* New York: HarperCollins.

Gray, J. A., & McNaughton, N. (2000). *The Neuropsychology of Anxiety* (2nd ed.). Oxford, England: Oxford University Press.

Grayson, J. & Kirby, H. (2003) Adding cognitive techniques to the treatment of OCD: Their use and misuse. Paper presented at Anxiety Disorder Association of America Annual Conference, Toronto, Ontario, Canada, March 28, 2003.

Greist, J. (1999). Unmet needs in the management of social phobia. *New Directions in Psychiatric Practice audiotape series, 1,* 3.

Heide, F. J., & Borkovec, T. D. (1983).Relaxation-induced anxiety: Paradoxical anxiety enhancement due to relaxation training. *Journal of Consulting and Clinical Psychology, 51,* 2, 171–182.

——— (1984). Relaxation-induced anxiety: Mechanisms and theoretical implications. *Behaviour Research and Therapy, 22,* 1, 1–12.

Heimberg, R. G., Dodge, C. S., Hope, D. A., Kennedy, C. R., Zollo, L. J., & Becker, R. E. (1990). Cognitive-behavioural group treatment for social phobia: Comparison with a credible placebo control. *Cognitive Therapy and Research, 14*(1), 1–23.

Hellhammer, D. (1992). Psychoendocrinology: The brain, hormones, and behavior. In A. Ehlers, W. Fiegenbaum, I. Florin, & J. Margraf (eds.), *Perspectives and promises of clinical psychology.* New York: Plenum.

Himle, J. A., McPhee, K., Cameron, O. G., & Curtis, G. C. (1989). Simple phobia: Evidence for heterogeneity. *Psychiatry Research, 28,* 25–30.

Hoekstra, R. (1989). Treatment of obsessive-compulsive disorder with rational-emotive therapy. Paper presented at the *First World Congress of Cognitive Therapy,* Oxford, England, 28 June–2 July 1989.

Hofman, S. G., & Barlow, D. H. (2002). Social phobia. In D. H. Barlow, *Anxiety and its disorders: The nature and treatment of anxiety and panic* (2nd ed., pp. 454–476). New York: Guilford Press.

Hofsiss, J. (director) (1982). *I'm dancing as fast as I can* [film]. Paramount Pictures.

Hollander, E., Kwon, J., Stein, D., Broatch, J., Rowland, C. T., & Himelein, C. A. (1996). Obsessive-compulsive and spectrum disorders: Overview and quality of life issues. *Journal of Clinical Psychiatry, 57* (Suppl. 8), 3–6.

Hope, D. A., & Heimberg, R. G. (1993). Social phobia and social anxiety. In D. H. Barlow (ed.), *Clinical handbook of psychological disorders* (2nd ed., pp. 99–136). New York: Guilford Press.

Infoxchange net. http://www.anxietydisorders. infoxchange.net.au/famous_people.html.

Izard, C. E. (1985, March). Anxiety and emotion theory. Talk given at the Phobia Society of America National Conference, New York.

Kagan, J. (1994). *Galen's prophecy.* New York: Basic Books.

Kessler, R. C., McGonagle, K. A., Zhao, S., Nelson, C. B., Hughes, M., Eshleman, S., Wittchen, H.-U., & Kendler, K. (1994). Lifetime and 12-month prevalence of DSM-III-R psychiatric disorders in the United States: Results from the National Comorbidity Survey. *Archives of General Psychiatry, 51,* 8–19.

Kirsch, I., & Lynn, S. (1999). The automaticity of behavior in clinical psychology. *American Psychologist, 54,* 504–575.

Klein, D. F. (1993). False suffocation alarms, spontaneous panics, and related conditions: An integrative hypothesis. *Archives of General Psychiatry, 50,* 306–317.

——— (1994). Testing the suffocation false alarm theory of panic disorder. *Anxiety, 1,* 1–7.

Krystal, H. (1993). *Integration and self-healing: Affect, trauma, alexithymia.* New York: Lawrence Erlbaum.

Lazarus, A. A. (1977). *In the mind's eye: The power of imagery for personal enrichment.* New York: Guilford Press.

Leahy, R. L., & Holland, S. J. (2000). *Treatment plans and interventions for depression and anxiety disorders.* New York: Guilford Press.

Leary, M. R., & Kowalski, R. M. (1995). *Social anxiety.* New York: Guilford Press.

Leckman, J. F., Grice, D. E., Boardman, J., Zhang, H., Vitale, A., Bondi, C., Alsobrook, J., Peterson, B. S., Cohen, D. J., Rasmussen, S. A., Goodman, W. K., McDougle, C. J., & Pauls, D. L. (1997). Symptoms of obsessive-compulsive disorder: *American Journal of Psychiatry, 154,* 911–917.

LeDoux, J. (1996). *The emotional brain: The mysterious underpinnings of emotional life.* New York: Simon & Schuster.

Lenderhendler, I. I. (1995). Neural regulation of behavior. In S. H. Koslow (sr. ed.), *The neuroscience of mental health II: A report on neuroscience research* (pp. 59–77). Rockville MD: U.S. Department of Health and Human Services, National Institute of Mental Health.

Lycos Health Online with WebMD, article 1680.51097.; ibid., p. 273.

Lydiard B. (1996, Fall). Anxiety and the gastrointestinal system. ADAA *Reporter.* Rockville, MD: Anxiety Disorders Association of America.

Lynn, S. J., & Kurzhals, R. (2000). Ironic processing in simple phobia. Unpublished manuscript, Binghamton University.

Marks, I. M., & Gelder, M. G. (1966). Different ages of onset in varieties of phobia. *American Journal of Psychiatry, 123,* 218–221.

Mattick, R. P. (1990). Social phobia: An overview of psychological concepts and treatments. In N. McNaughton & G. Andrews, (eds.), *Anxiety* (pp. 179–85). University of Otago, Dunedin, Scotland.

McLean, P. D., and Woody, S. R. (2001). *Anxiety Disorders in Adults: An evidence-based approach to psychological treatment.* New York: Oxford University Press.

McNally, R. J. (1994). *Panic disorder: A critical analysis.* New York: Guilford Press.

—————— (2002). Disgust has arrived. *Anxiety Disorders, 16,* 561–566.

—————— (2002, March). Personal communication.

—————— (2003, April). Personal communication.

Merck Manual: Home Edition (Internet edition) (accessed March 2002).

Meyer, V. (1966). Modification of expectations in cases with obsessional rituals. *Behaviour Research and Therapy, 4,* 273–280.

Mick, M. A., & Telch, M. J. (1998). Social anxiety and history of behavioral inhibition in young adults. *Journal of Anxiety Disorders, 12,* 1–20.

Milestones at the Millennium Lectures and Symposia. ADAA *Reporter* (Spring 2000).

Morrow, J., & Nolen-Hoeksema, S. (1990). Effects of responses to depression on the remediation of depressive affect. *Journal of Personality and Social Psychology, 58,* 519–527.

Mowrer, O. H. (1960). *Learning theory and behavior.* New York: John Wiley.

Narrow, W. E., Rae, D. S., & Regier, D. A. (1998, July 1). NIMH epidemiology note: Prevalence of anxiety disorders. One-year prevalence best estimates calculated from ECA and NCS data. Population estimates based on U.S. Census estimated residential population age 18–54. Unpublished.

National Institute of Health (NIMH) website: Online at www.niaaa.nih.gov.gallery/endocrine/organ.jpg.

—————— (2001). Best estimate 1-year prevalence rates based on ECA and NCS, ages 18–54.

—————— (accessed April 2002). Mental health: A report of the surgeon general—epidemiology of mental illness. www.nimh.nih.gov.

Newsweek, August 28, 2000. Hikikomori, p. 37.

Ohman, A., Dimberg, U., & Öst, L.-G. (1985). Animal and social phobias: A laboratory model. In P. O. Sjoden & S. Bates (eds.), *Trends in behavior therapy.* New York: Academic Press.

Ohman, A., Eriksson, A., Fredriksson, N., Hugdahl, K., & Oloffson, C. (1974). Habituation of the electrodermal at orienting reaction to potentially phobic and supposedly neutral stimuli in normal human subjects. *Biological Psychology, 2,* 85–92.

Öst, L.-G. (1987). Age of onset in different phobias. *Journal of Abnormal Psychology, 96,* 223–229.

Otto, M. W., Jones, J. C., Craske, M. G., & Barlow, D. H. (1996). *Stopping anxiety medication: Panic control therapy for benzodiazepine discontinuation.* Albany, NY: Graywind.

Peterson, R. A., & Reiss, S. (1987). *Test manual for the Anxiety Sensitivity Index.* Oakland Park, IL: International Diagnostic Systems.

Pigott, T., & Seay, S. (1997). Pharmacotherapy of OCD. *International Review of Psychiatry, 9,* 1, 133–147.

Pilkonis, P. A., & Zimbardo, P. G. (1979). The personal and social dynamics of shyness. In C. E. Izard (ed.), *Emotions in personality and psychopathology.* New York: Plenum.

Prochaska, J. O., Norcross, J. C., & DiClemente, C. C. (1995). *Changing for good.* New York: Avon.

Rachman, S. (1976). The passing of the two-stage theory of fear and avoidance: Fresh possibilities. *Behaviour Research and Therapy, 14,* 125–131.

——— (1977). The conditioning theory of fear acquisition: A critical examination. *Behaviour Research and Therapy, 15,* 375–387.

Rachman, S., & DeSilva, P. (1978). Abnormal and normal obsessions. *Behaviour Research and Therapy, 16,* 233–248.

Rachman, S., & Shafran, R. (1998). Cognitive and behavioral features of obsessive-compulsive disorder. In R. P. Swinson et al., op. cit., pp. 52 and 56.

Radomsky, A. S., Rachman, S., Teachman, B. A., & Freeman, W. S. (1998). Why do episodes of panic stop? *Anxiety Disorders (12)* 3, 263–270.

Rapee, R. M. (1998). *Overcoming shyness and social phobia: A step-by-step guide.* Northvale, NJ: Jason Aronson.

——— (1999). *He says, she says* (videotape). New York: Guilford.

Rapee, R. M., & Sanderson, W. C. (1998). *Social phobia: Clinical application of evidence-based psychotherapy.* Northvale, NJ: Jason Aronson.

Rapee, R. M., & Heimberg, R. G. (1997). A cognitive-behavioral model of anxiety in social phobia. *Behaviour Research and Therapy, 34,* 315–322.

Regier, D. A., Boyd, J. H., Burke, J. D. Jr., Rae, D. S., Myers, J. K., Kramer, M., Robins, L. N., George, L. K., Karno, M., & Locke, B. Z. (1988). One-prevalence of mental disorders in the United States: Based on five Epidemiologic Catchment Area sites. *Archives of General Psychiatry, 45,* 977–986.

Reiss, S., & McNally, R. J. (1985). The expectancy model of fear. In S. Reiss & R. R. Bootzin (eds.), *Theoretical issues in behavior therapy* (pp. 107–121). New York: Academic Press.

Rescorla, R. A., & Wagner, A. R. (1972). A theory of Pavlovian conditioning: Variations in the effectiveness of reinforcement and nonreinforcement. In A. H. Black & W. F. Prokasy (eds.), *Classical conditioning: Vol. 2. Current research and theory* (pp. 64–99). New York: Appleton-Century-Crofts.

Riggs, D. S., & Foa, E. B. (1993). Obsessive compulsive disorder. In D. H. Barlow (ed.), *Clinical handbook of psychological disorders*. New York: Guilford Press.

Robins, L. N., Helzer, J. E., Weissman, M. M., Orvaschel, H., Gruenberg, E., Burke, J. D., & Regier, D. A. (1984). Lifetime prevalence of specific psychiatric disorders in three sites. *Archives of General Psychiatry, 41,* 949–958.

Rostand, E. (1897). *Cyrano de Bergerac.*

Roth, D., Antony, M. M., and Swinson, R. P. (In press.) Interpretations for anxiety symptoms in social phobia. *Behavioural Research and Therapy.*

Rycroft, C. (1968). *Anxiety and neurosis.* London: Karnac Books.

Salkovski, P. M. (1985). Obsessional-compulsive problems: A cognitive-behavioral analysis. *Behaviour Research and Therapy, 25,* 571–583.

Sanderson, W. C., DiNardo, P. A., Rapee, R. M., & Barlow, D. H. (1990). Syndrome comorbidity in patients diagnosed with a *DSM-III Revised* anxiety disorder. *Journal of Abnormal Psychology 99,* 308–312.

Schwartz, J. M., & Bayette, B. (contributor) (1996). *Brain lock: Free yourself from obsessive-compulsive behavior: A four-step self-treatment method to change your brain chemistry.* New York: HarperCollins, pp. 209–210.

Seligman, M. E. P. (1971). Phobia and preparedness. *Behavior Therapy, 2,* 307–320.

Selye, H. (1950). *The physiology and pathology of exposure to stress.* Montreal: ACTA Press.

Sheehan, D. V. (1983). *The anxiety disease.* New York: Charles Scribner's Sons.

Shiovitz, T. (2001). Personal communication.

Soifer, S., Zgourides, G. D., Himle, J., & Pickering, N. L. (2001). *Shy bladder syndrome.* Oakland, CA: New Harbinger.

Stanley, M. A., & Averill, P. M. (1998). Psychosocial treatment for obsessive-compulsive disorder: Clinical applications. In R. P. Swinson, et al., op. cit.

Steketee, G., & Barlow, D. H. (2002). Obsessive-compulsive disorder. In D. H. Barlow, *Anxiety and its disorders: The nature and treatment of anxiety and panic* (2nd ed., pp. 516–550). New York: Guilford Press.

Steketee, G., & Pigott, T. (1999). *Obsessive compulsive disorder: The latest assessment and treatment strategies.* Kansas City, MO: Compact Clinicals.

Steketee, G., & Pruyn, N. A. (1998). In R. P. Swinson et al., op. cit., p. 121.

Steketee, G., & White, K. (1990). *When once is not enough: Help for obsessive-compulsives.* Oakland, CA: New Harbinger.

Stopa, L., & Clark, D. M. (1993). Cognitive processes in social phobia. *Behaviour Research and Therapy, 31,* 255–267.

Summerfeldt, L. J., Huta, V., & Swinson, R. P. (1998). Personality and obsessive-compulsive disorder. In Swinson et al., op. cit., pp. 79–119.

Susann, J. (1966). *Valley of the dolls.* New York: Grove/Atlantic.

Swinson, R. P., Antony, M. M., Rachman, S., & Richter, M. A. (eds.) (1998). *Obsessive-compulsive disorder: Theory, research, and treatment.* New York: Guilford Press.

Taylor, S., & Cox, B. J. (1998). An expanded Anxiety Sensitivity Index: Evidence for a hierarchic structure in a clinical sample. *Journal of Anxiety Disorders, 12,* 463–483.

Turk, C. L., Lerner, J. L., Heimberg, R. G., & Rapee, R. M. (2001). In S. G. Hoffman & P. M. Dibartolo (eds.), From social anxiety to social phobia. Boston: Allyn & Bacon.

Turner, S. M., Beidel, D. C., & Stanley, M. A. (1992). Are obsessional thoughts and worry different cognitive phenomena? *Clinical Psychology Review, 12,* 257–270.

"Tyramine-Free Diet." www.puritan.com/healthnotes1/Diet/Tyramine_Free_Diet.htm. Accessed April, 2003.

Van Oppen, P., & Arntz, A. (1994). Cognitive therapy for obsessive-compulsive disorder. *Behavioural Research and Therapy, 32,* 1, 79–84.

Watson, J. B., & Rayner, R. (1920). Conditioned emotional reactions. *Journal of Experimental Psychology, 3*(1), 1–14.

Webster's Universal College Dictionary (1997). New York: Random House.

Wegner, D. M. (1989). *White bears and other unwanted thoughts.* New York: Viking.

Wells, A. (1997). *Cognitive therapy of anxiety disorders: A practice manual and conceptual guide.* Chichester, West Sussex, England: Wiley.

Wells, A., Clark, D. M., and Ahmad, S. (1998). How do I look with my mind's eye: Perspective taking in social phobic imagery. *Behavior Research and Therapy, 36,* 631–34.

Wilson, K. G., Sandler, L. S., Asmundson, G. J. G., Larsen, K. K., & Ediger, J. M. (1991). Effects of instructional set on self-reports of panic attacks. *Journal of Anxiety Disorders, 5,* 43–63.

Wilson, R. R. (1996). *Don't panic: Taking control of anxiety attacks* (2nd ed.). New York: HarperCollins.

——— (2000). More about social anxieties and phobias. Online at www.anxieties.com.

Wolpe, J. (1958). *Psychotherapy by reciprocal inhibition.* Stanford, CA: Stanford University Press.

——— (1990). *The practice of behavior therapy.* New York: Pergamon Press.

Woody, S. R., & Tolin, D. F. (2002). The relationship between disgust sensitivity and avoidant behavior: Studies of clinical and nonclinical samples. *Anxiety Disorders, 16,* 543–559.

Zimbardo, P. G., Pilkonis, P. A., & Norwood, R. M. (1974). *The silent prison of shyness.* Stanford, CA: Office of Naval Research Technical Report No. 2-17. Stanford University.

Zinbarg, R. E., Craske, M. G., and Barlow, D. H. (1993). *Therapist's guide for the Mastery of Your Anxiety and Worry program.* Albany, NY: Graywind.

Index